PRESSURE

POINTS

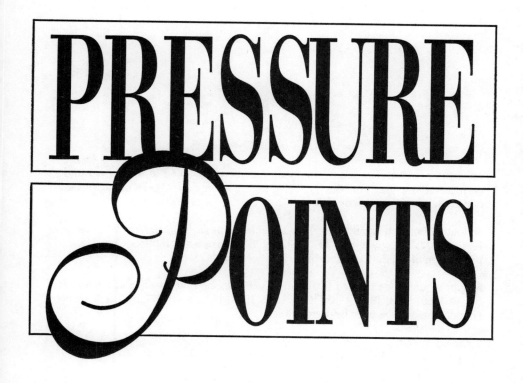

GARY J. OLIVER, Ph.D.
and H. NORMAN WRIGHT

MOODY PRESS

CHICAGO

Contents

Foreword

Anger! A force that can be either maliciously destructive or powerfully energizing. Throughout life, how we come to understand and deal with anger may determine success or failure in all areas of life.

Christians have a particularly difficult time dealing with anger. They tend to see only the "gentle Jesus, meek and mild." Those occasions when He railed at the hypocrites and sped through the holy temple dumping tables and driving out livestock are easily overlooked. Yet the God of the Old Testament, often angry with His wayward children, still reigns.

One thing is certain today—anger *is*. Simply stated, it exists, and it will be expressed one way or another. Gary Oliver and H. Norman Wright have tackled an extremely important and sensitive issue, and they have done it well.

With amazing empathy, these two men have entered our women's world—the world of today. And they have expressed for us focused concepts that many of us have never fully clarified for ourselves. With a few well-selected words, they explain the reality and comprehensibility of our emotions.

As carefully as I searched, nowhere could I find old clichés or ancient expectations so often used in the past for accusing women. Instead, through a vast number of careful interviews with women, they have accumulated remarkable insights. These they have sifted, interpreted, and reflected back to us for our enhanced understanding and enrichment.

My experience reinforces their findings. Anger is the constant accompaniment of pain or fear. When we most fear our weaknesses, then we are at the greatest risk of explosive anger. When exhaustion or illnesses drain our resources, then we are most vulnerable to angry emotional storms.

The authors offer us the tools of insight and awareness. These tools provide the means of expressing our anger appropriately and constructively. Neither suppressing nor repressing anger, they teach us, will work. Anger expressed violently and without control is equally damaging or worse.

It is through the early recognition of our feelings that we can express them honestly and even forcefully, but without danger to others or later embarrassment to ourselves. A sample of some excellent directives they list are these:

1. Acknowledge that you are angry.
2. Ask, "Have I put first things first?"
3. Decide what are the causes.
4. Find out what is the healthiest way for you to respond.
5. Determine, "Now that I've decided what to do, where do I begin?"

Each step is thoughtfully defined and explained.

Once we have gained mastery over our own anger, we can learn to cope with aggression in others. And, by the way, the authors nicely distinguish between assertiveness and aggression in expressing anger. Knowing that angry people are often bullies, inwardly frightened themselves, alleviates our fear of them. In fact, we can even offer such threatening people the priceless gift of compassion and understanding.

It will surprise many of you that all of this work on anger is strictly biblically based. The writers have carefully researched the wisdom in the Bible and related it to everyday struggles. Without being simplistic, they emphasize the profoundly simple reality of prayer and reliance on our powerful God.

The section on being a mature, or assertive, responder is especially useful. The authors define her.

> The mature responder is an assertive woman who has a clear sense of who she is in Christ. Her emotions, mind, and will work together and function in a balanced way. She can express her opinions but doesn't need to put others down. She delights in serving but is not servile. She can be tough and tender. She isn't reactive; she is proactive. She has taken the time to look at, understand, and develop a healthy plan for dealing with her God-given emotion of anger.

In every arena of life, anger occurs—on the job, in the home, in social situations, in the church, in others, and, yes, in you. You can now successfully cope with anger, becoming more than a conqueror.

GRACE KETTERMAN, M.D.
Crittenton
Kansas City, Missouri

Acknowledgments

We owe a debt of gratitude to the many women (and a few men) across the country who contributed to the research for this book.

Much of our information regarding the kinds of pressures women face and how they deal with it came from more than 3,000 surveys of women across the United States. Those who helped us collect those surveys include:

Virgil and Evelyn Ediger   Jolene Kelley
Steve and Twila Lee   Paul and Kathy Nauman

Early in our research process we sent more extensive survey to a variety of women who have been involved in ministry to women on a denominational and/or national level. All of these women, though busy, were kind enough to take the time to respond to our questions. Their insights, concerns, and questions were very helpful. Their gracious participation in our research does not imply an endorsement of what we have written.

Elisabeth Elliot	Karen Mains
Ruby Friesen	Carol Mayhall
Diana Garland	Lee McDowell
Pamela Heim	Shirley Stevens
Kay Lindskoog	Sandra Wilson

Additional thanks goes to Carrie Oliver, Lanell Schilling, Carol Golz, Lynn Trathen, Naomi Gade Penner, and Marilyn McGinnis for helpful discussions and contributions. Thanks go as well to Judy Coddington and Kristi Buhler for typing the manuscript; to Bryn Edwards for her efficient orchestrating of a multitude of details in the office; and to the Moody Press staff, including editors Jim Bell and Anne Scherich.

A special word of thanks to Maryellen Stipe, who gave many hours helping in literature reviews and tracking down hard-to-find articles in journals and magazines—and remained joyous throughout the process. In addition to her contribution to our research, her group of more than two hundred women at the Crossroads Church in Denver provided invaluable feedback to some of the ideas presented in this book.

We are grateful to the women who have trusted us with their stories and to Moody Press for believing that two men could meaningfully write about how women can understand and more effectively deal with the pressure points in their lives.

CHAPTER ONE

Anger—
Friend or Foe?

I'm a yeller. When I get angry, you better watch your step around me, because I'll let you know in no uncertain terms that I'm angry. It could be my husband, my daughter, or the dog that's going to hear me. I guess I want others to know that I'm angry. It's only fair to warn them. We had no warning in my home when I was younger. We were always ambushed by Mom or Dad. Maybe anger isn't always the best, but when it's there and I have to feel it, you're going to feel it as well."

As the woman who said this sat down, many of the other women in the group were nodding their heads in agreement. What they had heard was familiar to them. They too were yellers.

Another woman stood up and said, "I'm different. I let my anger out but in a different way. And I guess it confuses my family. I'm a crier. When I get angry, I start crying. I don't know why. My husband tells me he would rather I threw things, or yelled, because he can't out whether I'm angry or hurt. You know, sometimes its hard for me to decide which it is too."

The women in this group were completing the sentence "When I get angry I . . ." They were among the more than twenty-four-hundred women who responded to a survey endeavoring to discover more about this emotion so many women struggle over. If you were asked to complete the same sentence, what would you say? Here is what a number of others said:

When I get angry, I . . .

- Usually keep my anger inside and let it build up until I'm basically fed up.
- Don't immediately express it. I rationalize the situation or I contemplate the cause and validity of my reaction to the cause.
- Get sarcastic and biting in my comments. I fish for someone to ask me what is wrong.
- Find it easy to stuff it and get depressed.
- Fume inside and snap at people. I do use words to express it, but I become snappy and impatient.
- Drive myself crazy.
- Get ugly. If I happen to walk by a mirror, I am surprised at how hateful I look. I want to hurt back with words. I want that person to be sorry they hurt me. And then I am sorry at my own selfishness.
- Probably am more negative. I tend to clam up, and I know that is wrong.
- Scream.
- Yell, then cry.
- Feel sad for feeling that way—then I lose my patience.
- Feel out of control and lash out—I regret my behavior later. I even hate myself at the time, but I can't seem to stop.
- Either button up for awhile, or I rage like a crazy person; or I express myself passionately but controlled.
- Hit a wall, throw something, yell, say something I regret, slam a door.

- Tend to yell and want to hit someone.
- Tend to draw inward with my emotions and then feel very guilty.
- Sometimes I walk away and let it simmer underneath. Sometimes I raise my voice and express it. Sometimes I yell. Sometimes I take the person aside and talk calmly about it.

Anger. That strange feeling. That puzzling response. It's a strong feeling of irritation. It's a signal and a warning system telling us that something more is going on in our life than we are paying attention to. It's not a signal to be ignored, either, or a postcard sent at a bulk rate. It's more like a special delivery letter telling you that you're being hurt, your rights are being trampled, you're living in fear, you're frustrated, or you're ignoring something significant in your life. You could be feeling anger because you are trying too hard to please others and are neglecting yourself; or you could be doted on too much by others, and that too is depriving you of growing and becoming more independent.

But is this what you were taught about anger as you were growing up? Did your mother or father sit down with you and say, "Let me tell you about anger?"

WHO TAUGHT YOU TO BECOME ANGRY?

We asked the question, "Who taught you to become angry?" Here are some of the responses:

- Both parents. My father was slow to anger, but more to be feared when provoked. For my mother, it was a daily, frequent ritual of outbursts.
- Born a sinner—don't think I needed to be taught.
- Myself from watching my sister and mother and sometimes my dad because he stuffs his feelings deep (for years) until one day he would explode.

- My family taught me how *not* to become angry, and I hope God's Word and His Holy Spirit taught and are teaching me how to become angry.
- I think there was lots of anger stuffed in marriage, a hard marriage. Husband gone all the time and left me with full responsibility. Lots of anger came from him—men in general.
- Some book about two kinds of anger—righteous and unrighteous (after I was an adult).
- My father.
- No one taught me how to become angry. I think anger is a natural human emotion.

These women also responded to the statement, "If there is any one question that I could have answered about anger, it would be . . ." Here are some of their responses:

- Why do I take on the anger of an angry person after they're over the emotional part of it? It seems to stay with me for a period of time.
- Why do women in the South have such an incredibly tough time with emotional expression—especially anger? My experience indicates there must be a cultural factor involved.
- How can I stop before I get to the point in which I become so confused and hurt, resulting in what I feel is a loss of control over my hurting the closest person to me—my husband?

(Appendix 1 contains a sampling of many of the other questions the respondents answered.)

You are going to experience anger in your life for many reasons. And when you do it's important that you face your anger, accept it, hear the message that it is conveying to you, and learn to express your anger in a healthy way. Your anger needs your respect and attention. It's all right to be angry because it can help you improve relationships and correct some of the wrongs in your life. Anger can be expressed in a healthy way so that others can hear your anger.

We doubt that was the message you heard when you were growing up. If you are like many women, you probably heard, "Don't rock the boat. Be a peacemaker. Your job is to nurture others. And don't show a man your anger. It will drive him away."

Over the past decades when women became angry they were looked on as unfeminine and were usually given uncomplimentary labels. Look at the language often used against a woman who is angry. She's called a "witch," "nag," or "man-hater," just to name a few. But what are the uncomplimentary labels for men when they are angry? You won't find them. There have been so many restrictions against women feeling and expressing anger it is difficult for many women even to know that they are angry. I've heard the phrase, "She's just irrational," used many times when a woman was expressing her anger, as though a label could explain it away.

Harriet Goldhor Lerner describes the problem well:

Why are angry women so threatening to others? If we are guilty, depressed, or self-doubting, we stay in place. We do not take action except against our own selves and we are unlikely to be agents of personal and social change. In contrast, angry women may change and challenge the lives of us all, as witnessed by the past decade of feminism. And change is an anxiety-arousing and difficult business for everyone, including those of us who are actively pushing for it.

Thus, we too learn to fear our own anger, not only because it brings about the disapproval of others, but also because it signals the necessity for change. We may begin to ask ourselves questions that serve to block or invalidate our own experience of anger: "Is my anger legitimate?" "Do I have a right to be angry?" "What's the use of my getting angry?" "What good will it do?" These questions can be excellent ways of silencing ourselves and shutting off our anger.[1]

Traditionally, women have expressed their anger in indirect ways. Those could take the form of acting hurt, or being wounded, or sulking—all of which fit the image of being "nice." But being a placater and overriding one's true feelings, hopes, desires, and dreams leads to an accumulation of anger. I've talked to a number of women in counseling over the years who have had this experience. They say, "I really don't do too well getting angry but I'm quite adept at feeling guilty. At least then I'm the only one that gets hurt." But that isn't really true either, for that guilt leads to anger—and one way or another your anger is going to find an outlet, whether you want it to or not.

SOCIAL INJUSTICE AND WOMEN'S ANGER

Many women today are fed up and will not put up with the inequality and harassment that they usually have just accepted and remained silent about. Many women are tired of being quiet and compliant, as evidenced by their response to the Clarence Thomas–Anita Hill hearings held before the US Senate Judiciary Committee—all of whose members were male and who represented a predominantly male legislative body.

I even heard a man in our racquetball club locker-room say, "What's the big deal over what he did? That's common. Why's she so angry? Probably just trying to get some free publicity." I'm sure that type of statement is not uncommon. But women are now less tolerant of some things they have tolerated for way too long.

Reflect with me over some of the beliefs, statements, and situations that have been common over the past century. President Grover Cleveland said in 1905, "Sensible and responsible women do not want to vote." In 1912 the president of Harvard said that women were physically too fragile to endure the demands of higher education.

In 1930 laws banning women's employment were proposed in half of the nation's state legislatures. Twenty-six of the states prohibited married women from working. Yet during World

War II women were urged to go to work in the factories—but unlike the women in Great Britain, they did not receive any housekeeping or child-care assistance from the government. In 1945, when the war ended, women pilots who flew risky non-combat missions were not eligible for military or veterans' benefits nor any of the honors.

In 1961 the Supreme Court ruled unanimously that each state retained the right to exclude women from jury duty so that their main work as wives, homemakers, and mothers would not be hindered. In 1962 businesses were polled, and 28 percent admitted that a woman's sex appeal was a qualification for certain jobs. In 1971 President Nixon vetoed federal day-care legislation because he believed it would threaten the sanctity of the family. In 1974 the Supreme Court ruled that the denial of disability benefits to women unable to work because of pregnancy-related disabilities was not unconstitutional. In that same year the mayor of Davenport, Iowa, was required to have her husband sign before she could obtain a BankAmericard.

In 1983 a woman was gang raped on a barroom pool table in a town in Massachusetts as the crowd watched and cheered. The defense argued that she was dressed provocatively and had gone there looking for a good time. As recently as 1991, in an article about the woman who charged she was raped by William Kennedy Smith, the *New York Times* said, "She had a little wild streak," implying that she got what she asked for.

How have women fared financially over the years? In 1903 women earned some 33 cents to the dollar earned by men; in 1922 the figure had climbed to 53 cents to the dollar; and in 1983 it reached 66 cents to the dollar. In 1984 Clarence Pendleton, of the US Civil Rights Commission, stated that equal pay for equal work was, in his words, "the looniest idea [he had heard of] in years." Perhaps these and hundreds of other examples of bias against women have had something to do with the intensity of the anger that is now being released.[2]

Put another way, what we see today is cumulative anger that reflects the still existing and even increasing negative treatment of women, including sexism and incidence of rape.

19

Sometimes the anger a woman feels over societal injustice is unleashed at her boyfriend or her husband, who is immediately put on the defensive because he doesn't feel he is the enemy. When a woman works in an environment where men are insensitive about the jokes they tell and engage in put-downs and even sexual harassment, it may be difficult for her to separate the good guys in her life from the bad guys.

SEXISM AND WOMEN'S ANGER

The anger is there for a number of reasons. It could be caused by a woman's feeling that she must live up to male expectations that she be fragile, dependent, helpless, and willing to follow a man's dictates.[3] It may be caused by her not being taken seriously in meetings when she voices her opinion, or by her being asked to take notes or get the coffee in the meeting because she is a woman. It could be caused by her having to put up with male behavior that is rude and rejecting simply because she is a woman. I have seen some pastors treat women speakers or leaders in this way. I have also observed similar behavior many times in phone conversations and even at my office. A man will be rude to one of my secretaries, whereas he wouldn't think of talking to me in the same manner. On occasions when I have confronted a caller about this issue, his change in attitude toward my secretary the next time he calls is amazingly different. The discrepancy in the way men and women are treated can also be seen when a man voices a complaint and gets more response to it than a woman would if she were to make the same complaint.

The labels men apply to women are another source of anger. "She's just hysterical, she'll calm down," a man might say. Another put-down: "Here comes the PMS again. It's time to avoid her for a few days."

SAFETY AND WOMEN'S ANGER

Many women feel powerless to do much about their situation. They engage in blame, and whenever blame is alive it leads to anger. Fear is another major cause of anger, and, consequently, we see anger on the increase because of the decreasing safety in our society for women. I (Norman Wright) have a friend whose daughter was almost raped. My wife and grown daughter both carry a protective spray whenever they are out, and there are certain places my wife will not go in the evening. I have worked with assault victims, and I have seen the fear and rage they have experienced because of what has happened to them. We can expect a steady increase in women's anger over the next few years because women are becoming more self-confident, have gained in power and influence, and have developed a feeling of entitlement, and are thus not so likely today to bury their feelings about the way they are treated.

A rallying point for women occurred in the Clarence Thomas –Anita Hill hearings, in which a familiar scenario was played out. The accused became the victim, and the victim ended up being the accused and portrayed as vindictive and unstable.

UNEQUAL WORK LOAD AND WOMEN'S ANGER

We see more anger at home and at work. Within the home much of the anger stems from the division of the work load. Women who work outside the home must spend many additional hours in housework each week compared to men, and both men and women are angry at the lack of appreciation they receive from their partner.[4] At work one of the continuing frustrations is the inequality in pay in certain professions, although fortunately there are a number of professions where one's gender does not matter.

We wondered what caused women to respond in anger. In our national survey, we asked the question, "What are some of the factors which increase your vulnerability to anger?" The respondents were given four spaces in which to give their response (not in order of importance.)

In a sampling of 722 surveys in which this question was answered, we discovered the following:

48% identified fatigue or being tired
28% mentioned stress
20% said injustice
14% mentioned children
13% said PMS
11% said pain or illness
 9% stated feeling out of control or helplessness
 8% identified frustration
 7% said communication with their husbands
 7% said it was a spiritual problem

But are women angrier today than they were decades ago? Perhaps not. What is occurring is more that anger that had been hidden in the past is now coming into the open. Women are no longer willing to be passive reactors. And as this occurs you can expect to witness more anger in men as they face having less control over women.[5]

PASSIVE-AGGRESSIVE EXPRESSION OF ANGER

One of the ways of going underground and being a passive reactor in your anger is by being passive-aggressive in expressing anger. This allows you to be angry but express it in a disguised way. Some people are clever at this. They may consciously know they are angry or they may not, but whatever their level of awareness, they are able to convey their anger. They may release it under the guise of critical comments, or they may harbor well-camouflaged resentment. If they are confronted they proclaim their innocence. Their response is similar to what we find in Proverbs 26:18–19: "As a madman who casts firebrands, arrows and death, so is the man who deceives his neighbor and then says, Was I not joking?" (AMP).

How might you respond if you're a passive-aggressive?

Letting out your anger by procrastinating is one tactic.[6] Putting off responsibilities or delaying doing something for someone else is another excellent way to vent your anger. But it's not obvious and it feels safe, because it's difficult for others to label the action as anger.

You're more comfortable being called "irresponsible" or "lazy" than being labeled "angry." Subtle stubbornness is another expression. So is forgetting or avoidance. These behaviors usually reflect anger that you wouldn't dare express openly.

Forgetting is another handy way to express anger, because the responsibility can be turned back against the other person. "Are you *sure* you asked me?" Or, "Are you *sure* that was the time we agreed upon?" "I'm so sorry you had to wait in the rain. But I was *sure* you said to pick you up at ten-thirty and not at ten. Well, anyway, you can get some dry clothes at home." When people say things like this to you, you begin to doubt yourself. You end up feeling responsible. But the truth is, you were set up.

How else might you express anger indirectly? Using your spouse's car and leaving it a mess along with an empty gas tank works well. Paying a bill but conveniently forgetting to mail it can bring a call from the gas company. You take money out of your partner's wallet and fail to let him know about it. During the viewing of her husband's favorite TV program a passive-aggressive woman will walk over and turn the channel to something she wants to watch.

Sarcasm is a "nice" way to be angry. Two messages are given at one time, a compliment and a put-down. "You look so young I didn't recognize you." "Your new suit is radical, but I like it."

I've seen passive-aggressives act as though they didn't understand the simplest instructions. You may even have noticed a slight smile or smirk on their faces, but confronting them usually doesn't work. They play innocent, and if you ever suggest that they might be angry you are likely to get a "Who me? I'm not angry at all!" response. You'll end up wondering if you're not the one with the problem.

Is burying anger worth it? Is there something underneath anger? If anger contains a message, what is it saying to you?

What is the purpose of anger in your life? What keeps you from opening up with your anger?

Many women think, *If I become angry, won't I become aggressive too?* I don't think so. For many years we connected anger and aggression. But there actually is not as much connection between anger and aggression as there is between anger and blame. We don't tend to become as angry when we understand the what and why of another person's response. That is especially important in significant relationships. When you lack an object of blame, do you become angry? Not usually.

ANGER AS A PROTECTOR AND A DEFENSE

Another often overlooked characteristic of anger could be operating in your life at this time. Anger acts as a protector and a defense. When the hormonal changes of anger kick in you will find that you can defend yourself better for three reasons:

- *Your anger gives you a feeling of empowerment.*

The doubts that you had about yourself are disappearing. You now have sufficient energy to cope. You discovered a new-found source of strength to mobilize yourself.

- *Your anger helps you to block out fear and guilt.*

Anger tends to drive away any feeling that might inhibit you. Unless you turn your anger back against yourself it will push you ahead to attack.

- *Your anger helps you to focus on your own needs rather than the other person's.*

Your pain and needs are the focus, not the other person's. When we are prompted to anger we also have the conviction of being right. Anger itself strengthens this belief. That is why some men and women become addicted to anger, for at no other time do they have these feelings.

EXAMPLES OF HOW WE USE ANGER AS A DEFENSE

Perhaps the best way to illustrate how we use our anger as a defense is by giving examples.

- *We use anger to alleviate the pain of guilt.*

Are you familiar with guilt? If so, you know how uncomfortable it is. To alleviate the pain of guilt you can defend yourself against it by becoming angry against what another person is making you feel guilty about. It works for a while, but doesn't resolve the problem.

- *We use anger to defend against hurt.*

That hurt could be the hurt stemming from an unkind remark, a rejection, or an injustice. In lashing out we cover the pain of the hurt.

- *We use anger to defend against a loss.*

I've seen people react with anger when a son or daughter goes off to college or to work in another part of the country, or when a friend moves away. Anger often arises when we lose a loved one in death. We find something to blame in the person and focus on the hurt we are experiencing instead of the delight he or she may be experiencing.

- *We use anger as a defense against the feeling of being trapped or helpless.*

You may be working overtime to pay for your children's braces. You didn't realize how long it would take nor the overall cost, and now you're stuck on a treadmill for the next two years. You don't have any alternative but to stick it out, so you begin to think, *They don't even appreciate what they're getting,* and you focus on your exhaustion and lack of time for yourself.

So it's no wonder that quarrels between you and your children have increased as you find more and more to become angry about. They see you as being overly critical, which you

25

may be, but it's your outlet against being trapped.

- *We use anger as a defense against fear.*

You've probably seen this in others or have experienced it yourself. A child runs into the street, and fear propels the mother into the street to grab her child from in front of a car. She yells at the child and spanks him in anger, which covers the feeling of fear.

- *We use anger to defend against painful feelings.*

Using anger to defend against painful feelings is normal. The problem arises when we make anger a habit or when the frequency and intensity of our anger begins to affect us and our relationships.

I've met anger addicts. They have used anger as a defense for so long they know no other way to respond and feel empty without the rush of anger.

That is the down side of anger. If you have used anger over a period of time as a defense, it is hard to let go of it, especially if it's easier to feel anger than to feel fear, hurt, guilt, or emptiness. Anger can become an addiction. All addictions feel good for the moment, but the problem is that unless you are immediately facing a situation in which you are directly threatened, your anger will probably direct you away from appropriate action that would help you resolve the problem.

WHAT ANGER KEEPS US FROM ACCOMPLISHING

If anger has the capacity to help to block out painful feelings, why should we deal with the original pain and its cause? We should do so because confronting the original pain and its cause is essential if we are to become whole.

- *Anger keeps us from confronting the source of our fear.*

Anger will keep you from separating actual threats from distortions that create fear. It will keep you from confronting negative messages you say to yourself that you may have learned from poor experiences with your parents or other significant individuals in your life. You may have a self-critical voice going off inside your head from time to time, so to silence it you use your anger to override it. But will anger help you confront that critic and evict it from your life? Not usually.

- *Anger keeps guilt alive.*

When you use anger as a defense, you will never come to the place where you deal with the source of your guilt. Your guilt may arise from false beliefs, or it may be the result of your giving need fulfillment priority over your value system. You become angry at yourself when you know you are violating your values, but that doesn't stop you from doing it again and again.

- *Anger keeps grief alive.*

Many times I have seen anger keep grief alive over a major loss in a person's life. Anger keeps him from saying good-bye to whatever was lost. Often the person keeps reliving the hurts, harsh words, and wrongs of the relationship, which just reinforces the pain, guilt, and intensity of the loss.

- *Anger closes off communication.*

I've rarely met an angry person who is able to talk about what pains him when he is angry. Yet if you are unable to talk about what is hurting you when you are angry, how can other people know what is bothering you? How can they change their response to you if you don't let them know how you felt wounded by what they said or did?

- *Anger keeps us feeling like victims.*

You feel helpless in spite of the strength of your anger because your anger doesn't let you fix what's wrong. When you blame or defend, your energy is diverted from resolving the original problem.

27

All of this is not to say that you should never become angry. Quite the contrary. It's when anger becomes your main line of defense that it becomes a difficulty. Every concern and issue has a solution, but anger doesn't usually lead you to that solution.[7]

SILENT PAIN

Anger within a woman that goes unrecognized, unadmitted, and untouched becomes an unwanted resident that soon affects the totality of her life. Recently a book for women was released with the title *Silent Pain,* referring to a submerged sadness or a deep ache that is always there just underneath the surface, taking the edge off of life. That pain could reflect deep unfulfilled longings, disappointments in your relationships, or lingering unhealed hurts.[8]

There are many reasons for silent pain. It could be a residual grief from the past that has never been resolved. Years ago I learned to ask my counselees the question, "What is there in your life that you've never fully grieved over?" In time most identify some loss—and with each loss there is usually a residue of anger.

It could be pain over a current situation that reminds you of a similar past heartache, but you don't feel free to talk about it. You're angry that it still exists, but you can't talk about the anger either.

It could be connected to a sense of shame over a past or present sin, real or imagined. You believe what you did was so wrong you cannot be forgiven, so you live with your pain. Underneath may be a residual anger over the unfairness of the continuation of that pain.

Some of the pain may be caused by the low-grade fever of suppressed or repressed anger that festers until it comes to a boil. In *Silent Pain* Kathy Olson talks about how her son, Brian, was born with spina bifida, a major birth defect. Several years after his birth Kathy was diagnosed with multiple sclerosis. "With my old pattern of suppressing sadness," she writes, "I rushed past the normal emotion of sorrow."[9] In time she began to face the ramifications of her disease. She describes her discovery:

> It took the specter of a nerve-rotting disease to awaken me to the way I was crippling myself with a soul-rotting pattern of emotional repression . . . in the name of faith. Not only my body had suffered, but my marriage had careened on the brink of indifference and deadly neglect. Our two sons trembled when I kicked the kitchen cabinet door so hard it cracked down the middle. I, Kathy Olson, always known for her gentle, calm spirit had become a gentle, calm volcano.[10]

When you bury any emotion, there is a loss. When you bury your sorrow and don't allow yourself to feel your sadness, you don't realize your need for comfort and consolation. When you bury your anger, you ignore what it's trying to tell you. In so doing you may create another nemesis more common to woman than to men—depression.

Some women take a long time to feel angry after an unpleasant event has occurred. The amount of control these women exercise also means that they are slow to recognize that they have just experienced something that might have prompted anger. Usually women like this have been taught that "an adult should be in control of her emotions," and that it's childish to let another person irritate you. If you become angry, you're just letting another person control you. Often this belief has been reinforced by observing uncomfortable angry scenes at home or work. The women equate anger with negative results. So when feelings of anger begin to emerge they experience a tremendous struggle to banish the feeling itself. They won't allow anger to take shape.[11]

But the fuel for the anger is there. The ingredients, the shape, the structure, and the energy are all there, whether ignored or not. What happens to all that energy? Where does it go?

ANGER AND DEPRESSION

Many women, after thinking about unfair events and experiences they have encountered, finally experience their anger and accept the fact that they are angry. But immediately they feel guilty for being angry. Sometimes they remain angry for an extended period of time, but regardless of the duration in time, they turn both the blame and the anger back on themselves.

What happens to that anger? Where does it go? In many cases it results in depression.

Why is it that women experience depression more than men? Why is it that one in every four women will suffer a serious clinical depression at some time in her life, whereas only one in eight men will? According to a 1990 study by the American Psychological Association, it is not because women are more willing to share their feelings, to complain, or go for counseling. It is instead because women have not been culturally condition to combat depression.[12] A chain reaction toward depression is involved. Women's vulnerability to depression may be connected to their tendency toward passivity and dependency, which they confuse with being feminine. This leads to a hesitation to admit, face, and resolve their anger. Men are given permission by society to be angry, whereas women are not, which in turn leads many women to feel it necessary to suppress their anger. Since anger that is suppressed does not just go away, suppressing anger makes women more prone to anger. That in turn leads to depression, for suppressed anger is often channeled into depression.[13]

Unfortunately, many women learn this pattern as young children. Growing up in a dysfunctional family retards emotional expression, whether the dysfunction is divorce, alcoholism, abuse, or perfectionism. What happens between a woman and her father is a key factor. Any type of abandonment is damaging, whether it be by emotional withdrawal, death, or divorce. Divorce is especially experienced as a form of abandonment, and a girl's emotional pattern and relationship with her father may be affected. A major study revealed the following:

Daughters felt they received less affection from their mothers after the separation, and that too much was expected of them. They understood that their mothers didn't have sufficient time for them because of work. But many of them felt emotionally trapped in the situation. They were angry at their fathers for abandoning them, but he wasn't available to be the target of their anger. So a daughter often felt like venting her anger on her mother, blaming her for the father's absence. At the same time, the girl felt the need to squelch her anger because Mom was all she had left, and she needed her more than ever. The pattern of daughters of divorce repressing their emotions is prevalent.[14]

This learned repression of emotions is what keeps a woman stuck in her pain. Some believe that emotional distress is caused not so much by the painful events of life but by silence about those events and the feelings underneath them. I've seen this tragedy in the counseling office with women in their thirties and forties, who for the first time in their lives are taking the cap off their repressed emotions and beginning to face them. It is interesting to see the transformation that occurs. As they let their feelings out, especially anger, they discover a newfound source of energy.

Kathy Olson suggests that when you face, accept, and feel your anger it is a step toward removing the barrier that has kept you from the vulnerability that you've been afraid to feel.

The author of *The Wounded Woman* writes:

Behind the rage are often tears . . . underneath the anger is vulnerability and the possibility for tenderness and intimacy . . . so if a woman can learn to relate to her rage, this may open up her tender side and the possibility for an intimate relationship. Frequently when women express their anger with their lovers, they open up more sexually as well. So rage can allow a fuller love experience on both the physical and emotional levels.[15]

Women have told us of their fear of repercussion from God if they were to admit their anger, and especially their anger toward God over the unfairness of life. Sometimes I reply, "But if God is God and who He says He is, doesn't He already know?" Perhaps the response of one woman's journey of anger and tears will illustrate why you don't need to be afraid of God with regard to your anger.

>And as I recalled that gray morning when I had wanted to throw something at Jesus, I began to cry.
>
>I sank to my knees and pounded on the bed.
>
>"Lord, I was so angry!" I sobbed. "And I hated You! I hated You! I hated You!"
>
>Then silence. A peaceful silence, as if the Lord had spoken and calmed a stormy sea. My bitter tears of anger became the soft tears of grief. I knew that I hadn't really hated the Lord with my whole heart, but speaking those words to Him released my honest pain. Even though I had beaten on His chest in fury, the Lord still folded His compassionate arms around me.
>
>In time, my view of those awful days began to change. I gradually realized that if Jesus Christ had been visible in our living room that morning, He wouldn't have been sitting in the easy chair watching. That was my distorted view of Him as someone separated from my suffering. The real Jesus would have been doing what I was doing and feeling what I was feeling. "In all their distress," the prophet wrote, "he too was distressed" (Isaiah 63:9 NIV).
>
>I knew then that Jesus Christ—who lives in me—had taken my anger, grief, and fear inside Himself. He absorbed it on the cross. His passion was united with His promises.[16]

POSITIVE WAYS OF DEALING WITH ANGER

What can you do about anger? First of all, accept it. Break out of the repressive mode. It has a message for you, and it isn't to be denied. It's there for a reason: to point out the need to resolve the cause.

So discover the reason for your anger. What is the real cause in each situation? As you look at each situation or encounter in which you are angry, ask yourself, "What is bothering me, and what would I like to change?" Then ask, "What can I do to change?"

Sometimes our anger response is different with different individuals. You may argue with one individual, yell at another, use silent withdrawal from another, push intensely toward another, and distance yourself physically and emotionally from someone else. Which do you do with whom, and why? Who sees you as angry? Who never sees your anger? Which persons do you want to know about your anger?

You can learn the difference between expressing your anger aggressively and expressing it assertively. You can learn when you are using anger to defend and when you are using it to blame. Once you are able to express your anger without yelling, blaming, or attacking, you will feel better about what you are saying, and others will hear you more clearly. Later in this book you will learn the steps involved in the process.

When you express your hurt and disappointment in honest, controlled, and constructive ways, other people will be freed to be just as honest with you. Then growth in your relationships can occur. Relationships can survive and even improve when disagreements are handled properly. When you express anger properly it will have the effect of exposing you to the criticism and challenges of others. It will force you to stop blaming other people and consider your own responsibilities for change. If you suppress anger or explode it won't provide the advantage of constructive expression that opens you up to an evaluation of your own behavior. Suppression and constant defensive anger are ineffective ways of dealing with anger.

Don't apologize for your anger. If it's there, accept it. It's yours. Use it for change. As a woman, you need not be uncomfortable with the anger you feel. Instead, see it as a messenger telling you about the cause. Then, with God's love and help, tackle the cause.

NOTES

1. Harriet Goldhor Lerner, *The Dance of Anger: A Woman's Guide to Changing Patterns in Intimate Relationships* (New York: Harper and Row, 1985), 3.

2. Adapted from Jon Tevlin, "Why Women Are Mad As Hell" *Glamour,* March 1992, 207–9.

3. This paragraph and the next are adapted from *When Anger Hits Home,* p. 149.

4. Ibid., 209.

5. Adapted from Herb Goldberg, *The Hazards of Being Male: Surviving the Myth of Masculine Privilege* (New York: Signet, 1976), 10–16.

6. This and the next five paragraphs closely follow Gary Jackson Oliver and H. Norman Wright, *When Anger Hits Home: Taking Care of Your Anger Without Taking It Out on Your Family* (Chicago: Moody, 1992), 20–21.

7. Adapted from Matthew McKay, Peter D. Rogers, and Judith McKay, *When Anger Hurts* (Oakland, Calif.: New Harbinger, 1989), 207–25.

8. Adapted from Kathy Olson, *Silent Pain* (Colorado Springs: NavPress, 1992), 11–13.

9. Ibid., 26.

10. Ibid., 26–27.

11. Adapted from Jeanne Plas and Kathleen Hoover-Dempsey, *Working Up a Storm: Anger, Anxiety, Joy and Tears on the Job* (New York: Norton, 1988), 41–42.

12. "Depression Strikes Women More," *Tyler Morning Telegraph,* 12 December 1990.

13. Adapted from Olson, 62–63.

14. H. Norman Wright, *Always Daddy's Girl: Understanding Your Father's Impact on Who You Are* (Ventura, Calif.: Regal, 1989), 92.

15. Linda Schierse Leonard, *The Wounded Woman: Healing the Father-Daughter Relationship* (Boston and London: Shambhala, 1982; Athens, Ohio: Ohio Univ. Press, 1982), 120.

16. Olson, 58–59.

CHAPTER TWO

Women and Their Emotions

For close to a year I've been frustrated, confused, discouraged, and dejected," Ann said as she began her first couneling session. "I've been able to handle those emotions," she continued, "but the reason I've come to see you is that in the last couple of months I've found myself experiencing a lot of anger."

She looked down at the floor, and after a pause she continued. "To be totally honest, in the past couple of months I've lost control several times. I've yelled at my husband and the kids. I've thrown things. I've stomped out of the house. And it really scares me to death. I don't understand it, and I don't know what to do about it. What's worked in the past isn't working anymore."

For most of her life Ann had prided herself on her ability to control her emotions. She saw herself as a strong and stable person. She rarely let things bother her, and she valued this ability as a sign of spiritual maturity. From Ann's point of view her only problem was the seemingly sudden appearance of anger and her inability to control it.

As she talked about her concerns over her anger it became clear that her problem wasn't only with the emotion of anger. Her difficulty with anger was merely a surface manifestation of a deeper problem. Like many people we've worked with, she had a limited understanding of and many misconceptions about emotions.

"As women we're supposed to be the experts on emotions. But I feel like I'm anything but an expert," Ann said with a tone of dejected resignation. "It seems to me that I experience more emotions than my husband does. I know I talk about them more than he does. But I sure don't understand them!"

Several weeks after Ann had first come in to see me, a recently divorced mother of two asked me during a counseling session, "Dr. Oliver, I know I'm supposed to be an expert on emotions, but right now I have no idea what I'm feeling—except bad."

"Carol," I asked, "who told you that you are supposed to be an expert on emotions?" She pondered my question for a few seconds and then responded, "Well, everyone knows that women are more emotional than men."

Ann and Carol are representative of the thousands of women Norman Wright and I have worked with and surveyed. They believed that because they were women they should somehow understand and be experts on their emotions—and not just their emotions, but also the emotions of everyone around them.

They were the subtle victims of some of the widespread misbeliefs about women, men, and emotions. In their extreme form some of these misbeliefs include the following:

- God designed women to be more emotional than men.
- God designed women to have different emotions than men.
- God designed women to feel but not think. He made men to think but not feel.

- God designed women to be right-brain. He made men to be left-brain.
- God designed women to be nurturing. He made men to be competitive.

Although most of these misbeliefs are unconscious, they can have a powerful influence on how women act and the kinds of expectations women place on themselves.

WHAT EXACTLY ARE EMOTIONS?

In the first chapter we introduced the issue of anger, its causes, and some of the ways we can handle it. But in order to understand and deal with anger, we must first understand what emotions are, where they come from, how God designed them to function, how sin has damaged them, and what we can do about them. We need also to know the relative importance of emotions and when we can trust them and when we cannot. We need to know how feelings relate to thinking and how much weight we should give to each one in making our decisions. These are some of the matters we will deal with in this chapter.

Webster's defines *emotion* as "a psychic and physical reaction subjectively experienced as strong feeling and physiologically involving changes that prepare the body for immediate vigorous action." The English word *emotion* is derived from the Latin word *emovare,* which means "to move," or having to do with motion, movement, and energy. I have heard one speaker say that emotion could be spelled "E-motion," since emotions are energy in motion.

Dorothy Finkelhor, author of *How to Make Your Emotions Work for You,* says that emotions are the

motivating forces of our lives, driving us to go ahead, pushing us backward, stopping us completely, determining what we do, how we feel, what we want, and whether we get what we want. Our hates, loves, fears, and what to do about them are determined by our emotional structure. There is nothing in our lives that does not have the emotional factor as its mainspring. It gives us power or makes us weak, operates for our benefit or to our detriment, for our happiness or confusion.[1]

The psalmist states in Psalm 139:14, "I am fearfully and wonderfully made" (NIV). Nowhere is the delicate complexity of God's creation more evident than in our emotional makeup. Our emotions are complex. The experience of emotions involve sensory, skeletal, motor, autonomic, and cognitive aspects. Our emotions influence the spiritual, social, intellectual, and physical parts of our lives.

WHAT ARE SOME OF THE MOST COMMON EMOTIONS?

Whereas some people find it hard to define what emotions are, others find it difficult to name more than five or six emotions. In seminars and workshops I've asked participants to make a list of frequently experienced emotions. The lists that various groups have come up with have had as few as eleven and as many as eighty-two different examples of what they considered emotions. I might add that the group that came up with only eleven was a group of men and the group that came up with eighty-two was a group of women. Here are some of the most frequently listed emotions.

loved	happy	pleased
surprised	confused	confident
anxious	concerned	indifferent
fearful	hurt	frustrated
embarrassed	frightened	humiliated
angry	appreciated	accepted
excited	grieved	confused
scared	lonely	proud
bored	glad	elated
worried	delighted	uncomfortable
shamed	generous	depressed
ticked	sad	terrified

CHARACTERISTICS OF EMOTIONS

If we are to move toward emotional maturity, there are certain characteristics of emotions we need to be aware of. One of the most helpful ways to understand emotions is to look at what they have in common.[1]

- *All emotions were created by God.*

The best place to start is where the Bible starts. And that's with Creation. Genesis 1:26–27 (NIV) reads:

> Then God said, "Let us make man in our image, in our likeness, and let them rule over the fish of the sea and the birds of the air, over the livestock, over all the earth, and over all the creatures that move along the ground." So God created man in His own image, in the image of God he created him; male and female he created them.

When God made us in His image He gave us a mind, a will, and emotions. Our mind gives us the ability to think. Our emotions provide the ability to feel. Our will allows us the opportunity to choose. God intentionally designed the three parts of our person to work together in balance and harmony. Like the legs of a three-legged milking stool, each dimension of our personality is important and necessary.

Although we can talk about the mind, will, and emotions as separate entities, it is critical for us to remember that, by God's design, they are intricately interrelated. The choices we make influence what we feel. Our emotions influence what we think and the decisions that we make. Our thoughts, or the mental interpretations we make of events around us, influence how we feel and the choices we make.

It is helpful to understand that the Bible uses the word *heart* to refer to personality as a whole as well as to all three of its components. Here is an analysis of some of the various ways and the number of times the Hebrew and Greek words for heart are used:[2]

Sense	Old Testament	New Testament
Personality	257	33
Emotional State	166	19
Intellectual Activity	204	23
Volition	195	22

Most of the decisions we make are based on certain kinds of information. That information comes from two primary sources. Our emotions and our mind are two different yet equally valuable ways of experiencing and understanding life. They provide us with two different kinds of information about ourselves and the world around us. They can balance each other out. When our mind and emotions work together we are more likely to make wise choices.

Although God designed our mind, will, and emotions to work in harmony, sin has seriously complicated the picture. Sin brought a division between God and humanity. It brought disharmony between male and female into the picture. And it produced a division within each one of us.

• Mind and emotions are both important.

As a consequence of the Fall and the effect of sin in our lives, our mind, will, and emotions have become damaged and distorted. This damage is especially evident in relation to our mind and our emotions. God designed them to work together in a complimentary relationship, but they are often seen as opposing one another. One of the many effects of sin has been to produce in each of us a tendency to prefer one over the other, sometimes even to the exclusion of the other.

Error #1: Mind is more important than emotions. Those who fall into this error emphasize the mind and believe that emotions are untrustworthy and unreliable. I once heard a well-known preacher say, "You can't base your decisions on your emotions. Emotions change, but God's Word never changes. There is no room for emotionalism in the mature Christian life." This pastor had good intentions, but he built an artificial and unbiblical dichotomy between the mind and emotions, saying that the mind is good but emotions bad.

That pastor, and others like him, see emotions only as a necessary evil. It is good to be aware of emotions, they say, but one shouldn't take them too seriously. When it comes to making decisions, ignore your feelings. They are fickle, changeable, unreliable, and only get you into trouble. Only flakes or people who don't know how to think rely on their emotions.

Unfortunately, many evangelicals have bought into this error. They see the mind as good, emotions as bad. Emotions are the "black sheep" of our personality. I have heard emotions described as something "caused by the Fall, and a cause of many people's downfall." Emotions are seen at best as unimportant and at worst as a mark of immaturity.

In our experience, men are more likely to fall into Error #2. This can bias many men's perspective. I have worked with many men who believe that if they feel strongly about what they're saying, even if they can't give good reasons for it, they're being rational. Or course, from their perspective if a woman does the same thing, she is being irrational, illogical and, even worse, emotional. Why? Because she is a woman.

If you carry Error #1 a bit further you can end up with the even more absurd conclusion that, since the mind is more reliable than emotions, and since men are better at thinking than feeling, the gender orientation known as masculinity is by definition better and more reliable than femininity. It is hard to believe that people actually believe this, but they do.

When we elevate the mind to a position of superiority and relegate the emotions to the servants' quarters we are splitting our personality in a way God never intended. We are trading in our emotional birthright for an intellectual mess of pottage. That is a trade God never asks us to make.

Error #2: Emotions are more important than mind. For people who succumb to the error of emphasizing emotions over matter, emotions are the measuring stick of life. All feelings are factual and valid. They have the final word. The motto of this group: "If I don't feel like it, I shouldn't do it. God doesn't want me to be a phony."

Whereas Error #1 involves downgrading the emotions, Error #2 involves downgrading the mind. Those who emphasize the mind are viewed as hard, cold, insensitive, unkind, and uncaring. Their only concern is for the "bottom line." For them, things are much more important than people.

This error was well illustrated by a cartoon showing a husband and wife in an argument. The wife turns to the husband and says, "Anyone who has to resort to logic must be pretty unsure of himself."

Feelings are important. But they were never meant to be the absolute standard of truth, the infallible guide to what is right, the source of all our decisions and actions. C. S. Lewis wrote that "no natural feelings are high or low, holy or unholy in themselves. They are all holy when God's hand is on the rein. They all go bad when they set up on their own and make themselves into false Gods."[3] It is important to be aware of and acknowledge our emotions but they are only a part of who God made us to be. In a different essay Lewis observed that "feelings come and go, and when they come a good use can be made of them: they cannot be our regular spiritual diet."[4]

Although both men and women can fall prey to Error #2, most would agree that women are more likely to fall into this category than men. In her book *Women and Their Emotions* Miriam Neff has written:

> I've heard it said that women are more in tune with their feelings and more sensitive than men. I'm not so sure about that. I am sure about one thing: we more frequently allow our emotions to lead us. While men are thinking about what should be done, we're sorting out how we feel about it. We're likely to act based on those feelings before we've applied our minds to the issue at hand. The marriage of our minds and our emotions equals what Scripture refers to as the heart. Bridging the gap is

marrying the mind to the emotions and placing them both under God's control.[5]

Which of the two errors is most characteristic of how you function? Where did you learn that this was the "right" way to be? How about your same-sex parent and your opposite-sex parent? If you are married, which is most characteristic of your spouse?

Both Error #1 and Error #2 reveal a major misunderstanding of the biblical teaching on how God designed us to function. In the last two sentences of the quote above Neff captures the challenge that faces each of us: the marriage of our minds and our emotions so that they work together to give direction to the choices we make.

True spiritual maturity involves the whole person. It is impossible to be spiritually mature and emotionally or intellectually immature. It is not a matter of mind over emotions or emotions over mind. True maturity involves a balance of heart, head, and will; of feeling, thinking, and doing. Each is important. Each was designed by God for our good. Each is a manifestation of the image of God in us.

William T. Kirwan says:

> "Facts" and "feelings" are part of the same process. The brain does not separate feelings from facts or facts from feelings. There is little distinction between the two: all feelings are psychological and neurological arousal attached to facts. . . . Nor does the Bible make a distinction between facts and feelings. . . . We deal not with facts or feelings, but with facts and feelings. . . . By seeing emotions or feelings as a key aspect of the heart we see that they are also a key part of one's being. As a key to being, they are of vital importance in the life of the Christian.[6]

• *Everyone (including men) has emotions.*

Everyone has emotions. It doesn't matter if you are male or female, young or old, black or white, rich or poor—we all experience and, to a greater or lesser degree, express emotions. Not only do we all have emotions, but we all have the capacity to experience the full range of emotions.

One of the misbeliefs about emotions is the idea that there are male and female emotions. Recently I have had several women tell me, in a humorous vein, that men have only two emotions: lust and anger. At the same time I have had several men, in a more serious vein, tell me that there are male emotions and female emotions.

Although men and women are different, we aren't as different as some would have us believe. Carol Tavris notes that while both sexes go through certain developmental phases at different ages, the differences between them eventually disappear. As adults, men and women do not differ significantly in maturity of thought, complexity of reasoning, or in moral reasoning.[7]

- *Emotions aren't good or bad, healthy or unhealthy.*

One of the most dangerous misconceptions about emotions is the idea that some emotions are good and some are not. In reality, emotions can be experienced as negative or positive, painful or pleasurable, but there aren't any "bad" emotions. There are only "bad" or unhealthy expressions of them.

- *Emotions have a physical effect.*

I can't count the number of times I have heard a sincere (though sincerely wrong) person say to his or her spouse, "Honey, it's all in your head." That is one of the most common misbeliefs about emotions. It is true that emotions are in our heads, but they are also in the rest of our bodies as well.

The experience of emotions involves changes in our central and peripheral nervous systems that include a variety of chemicals and neurotransmitters. When you experience emotions, your heart may beat faster, the pupils in your eyes may dilate, you may experience an increase in perspiration, you may tremble, tears may come to your eyes, you may get goose bumps, and you may experience a tremendous surge of energy or feel totally drained.

Not only is there a powerful physiological component to our emotions, but how we deal with our emotions can have a positive or negative effect on our health. For many years medical research has documented the role that a misuse of emotions can play in the disease process. However, up until now little had been said about the potential role emotions can play in the process of healing.

In *Anatomy of an Illness As Perceived by the Patient* Norman Cousins describes how he was healed from a painful disease in part through positive emotional experiences.[8] Specifically, he increased his laughter and optimism by watching Marx brothers movies. His conclusion was that there is more to medicine than expensive pills and sophisticated equipment.

Although Cousins's book was a best-seller and he became popular on the speaking circuit, many wrote him off as a kook. When in 1978 he accepted a position as adjunct professor in the School of Medicine at the University of California at Los Angeles, there was grumbling in some quarters of the medical profession. And when he published a survey of Los Angeles residents in the New England Journal of Medicine that emphasized the importance of a doctor's compassion and communication to a patient's well-being, some physicians were furious.

Now Cousins has moved past testimonies and anecdotes. In *Head First: The Biology of Hope,* he documents research being done at UCLA, as well as at a dozen other US universities, that demonstrates the role emotions can have in the war against disease.[9] The findings of an increasing number of studies are showing that the healthy use of emotions can aid in the healing and recovery process.

In *Redbook* magazine Henry Dreher discusses the results of research that suggests that the inability to express emotions may play a role in weakening the body's defenses. People prone to this problem tend to be self-deprecating, nice to a fault, and unable to express their frustration and anger. He notes that "many people who contract cancer seem to be out of touch with their emotions and their own needs and desires as individuals."[10]

- *If we understand and control our emotions, we can make them work for us rather than against us.*

It doesn't matter how important or unimportant we think they are. It doesn't matter how much we are aware of them. Whether we like it or not, for better or for worse, our emotions play a major role in our lives. One thing is clear: If we don't understand and control our emotions they will control us.

Carol came into my office and with a heavy sigh began to describe what had been happening to her. I could tell that she was discouraged and frustrated, but for the first twenty minutes the conversation was about everyone else but her. Finally I asked, "Carol, what are you feeling?" My question clearly caught her off guard.

She paused for a moment and then continued, "I wish I knew what I could do to help Susan [her good friend] get over her depression." After a few more minutes I repeated my question, "Carol, what are *you* feeling?" She had been so focused on trying to understand everyone else she had forgotten to take a look at herself. She was one of those dependent individuals who had become sensitive to everyone's feelings but her own.

The emotionally overcontrolled person. Some people suffer from the disease of overcontrolled emotions. When we are out of touch with our emotions we are out of touch with our true needs. We become "other-focused" in the unhealthy sense of the word. Gradually we loose a sense of ourselves and can become emotionally dependent on and addicted to others.

It can get to the point that we allow others to define who we are. In these kinds of relationships our significance and security are determined not by who we are in Christ, nor by what He accomplished for us on the cross, nor by what God has to say about us. The basis for our sense of significance and security is determined by the "significant other" in our lives.

People in this condition tend to gravitate towards dependent/independent relationships. Here are some of the characteristics of these individuals:

The Self	**The Other**
is emotionally overavailable	is emotionally unavailable
focuses on others	focuses on themselves
gives encouragement, support, money, time, etc.	gives little, if anything, to anyone
their needs are rarely met	their needs are being met
gives much more than 50 percent	gives much less than 50 percent
gives up or loses power	maintains and gains power
validates the other	is validated by others
tolerates inappropriate behavior	often engages in inappropriate behavior
attaches or becomes enmeshed with the other	detaches or moves away (disengaged) from the other[11]

According to women leaders we surveyed, this is a special problem for women. In the dependent/independent relationships who do you suppose is most often in the "dependent" role? That's right. The woman. Some women have an advanced case of overcontrolled emotions.

With the best of intentions these women become sensitive to everyone's feelings but their own. Even if they are encouraged to be aware and sensitive, it is usually to tune into the emotions and reactions of others. But then they become diverted from examining and expressing their own emotions. Women need to apply their highly developed capacity for understanding to themselves as well as others. They need to be in touch with their own God-given emotions.

The emotionally out-of-control person. The opposite of the overcontrolled individual is the emotionally out-of-control person. These are the ones we tend to hear about on the news and read about in the paper. When we let the river of emotion get out of control it can flood its banks and wreak havoc.

It was the summer of 1981. My wife, Carrie, and I had only been married about six months. Our first home was a delightful old farmhouse near Grand Island, Nebraska. It wasn't that unusual to have a tornado watch, which means that a tornado is possible. However, it was much rarer to have a tornado warning, which means that a tornado is probable so take cover.

That night there was a tornado watch that turned into a tornado warning. Before going down to our basement I went out on the front porch. The sky was a greenish tint, and there was an eerie stillness in the air. After about an hour the all-clear sounded, and we came upstairs. We looked outside and didn't see anything, so assumed that nothing had happened.

Little did we know that only five miles away a family came up from their basement at the sound of the all-clear to find that their entire two-story home had been lifted off of its foundations and blown away. A few miles away in Grand Island several tornados had created massive destruction.

If you see a tornado you know it is probably going to hit land at some point. You may not know where or when it's going to land, but you do know that when it does, you don't want to be anywhere close to it. That's what being around an out-of-control person is like.

The overcontrolled/out-of-control person. Some people are both overcontrolled and out of control. Most of the time they are overcontrolled, but every now and then they get out of control. Being close to a person like that makes life, at best, chaotic.

I grew up in Long Beach, California. When I was a teenager there was an amusement park downtown called "The Pike." The Pike had was what was billed as the "World's Largest Roller Coaster," the "Cyclone Racer." It only cost a quarter to ride it. One Saturday, after saving up as many quarters as we could, a friend and I took the bus downtown and rode the "Cyclone Racer" over twenty times. It was great!

A roller coaster is a lot of fun to ride on. But I wouldn't want to try to live on one of them. Being married to a person who swings from overcontrolled emotions to out-of-control emotions is like trying to live on a roller coaster.

- *Emotional maturity can increase our effectiveness.*

Dr. Alice Isen, a psychologist at the University of Maryland, has spent more than seventeen years studying the ways in which positive emotions affect the way people think. Her research suggests that positive emotions not only make people more helpful and generous toward others, but appear to improve thinking processes such as judgment, problem-solving, decision-making, and creativity.

> Good feelings seem capable of bringing out our better nature socially and our creativity in thinking and problem-solving. . . . They are a potential source of interpersonal cooperativeness and personal health and growth. Our studies have implications for classrooms, businesses, relationships or any situation where you want to bring out the best in someone. . . . Positive emotions encourage people to look beyond the normal problem-solving method to try different options.[12]

- *Shared emotions are the currency of healthy relationships.*

Our research has shown that women like to talk about emotions more than men do. That wasn't any big surprise. It simply confirmed the results of other research we've seen. Women reported that the emotional quality of a relationship seemed more important to them than to their husbands. They say that talking about their emotions helps them sort out their feelings and express closeness.

Actually, shared emotions aren't only important for women. For all of us, female and male, emotions need to be communicated.

- *"Emotional" is not a dirty word.*

What do you think of when you hear the word *emotional?* Is your first response a positive or a negative one? Has anyone ever called you "emotional"? Do you remember the last time it happened? What was the context? Were they giving you a compliment? Did you respond by saying "Thank you. I'm so pleased that you noticed." Or did you take it as a criticism or put-down? Was the person who labeled your behavior emotional a man or a woman? Does the gender of the person using the word emotional affect how you interpret its meaning?

When most people use the word *emotional* they are referring to someone's behavior. "Stop being so emotional." "You are starting to sound emotional." It's also used to describe an enduring characteristic of a person. "She is just an emotional person."

There doesn't seem to be any clear definition for the word *emotional.* Its definition seems to be influenced by the behavior of the person who is being described and the intentions of the one who is doing the labeling. Being labeled "emotional" has something to do with the frequency, intensity, duration, and appropriateness of a response.

What is clear is that the label "emotional" is most often used in a negative context. It is often used in an attempt to influence or control a person's behavior. An emotional person is often considered irresponsible, immature, and irrational. We have done a word association with several women's groups for the word *emotional* and some of the terms most frequently associated with it include *out of control, immature, irresponsible, irrational,* and *childish.*

Several years ago the *San Francisco Chronicle* conducted a survey of their male readers' opinions about women. The survey was designed to reveal what men want and don't want from women. When the men were asked what they disliked most about women, can you guess their major complaint? Was it that women work too hard? That they aren't social enough? That they are too rational? That they aren't involved enough at home?

What came out in front of the men's complaints were frustrations regarding women's emotional behavior. Women's nagging was first, with 44 percent of the men listing it as their major irritation. The second most common problem, with a 39 percent response, was that "women get too emotional when I argue."

One writer asked, "Why is it 'arguing' when he does it, but 'getting emotional' when she does it? Why does the word 'nagging' immediately bring to mind the picture of an unstable woman building toward an emotional tirade?"[13]

While ours wasn't a rigorous scientific survey it did tap into one of the most common gender stereotypes. Men are portrayed as calm, cool, and rational even in the face of great danger. Their emotional displays are limited to righteous anger and awh-shucks, tongue-tied expressions of love. Women, on the other hand, swoon with emotions at the slightest provocation. They'll even cry over television commercials. Emotions of all qualities and quantities are her trademark. It doesn't matter that there are numerous exceptions to the stereotype. It is still alive and well.

When did the term *emotional* get this bad reputation? If it's bad to "get all emotional," what is the problem? Is it with our emotions? Or is it with how we at times choose to express our emotions? Emotional maturity is not about whether or not we should experience our emotions. It's more about understanding what we are feeling, determining the appropriateness of that emotion, and then choosing how to express it.

In this book we will show you how to do that with the emotion of anger. How to understand it, determine it's appropriateness, and then how to express it in ways that help and heal rather than in ways that hurt.

TAKE ACTION

Here is the survey on anger beliefs that well over a thousand women completed. Before going on to the next chapter, please take a few minutes and complete it for yourself. You'll find it helpful in applying the information that follows.

ANGER BELIEFS

Please read through the following list of anger beliefs. If, at any time in your life, you have either outwardly agreed to a particular belief or, by your actions, have functioned according to it, circle the number that most accurately expresses the degree of your agreement with that belief.

1 = Strongly Agree   3 = Neutral   4 = Moderately Disagree
2 = Moderately Agree   5 = Strongly Disagree

1. God is love and anger is the opposite of   1   2   3   4   5
love. Therefore, God is against anger. Whenever we allow ourselves to be angry, we are sinning.

2. If a person never looks or sounds angry,   1   2   3   4   5
she doesn't have a problem with anger.

3. Anger always leads to some form of vio-   1   2   3   4   5
lence and, therefore, it is never good to be angry.

4. If you express anger to someone you   1   2   3   4   5
love, it will destroy the relationship. Anger and love don't mix.

5. The best way to deal with anger is to ig-   1   2   3   4   5
nore it. If you ignore it, it will go away.

6. The best way to deal with anger is to stuff   1   2   3   4   5
it. Expressing anger breeds even more anger and leads to loss of control.

7. The best way to deal with anger is to 1 2 3 4 5 dump it. Just get all of that anger out of your system. You and everyone else will feel better when you express it.

8. Nice people don't get angry. 1 2 3 4 5

* *

9. T F It is more acceptable for men to express anger than women.

10. T F I often feel guilty about my anger.

11. T F I don't know how to express my anger appropriately.

12. T F I wish I weren't such an angry person.

13. T F I'm afraid that if I get in touch with my anger I will lose control.

14. T F It's hard for me to know when I'm angry.

15. What are some of the factors that increase your vulnerability to anger?

1.   3.

2.   4.

16. When you hear the word *anger*, do you tend to have a positive or a negative response to that word?

☐ Positive   ☐ Negative

17. From your point of view, is anger primarily a positive or a negative emotion?

☐ Positive   ☐ Negative

18. When I get angry, I . . .

19. When someone around me gets angry, I . . .

20. When I was a child, the primary *times* in which I saw anger expressed were:

21. The *ways* in which I saw anger expressed were:

22. Who taught you how to *become* angry?

23. Who taught you how to *express* anger?

24. If there is **any** one question that I could have answered about anger, it would be:

NOTES

1. Dorothy C. Finkelhor, *How to Make Your Emotions Work for You* (Berkeley: Medallion, 1973), 23–24.
2. Cited in William T. Kirwan, *Biblical Concepts for Christian Counseling: A Case for Integrating Psychology and Theology* (Grand Rapids: Baker, 1984), 46–47.
3. C. S. Lewis, *The Great Divorce* (New York: Macmillan, 1946, 1978), 92–93.
4. "The World's Last Night," *The World's Last Night and Other Essays* (New York: Harcourt, Brace, Jovanovitch, 1962), 109.
5. Miriam Neff, *Women and Their Emotions* (Chicago: Moody, 1983), 13–14.
6. Kirwan, 46–53.
7. Adapted from Carol Tavris, *The Mismeasure of Woman* (New York: Simon & Schuster, 1992), 294.
8. Norman Cousins, *Anatomy of an Illness As Perceived by the Patient: Reflections on Healing and Regeneration* (New York: Norton, 1979).

9. Norman Cousins, *Head First: The Biology of Hope and the Healing Power of the Human Spirit* (New York: Penguin, 1990).

10. Adapted from Henry Dreher, "Do You Have a Type-C (cancer-prone) Personality?" *Redbook*, May 1988, 108, 109, 158, 160.

11. Adapted from Martha R. Bireda, "AACD Individual-Study Program," *Love Addiction: Developing Emotional Independence* (Alexandria, Va.: AACD, 1991), 3–4.

12. Alice Isen, quoted by A. J. Hostetler, "Feeling Happy, Thinking Clearly," *APA Monitor*, 6–7.

13. Stephanie A. Shields in Carol Tavris, ed., *Every Woman's Emotional Well-Being: Heart and Mind, Body and Soul* (New York: Prentice Hall, 1986), 131.

CHAPTER THREE

Why Is Anger
the Forbidden Emotion?

omehow, when I was a little girl I learned that anger was the forbidden emotion. Especially for little girls." With a halting voice and misty eyes Janet, a forty-two-year-old mother of four continued, "Whenever I expressed anger as a child my parents would emotionally withdraw from me." At an early age she learned that love was based on her performance. It was conditional. When she expressed anger love was removed. It didn't take long for her to associate expressing anger with abandonment and rejection. The unconscious lesson was "If I express anger I won't be loved."

As a child, Janet concluded that it didn't pay to express anger. And she learned to fear her anger. "I knew that any expression of my anger would bring the disapproval of those I loved." Instead of learning how to use her anger to clarify and strengthen her own identity, she learned how to pursue excellence in ignoring her anger. She discovered that what did pay was learning how to read people and give them what they wanted. She became a people-pleaser. She learned how to perform. Everyone referred to her as a "nice girl."

What brought Janet into counseling was that now, as an adult, she was finding it harder and harder to control her temper. "Things will go along great for several weeks, and then —sometimes over the tiniest provocation—I'll lose it," she told me. "At first it would build gradually. But lately, all of a sudden I find myself shouting, screaming, snapping at my kids, or lashing out at Larry.

"I look at the way I am traumatizing my family, and I feel guilt and shame. After each episode I feel terrible about myself. I bend over backwards to make up for what I've done. I ask them to forgive me. Yet with each succeeding episode it becomes harder for them to trust me. They're scared because they never know when I'm going to lose it. It becomes harder for me to trust myself. I feel like I'm doing damage to my husband, my kids, and myself."

Janet had spent a lifetime burying her anger, and now, like an emotional Mt. St. Helens, the pressure was getting too strong. It was erupting, and she was having a hard time controlling it. Because she had never learned how to understand and control or direct her anger it was now starting to control her.

Janet's experience is not unique. In our surveys we asked women, "What emotion is the most difficult for you to express?" To an overwhelming degree the number one response was "anger." For many years women have been discouraged from being fully aware of their anger and clearly expressing it. Anger has become, in Janet's words, "the forbidden emotion."

Harriet Goldhor Lerner says, "Sugar and Spice are the ingredients from which we are made. We are the nurturers, the soothers, the peacemakers, and the steadiers of rocked boats. It is our job to please, protect, and placate the world. We may hold relationships in place as if our lives depended on it."[1]

EIGHT MISBELIEFS ABOUT ANGER

Janet, like many of us, had been raised to accept certain beliefs about anger. Unfortunately, most of them were wrong. Of all the emotions, anger is the least understood and most misunderstood—and it's not just women who have been raised with misbeliefs and misunderstandings about anger. All of us have. Some misbeliefs, however, have had a much more negative effect on women. Based on our clinical experience and the results of our surveys and interviews we have identified eight misbeliefs about anger that have had a particularly damaging effect on women.

- *Misbelief #1: The Bible teaches that anger is a sin and something that should be "put away" or avoided. Whenever we allow ourselves to get angry we are sinning.*

This misbelief about anger is one of the most dangerous and absurd of them all. Yet many people believe it. I read it in books, I see it in the lives of people I know, I hear it on the radio and in the counseling room.

"I really don't have anything to be angry and depressed about," Patti said with a deep sigh. "That's why these emotions are so confusing. I know I shouldn't feel this way. But I do!" Patti had asked to see me for help in understanding and dealing with her increasing anger with and resentment toward her husband and children.

Patti and Roger had been married for eight years. They had two preschoolers and one seven-year-old. Roger was a committed husband and father. He held a good-paying job but was on the road a lot. As we talked it became clear that she was frustrated with her life. "I love being a wife and a mother, but is this all there is? There's got to be something more."

If you were the counselor how would you view Patti's situation? What would you see as the problem in her situation? What approach would you take toward it? What is the biblical perspective?

If you believe in lie #1, you would probably say that Patti's anger is unhealthy, inappropriate, and caused by her sin nature or spiritual immaturity. Patti had talked with a speaker at a women's conference who took this approach. The speaker told her that she should be grateful for a husband who was a good provider and for her three healthy children. Her anger and resentment were a natural part of the gift of motherhood, the speaker told her. If she would only "try harder" she would find victory over her anger. God made women to be responders. If she learned to respond better her frustration would decrease. "When you've totally given yourself to the Lord, when you have really laid your life on the altar, you will find your anger disappear," the speaker said. The implication: It's all your fault.

One well-known female Christian leader for whom I have a great deal of respect, though I disagree with her on this point, has written that God tells us that anger is to be "put away" and not "worked through," expressed, or given room. Confess it, give it to God, quit. Anger is a sin, and the church needs to be teaching us that it is not permissible. That's one point of view.

There is another way of looking at this situation. It is possible that much of Patti's anger is healthy, legitimate, appropriate, and realistic. One could argue that with the best of intentions Patti had slipped into a view of motherhood that relegated her to living vicariously through her husband and her children. Her experience of anger was a sign that something was wrong and needed to be discussed. Being a better wife and a better mother doesn't necessarily mean shaming oneself and "trying harder."

Patti had bought into the misbelief that a "good mother" always puts everyone's needs ahead of her own, even to the exclusion of her own. Serving does not mean selling out. Patti didn't have to exchange her God-given uniqueness and giftedness for the career of her husband and the growth and development of her children. She didn't have to settle for an either/or life. It could be both/and.

The apostle Paul challenges the misbelief that all anger is sin when he says: "Be angry, and yet do not sin; do not let the sun go down on your anger, and do not give the devil an opportunity" (Ephesians 4:26–27 NASB). The translators of the *New American Standard* version of the Bible accurately translated the meaning of the original Greek text of verse 26, in which we are given two commands: Do be angry, but don't sin. The first word Paul uses for anger (*orge*) refers to an attitude of anger that is slow in its onset.

When Paul wrote "do not let the sun go down on your anger" he used a word for anger (*parorgismos*) that referred to a stronger form of anger that is characterized by irritation and exasperation. Paul made clear that although it is normal to experience anger, we can choose to express that anger in ways that are not sinful.

It is not a sin to experience anger. However, sin can enter the picture when we don't acknowledge and deal with our anger. If we allow our anger to lead to bitterness, resentment, an unforgiving spirit, or the tendency to make someone else pay for their wrong, we are more likely to express our anger in sinful kinds of ways.

A basic error underlying the anger misbeliefs is the failure to make a distinction between experiencing the emotion of anger and the ways in which we choose to express it. This error plagues many people and keeps them from fully understanding, appreciating, and being able to use this God-given emotion in ways that help and heal rather than in ways that hurt.

In *When Anger Hits Home* we say:

> The experience of anger is a normal and natural one. As part of being made in God's image, humans have emotions, and one of those emotions is anger. Like all of God's gifts, anger has tremendous potential for good. [But because of the Fall and the effects of sin in our lives what God designed for good can be misused.] On the other hand, the expression of anger is optional. We can choose to express our anger in healthy or unhealthy ways—in ways that heal or in ways that hurt. We can allow our anger to dominate and control us, or we can, with God's help and with a little bit of work, learn how to make the emotion of anger work for us rather than against us. We can develop healthy and constructive expressions of anger.

The experience of anger is not optional, but the expression of anger is. I can be angry and sin, or I can be angry and not sin. The sin does not lie in the fact of my experience of the emotion of anger but rather in how I choose to express that anger.[2]

As we mature, God wants to teach us how to balance the emotion of anger with other emotions. In Exodus 34:6 God is described as "compassionate and gracious, slow to anger, and abounding in love and faithfulness" (NIV). The Bible reveals a God who experiences and expresses anger. But He also balances His anger with other emotions, such as gentleness, kindness, compassion, loving-kindness, and truth.

- *Misbelief #2: If you don't look or sound angry, you don't have a problem with anger.*

This misbelief makes the assumption that whenever we experience an emotion we are probably aware of it and cannot help but show it on our face. It is true that some individuals have a difficult time hiding what they feel. Even a stranger can look at them or listen to them and and tell what is going on inside. But there are a lot of people for whom this is not the case.

Over the years I have found that, at times, anger can be caught peeking out from other safer and more innocuous expressions. Here is a sample of some I've collected from my patients. They all have to do with what we say instead of "I'm angry!" Which of these expressions might imply an underlying anger in people who will deny angry feelings?

You always	You never
I'm down in the dumps	I wish that
I'm disappointed	I just don't understand why
It's not fair that	I'm depressed
You should/shouldn't	I'm feeling blue
I'm sick and tired of	When will you ever
I'm sorry	I'm fed up

There are people who frequently are unaware that they are angry, or when when they *are* aware of their anger, have learned to repress, suppress, deny, or ignore it. Do you remember Janet at the beginning of this chapter? She had learned not to admit anger. Anyone who knew Janet would say that she was not an angry person. In some ways that was true. But although Janet was not your typical angry person, she did have a problem with anger.

- *Misbelief #3: Nice girls don't get angry, and if they do get angry, they don't express it.*

Historically, women have been led to believe that it is wrong for them to experience anger. Victorian women, for example, were not supposed to even feel anger, much less express it. Anger and femininity were antithetical. One Victorian author, describing his angry wife, said, "Every womanly emotion—generosity, delicacy, honor—yielded before the demon that held her in his iron fold." Her temper, he said, "stifled the exercise of every womanly and gentle feeling."

The bottom line was that angry women were worse than angry men. As Carol Zisowitz Stearns and Peter N. Stearns put it in *Anger: The Struggle for Emotional Control in America's History:*

> Men, to become angry, certainly must display the justification of a patently unreasonable wife, but at least there were some discussions of the anger felt by decent men, who must, of course, struggle with their anger and overcome it. No such struggle was allowed a woman, for even in feeling anger she proved her bad character.
>
> Anger in women made the Victorians more uncomfortable than did anger in men. A thorough study of the literature of the era reveals that "it was almost impossible to write a story with a good but angry woman, for the Victorians had a failure of imagination in actually conceiving of a woman who could be both."[3]

Experiencing the emotion of anger has nothing to do with being naughty or nice. But when we talk about how we express the emotion of anger, that is a different story. We can choose to express our anger in ways that help, or in ways that hinder; in ways that build, or in ways that destroy. We can be irresponsible and allow the emotion of anger to control us and express that anger in cruel and violent ways. Or we can also be wise and not let the emotion of anger control us, but choose instead to express that anger in healthy and positive ways. That's what this book is all about.

The women we surveyed gave us some additional characteristics of "nice girls." Not only do nice girls not get angry, they are weak, don't have opinions, and don't disagree—especially with men and most especially with regard to theological issues.

The thread linking all these misbeliefs about anger is that being "nice" means staying in the background, being seen but not heard, not making any waves, and making men look good and appear to be smart and strong. All these ideas reflect our society's discomfort with strong women.

In my research for this book I came across an interesting illustration of the problem. The delightful musical *Annie Get Your Gun* is the story of Annie Oakley, a young and confident female sharpshooter. She doesn't believe that femininity is synonymous with inferiority and incompetence. Do you remember the song "Anything You Can Do, I Can Do Better"? When she meets world-class marksman Frank Butler in competition she defeats him. But she also falls in love with him and soon realizes that "you can't get a man with a gun." She deliberately loses her next competition with him, he realizes he loves her, and they live happily ever after. That was the musical version.

There was a real Annie Oakley and Frank Butler, but the true story is a bit different. In 1875, when as a teenager she defeated Frank Butler, he wrote, "It was her first big match—my first defeat. The next day I came back to see the little girl who had beaten me, and it was not long until we were married."[4]

For the next fifty years Annie was the featured sharpshooter in the Buffalo Bill Wild West Show. Frank worked as her manager. They traveled and worked together throughout the United

States and Europe, and they remained deeply in love. Frank was a sensitive man who continued to express his love and affection for Annie in love poems and press interviews. They died in 1926, within eighteen days of each other.

When I read the true story of Annie and Frank I was amazed. I found myself asking, "Why did the creators of the musical dramatically change the true love story?" The most obvious conclusion is that the real story didn't fit the current cultural gender stereotypes of romantic love. Men were supposed to be smarter, stronger, and more competent than women. Obviously the real Frank Butler didn't fit the stereotypic insensitive, inse- cure, and relationally brain-dead mold of masculinity, and so, for the story to be acceptable, what really happened had to be changed. What a sad commentary.

Nice people love. Nice people are compassionate. Nice people are concerned. Nice people can be discouraged. Nice people experience hurt, frustration, and fear. Nice people expe- rience anger. Nice people express their anger in healthy kinds of ways.

- *Misbelief #4: Getting angry is unfeminine.*

Therapist Celia Halas says:

[Anger] is an emotion that women express far less frequently than do men. In fact, men generally feel quite comfortable with anger, express it freely, and are reasonably careless about the problems it causes in other people. . . . Women are generally afraid to express their anger. They have been taught that to do so is unladylike. They fear the reaction they will get if their rage breaks forth.[5]

Men and women do differ in how they express love, anger, and other emotions. However, this difference isn't because women are naturally "emotional" and men naturally "rational," or, as one woman put it, "because women are naturally 'open' and men are by nature 'emotionally brain-dead.'" Research has found few differences between men and women in the kinds of emotions they feel or in how intensely they feel them. Many of the differences in the ways men and women express emotions are the results of cultural expectations. "Women are expected, allowed, and required to reveal certain emotions, and men are expected and required to deny or suppress them."[6]

For many people, expressions of anger and assertiveness are still considered masculine in men and unfeminine in women. There continue to be strong societal prohibitions against female anger. For many women, these prohibitions create deep unconscious anxieties about expressing themselves, disagreeing with men, or being assertive or competitive.

> Unlike male heroes who fight and even die for what they believe in, the angry or aggressive woman may, indeed, repel us all. For what images come to mind? The envious, castrating "man-hater" venting her rage and resentment against men? The passive-aggressive housewife who bitterly dominates and controls her husband from behind the scenes? The infantile, irrational, "hot-tempered" female who hurls pots and pans from across the kitchen and carries on like a hysterical bitch? These familiar images are more than just cruel, sexist stereotypes. They are neurotic positions that real women adopt when intrapsychic and cultural pressures combine to inhibit the direct and appropriate expression of legitimate anger and protest.[7]

It's not necessarily unfeminine, unmasculine, unbiblical or un-Christlike to be angry. The deeper questions are these: What is causing our anger, what we are going to do with that anger, and how will we choose to express it?

- *Misbelief #5: Getting angry is always selfish.*

Many women in our culture have been conditioned to be the caretakers, or custodians, of relationships. Their job is to think of, watch out for, and take care of others. If they do a good enough job taking care of everyone else then maybe, just maybe, someone will take care of them, provide for their happiness, and satisfy their needs.

Lerner writes:

> It is perhaps simpler for all of us to direct our energy toward
> seeking love and approval from others, to enter into relation-
> ships comprised of endless cycles of guilt and blame toward
> the person who is failing to provide for our happiness, and to
> preserve forever the fantasy that some other person can com-
> plete and fulfill us, as the nursing mother does for her child.[8]

Understanding and listening to our anger can make us
aware of danger and help us move out of a position of risk and
vulnerability to a position of safety. The healthy expression of
anger can protect the self. It can decrease the probability of
continuing to be unnecessarily hurt, walked on, taken advantage of, or victimized.

In Philippians 2:3 (AMP) Paul writes: "Let each regard the
others as better than and superior to himself—thinking more
highly of one another than you do of yourselves." Every person
is of infinite worth and value and deserves to honored.

The fact that others are important does not mean that we
are unimportant. God is not glorified when we trample and ignore
who He has created us to be. God "made Him [Christ] who had
no sin to be sin on our behalf, so that we might become the
righteousness of God in Him" (2 Corinthians 5:21 NASB) and
"partakers of the divine nature" (2 Peter 1:4 NASB). Moreover,
believers are "beholding, as in a mirror the glory of the Lord,
[and] are being transformed into the same image" (2 Corinthians 3:18 NASB).

Getting angry can be selfish. It is easy for anyone to get
angry for the wrong reasons. Pride, jealousy, selfishness, a pre-
occupation with "me" to the exclusion of or insensitivity toward "you" are all unhealthy causes of anger.

But anger isn't necessarily selfish. The healthy expression of
legitimate anger can be a statement of dignity and self-respect.
It can also be a statement that what I believe in is so important
that I am willing to take the risk of standing alone, even in the

face of disapproval, rejection, or the threatened lost of support from those I love.

- *Misbelief #6: Anger usually leads to some form of violence, and therefore it is never good to be angry.*

Erika was proud to be able to state that she was not an angry person and that, as far as she knew, she rarely even experienced the emotion of anger. Yet she did admit that she was frequently forgetful, tended to avoid problems, was often late, liked to change the subject, and was skilled in the use of subtle sarcasm.

In providing a brief history of her family-of-origin, Erika indicated that her father had been an alcoholic. She was quick to add that she didn't think that she had been affected by his alcoholism. As we discussed her family in greater detail, Erika began to talk about what it was like being the oldest child in a dysfunctional family—a type of family she had somehow never considered hers as being.

Erika told me how she would wait up for her father on weekend nights. "I would keep my bedroom window open and listen for how he would drive the car into the driveway, how he would slam the car door, the sound of his walking up the steps. . . . Then, of course, I would listen for the sound of his voice and a certain look on his face. Certain nonverbal signs always told me whether or not he would be beating Mom that night. I always knew if I had to gather my brothers and sisters up and get them out of the way." She went on to add, "Whenever Dad got angry he would either beat on Mom or one of us kids."

At an early age, Erika had learned to equate anger and violence. To her, the experience of anger and its expression through violence had become synonymous. Since she had vowed to herself that she would never be like her father, she simply denied any feelings of anger. She thought that if she never got angry she would never be violent. Over a period of several months Erika learned how to distinguish between the experience of anger and the various ways in which anger can be expressed.

She learned that she had indeed frequently experienced the emotion of anger, but had simply found different ways to express it. Although her passive and indirect expressions of anger were not as violent as her father's active and direct expressions of it, both ways of dealing with anger were unhealthy. Erika's denial of anger served to obscure and hide her deepest hurts, needs, and concerns from herself and from those she loved.

- *Misbelief #7: Since God is love, and anger is the opposite of love, it is clear that God is against anger. Anger and love don't mix.*

I have heard numerous people make the statement that anger is the opposite of love. I disagree. Anger isn't the opposite of love. We can choose to express our anger in ways that are unkind and unloving. The real opposite of love is indifference.

Indifference says that nothing is more important than my being safe. Nothing! Indifference doesn't care, or doesn't let itself care. It sits back, waits, watches, plays it safe. It doesn't give, doesn't invest, doesn't get involved, doesn't take risks. Indifference isn't hot or cold—it is lukewarm.

This misbelief says, "If you love me you won't get angry with me." The truth is that a loving relationship includes the freedom for both partners to experience and express their emotions. *All* of them. The fun ones and the painful ones. In a healthy relationship anger is not only permitted, it is encouraged.

Healthy anger can be a powerful, legitimate tool for communicating love. Healthy anger says that something or someone is valuable, important, and worth protecting. You can't have real love without some anger. People in a healthy relationship need to ask themselves, "Do we love and trust each other enough to believe that it's really OK to be angry?"

In the sometimes delightful process of two individuals becoming one it is inevitable that there will be differences. On one hand, those differences are what brought the two together. On the other hand, those differences are the source of their greatest frustrations and pains. Overall, they provide the strength and balance in the relationship. The process of negotiating their differences allows their hearts to be knit together as one and enables them to experience the breadth and depth of what true love can be.

Anger and love are separate emotions, but the deeper the caring the deeper the potential for frustration and hurt, and then anger. By not being in touch with and communicating our anger to one another we don't allow our family or friends to understand our hurts and frustrations. By not sharing our hurts and frustrations we rob each other of the opportunity to better understand the other and thus more effectively minister to him or her.

- *Misbelief #8: I'm afraid to express my anger. If I do I know I'll be shamed, punished, or rejected.*

Some women don't express their anger because they fear retaliation. They fear that admitting their anger will result in abandonment, loss of love, punishment, or revenge. One woman said, "If I express my anger, I'll pay for it. It may be sooner or later, but I'll pay for it." As a consequence, many women have never learned to understand their God-given emotion of anger and don't know how to express anger in healthy and constructive ways.

What are some of the fears or concerns you have in regard to the emotion of anger? Women in a workshop generated the following responses to the question "When I imagine being angry directly I fear . . ."[9]

losing control	losing my job
not being liked	scaring or hurting someone
getting physically hurt	losing my credibility

being called weak   being labeled defensive
being laughed at   feeling guilty
being called overemotional being labeled unprofessional

Many of the women we surveyed reported feeling shamed for even having their own needs and emotions, especially the emotion of anger. Many women said that they still feel guilt and shame when they experience anger. Those painful feelings increase when they assert themselves by saying no or by stating what they need or want.

Webster's defines *shame* as "a disturbed or painful feeling of guilt, incompetence, indecency or blameworthiness." In our experience, this emotion can range from a slight embarrassment to deep humiliation, self-depreciation, self-hate, and even suicidal thoughts.

Healthy shame tells me I did something wrong. Unhealthy shame tells me I am wrong. A person who evaluates his behavior from a healthy shame-base is motivated to learn from a mistake and do something different the next time. A person coming from a toxic shame-base sees his mistake as further evidence that he is a mistake. No matter what he does it will never be enough. Despair and discouragement replace hope.

At times the experience of anger can cause us to feel separate, different, or alone. The expression of anger involves stating the differences between people. Even a healthy expression of anger involves standing on your own two feet, being clear about what is important, and being separate from other people for a time.

When all is said and done, there is some truth to the mistaken idea about anger we are discussing in this section. If we allow ourselves to be vulnerable, we may be taken advantage of. If we show our concern and compassion for others and expose our emotions, someone may interpret that as incompetence and criticize us. If we express our anger we may be shamed, punished, or rejected. It is a real risk.

But it is probable that you have experienced shame, punishment, or rejection even when you haven't expressed your anger. Allowing your fear of those responses to control your behavior keeps you a prisoner of other people's irresponsible behavior. It reinforces their immaturity. And it removes any hope of meaningful communication, understanding, and growth.

Through a healthy expression of your anger you have a greater likelihood of accurately communicating what you really think and how strongly you feel about certain issues. An appropriate expression of anger is much more likely to move the issue into a place where it can be clearly seen, acknowledged, and understood. That provides a basis for resolution of conflicts and the ability to move ahead in a relationship.

THE TIMES, THEY ARE A-CHANGING

The past several years have been characterized by date-rape trials as well as harassment hearings in the judiciary and military arenas. The William Kennedy Smith date-rape trial, the Clarence Thomas–Anita Hill hearings, as well as the Tailhook scandal involving the navy's top-gun pilots have all brought to the surface the outrage many women have felt for years and are only now finally expressing.

A 1990 Virginia Slims poll conducted by The Roper Organization showed that many women are seething. At least half of them are resentful about their lives, their marriages, and their husbands' role and degree of involvement in the family. They are much less likely than before to view men as kind, gentle, and thoughtful, and far more likely to see them as selfish, self-centered, and not interested in their home life. They are "fed up" and even "angrier at men than they were twenty years ago." It's not so much that women are worse off today as that they are much less tolerant of sexism, double standards, various kinds of abuse, prejudice, and harassment—and they are willing to stand up and say so.[10]

The movie *Thelma and Louise* expressed the sense of powerlessness felt by many women today. The title characters were portrayed as victims in a male-dominated world; as used, abused, and taken advantage of by insensitive, arrogant, narcissistic men. In many theaters women in the audience cheered when the characters took revenge on the stereotypical male villains. Many men found the movie degrading and threatening. Some men have found the movie convicting. Whatever the response, a frustration and an anger were expressed that many men and women found shocking and that many of the women themselves didn't understand.

As Jon Tevlin put it in an article in *Glamour* magazine,

> this movie captured the raw emotion of the subjugated class, and feminism, for one glorious tequila-inspired moment, was a powder-blue Thunderbird careening through the American West, with all its intonations of masculinity. The pointed exaggeration of the film became a metaphorical catharsis for women's cumulative anger. "Take that!" it said.[11]

Some people believe that the showdown between Supreme Court nominee Clarence Thomas and Anita Hill most clearly revealed the depth of passion many women still feel about sexual discrimination in private and public life. The fact that a majority of women (as well as men) wound up disbelieving Hill did not change the significance of that event.[12]

Reflecting on those hearings, Toni Morrison, Pulitzer Prize-winning novelist and professor of humanities at Princeton University, observed that "people were upset, not so much about what happened to Hill, but that she talked about it, she spoke up. . . . Anita Hill crossed racial lines. Scratch a little bit and you'll find women share a powerful outrage over unequal treatment."[13]

Even when women's anger is expressed in healthy kinds of ways it is often misunderstood. When some people see the anger of women working for freedom and equal opportunity, they don't see past the anger to the anguish it represents. Patricia Gundry observes that "anger is the only healthy way many women know to express their pain. And it always represents pain: personal, searing, emotional pain."[14]

TAKE ACTION

Listed below are the eight common misconceptions about anger that may sneak into your thought-life or behavior. In the space underneath each misbelief write in your own words the truth about this aspect of anger.

1. The Bible teaches that anger is a sin and something that should be "put away," or avoided. Whenever we allow ourselves to get angry we are sinning.

2. If you don't look or sound angry, you don't have a problem with anger.

3. Nice girls don't get angry, and if they do get angry, they don't express it.

4. Getting angry is unfeminine.

5. Getting angry is always selfish.

6. Anger usually leads to some form of violence, and therefore it is never good to be angry.

7. Since God is love and anger is the opposite of love, God must be against anger. Anger and love don't mix.

8. If I express anger I will be shamed, punished, or rejected.

NOTES

1. Harriet Goldhor Lerner, *The Dance of Anger: A Woman's Guide to Changing Patterns in Intimate Relationships* (New York: Harper & Row, 1985), 2.

2. Gary Jackson Oliver and H. Norman Wright, *When Anger Hits Home: Taking Care of Your Anger Without Taking It Out on Your Family* (Chicago: Moody, 1992), 48.

3. Carol Zisowitz Stearns and Peter N. Stearns, *Anger: The Struggle for Emotional Control in America's History* (Chicago: Univ. of Chicago Press, 1986), 47–48.

4. Butler's memoirs, cited in Bonnie Kreps, *Subversive Thoughts, Authentic Passions: Romantic Love Reconsidered* (San Francisco: Harper & Row, 1990), 78.

5. Cited in Carol Tavris, *Anger: The Misunderstood Emotion* (New York: Simon & Schuster, 1983), 181–82.

6. Adapted from Carol Tavris, *The Mismeasure of Woman* (New York: Simon & Schuster, 1992), 263.

7. Harriet Goldhor Lerner, in *Women in Therapy* (Northvale, N.J.: Jason Aronson, 1988), 60.

8. Ibid., 72.

9. Tavris, *Anger: The Misunderstood Emotion,* 180.

10. Adapted from Jon Tevlin, "Why Women Are Mad As Hell," *Glamour,* March 1992, 206–7.

11. Ibid., 207.

12. Adapted from Nancy Gibbs, "The War Against Feminism," *Time,* 9 March 1992, 50–55.

13. Divina Infusino, "Toni Morrison: This novelist Challenges the Roles of Language, Race, and Gender," *VIS-à—VIS,* July 1992, 54.

14. Patricia Gundry in Alvera Mickelsen, ed., *Women, Authority and the Bible* (Downers Grove, Ill.: InterVarsity, 1986), 18.

CHAPTER FOUR

What Is Anger?

The voices arguing inside her head woke Laura up. This time it was Laura as a young girl arguing with her father. She was frightened by his gruff, raspy voice as he swore and put her down with his sword-like words. They were arguing because Laura was frightened by loud noises, especially ones that sounded like gunfire.

Lowell, her dad, always took advantage of such times. He was a master manipulator and would take advantage of any opportunity to frighten Laura. He seemed to relish the sense of power he had when his angry outbursts caused his youngest daughter to freeze in fear.

Laura loved to daydream, for the freedom she had in her mind, where no one could intrude, was marvelous. There she could be at peace. In the inner world Laura created anything could happen—including finding safety from an angry dad who yelled a lot and got red in the face. She needed her inner world in order to stay safe. Home was not safe when Lowell was there—unless he was asleep.

Since Lowell worked from six in the morning to six at night, Monday through Saturday, Laura had safe time with her mother, Ruth, but even then fear could intrude into her thoughts.

In the sticky spring air of that Texas night, the smell of honeysuckle hung in the air. The howling of mating cats woke Lowell from his tormented sleep. Years ago his back had been broken in a fall from a Santa Fe railroad water tank car that jerked into action before he could get down the ladder. He fell on a pile of rock and crushed his back, which cost him nine months in a body cast. That old injury prevented him from getting a good night's rest, but this night was noisy, too, and that meant trouble.

Lowell rose from his hard bed, cursed the cats under his breath, then went straight to the closet where he kept his .22 rifle. Since the house was in the country almost at the end of the road, there was a lot of open space and no ordinances. Lowell walked out into the backyard, listened for telling sounds, and fired into the darkness. A screech, then silence, as the bullet found its mark. He returned the gun to the closet and himself to the bed for a few more hours of fitful sleep.

When dawn broke Lowell pulled on his shirt and faded blue denim overalls and pushed his flat feet into the old brogues he wore daily. Outside, the dew hung heavy on the vines, grass, and flowers. On the edge of the garden near the rows of foot-high corn lay the cat, still and quiet. Its gray form was stiff from rigor mortis, its fur matted with dirt and thick red blood that oozed from the fatal wound. Lowell picked her up by the tail and walked toward the carport, intending to throw the cat into his truck and haul her away.

Ruth was up early, cooking breakfast, and the smells distracted Lowell from his task. He dropped the cat along the edge of the flower bed and came inside for the bacon-egg-biscuit-and-gravy breakfast that awaited him. By the time he left for work in the El Camino he had forgotten the events of the night before. With her husband fed and gone, Ruth washed the dishes and got ready for another hot day of housework.

Laura awoke, trying to remember if what happened last night was real or a dream. When she had heard the closet door open in the night while the cats fought in the yard, she had done what she had so many times before to "disappear." She pulled the pillow over her head and stuck her fingers in her ears, hoping not to hear the gun go off. How she hated that sound. This morning she was not sure if it had really happened.

Laura's usual routine before breakfast was to inspect the garden to see what miracles had appeared overnight. The holly-hocks were open wide—pink, white, red, and rose colored with big-bodied black and yellow bumblebees already at work inside them gathering nectar. There were giant golden squash blos-soms on the sprawling green vines and tiny white bean flowers in the garden. As Laura ran to the flower bed she spotted Patty's gray fur, the blood almost dried. Stunned, she stopped, caught her breath, then wheeled around and ran to the house, crying.

By the time she reached the back screen door Ruth heard her sobs. She thought Laura must have been stung by a bee as she investigated a flower too closely. If only that were all it was! Sobbing and screaming, Laura ran to her mother. "Why does he do that? Can't he stop shooting long enough to see?" Why had her dad had shot *her* cat and not the stray tom that came courting?

There were no answers then, or ever. Obviously, Lowell had forgotten the cat after breakfast, leaving it to be found by his heartbroken, terrified child. Laura never knew what would be his next target. One day her cat, the next a rabbit. When would it be her turn? Somewhere deep inside she knew her dad would like to turn her into a target also. She felt marked for death as surely as if she wore a red circle on her forehead. At a conscious level Laura did not remember being threatened with the same gun when she was three or four, but in her subcon-scious the threat was stark and real.[1]

Picture yourself as little Laura growing up in this environ-ment. Try to look out through her eyes and feel with her young heart. What kinds of lessons was she learning about life? About male/female relationships? About the role and place of women? About her value and worth? About emotions? About the emotion of anger?

This is a true story. Laura grew up learning that anger was harmful, dangerous, destructive, and something to avoid. And she tried hard to avoid it. For most of her life she repressed, suppressed, stuffed, denied, and ignored anything that even came close to anger. After all, she had learned well the effects of anger by watching her father, Lowell. She knew that nothing good ever came from being angry.

As she got older it became harder and harder for her to deny and stuff her anger. She didn't want it, didn't understand it, didn't know what to do with it, but it was there. She was concerned about her spirituality because she had been raised with the misbelief that "nice Christian girls don't get angry." She had also learned the "no talk" rule. Whatever went on at home should never be talked about to anyone outside of the home. Thus any kind of counseling was out of the question.

Over time she realized that her struggle with the emotion she didn't understand but could no longer deny was affecting almost every area of her life. The walls she had built and the emotional medication of busyness and denial that had for a time been helpful were no longer effective. God used a crisis or, what C. S. Lewis called "a severe mercy," to lead Laura to move beyond her fear and reach out for help.

"I was shocked to discover," Laura said, "that God wanted to use my anger to get my attention, to help me identify issues I needed to face, and to give me the energy to confront and resolve painful memories and corresponding behavior patterns that were keeping me stuck and hindering God's working through me." God used many of the insights we will share in this chapter to help Laura see the emotion of anger from God's perspective.

Laura is far from the only woman who has struggled with understanding anger. Do you remember Ann in chapter 2, who said, "As women we're supposed to be the experts on emotions. But I feel like I'm anything but an expert"? In our surveys and interviews we discovered that many women feel exactly as Ann did, especially when it comes to the emotion of anger. The emotion that women know the least about, feel the most insecure with, and are the most threatened by is—you guessed it —the emotion of anger.

One woman wrote, "I'm not even sure what I need to know about anger. I know the Bible says 'be angry and sin not.' I know that Jesus experienced anger. I also know that every experience I've had of anger has been negative." Another woman wrote, "I've spent most of my life avoiding anger. I've come to realize that has been a big mistake."

The last question in our survey was "If there is any one question that I could have answered about anger, it would be . . ." Here are some of the responses:

What is the emotion of anger?
Why did God create it?
How can anything good come from anger?
Where does my anger come from?
Why is anger such a difficult emotion to deal with?
Why are my anger responses so hard to change?
How can I make my anger work for me rather than against me?

In the following chapters we will be answering each one of those questions. (Additional questions from our survey are listed in the appendix of this book.) But before going any further we need to address the very first question and try to define what anger is. That's right, I said *try* to define it. Why do I say *try*? Because anger is one of the most complex and multidimensional emotions, and thus one of the most difficult to define.

When I have asked groups of people to define *anger*, I have received almost as many different definitions of anger as there were people in the audience. Given the nature of anger, I've found that the most helpful way to define it is by looking at both what it is and what it does.

Webster's defines *anger* as "emotional excitement induced by intense displeasure." *Anger,* the most general term, names the reaction but in itself conveys nothing about intensity or justification or the manifestation of the emotional state.

The English word *anger* is derived from an old Norse word *angre,* which means "affliction." In German, *Arger* is the noun of *arg,* which means "wicked"; thus *Arger* is the emotional response to *wicked* stimuli. In Spanish, *enojar* (to get angry) derives from *en* and *ojo*—"something that offends the eye." In these languages anger refers to uneasiness, displeasure, and resentment.

Here are some additional definitions of anger people have found helpful:

- Anger involves physiological arousal, a state of readiness. When we are angry our body has increased energy that can be directed in whatever way we choose.
- Anger is an intense emotional reaction that sometimes remains largely unexpressed and kept inside, and at other times is directly expressed in outward behavior.
- Anger is a state of arousal that can be experienced differently depending on how the source is perceived.
- Anger is one of many God-given emotions that can be a potentially powerful and positive force for good in our lives.
- Anger is a secondary emotion usually experienced in response to a primary emotion such as hurt, frustration, or fear.
- Anger is a natural and normal response to a variety of life's situations and stresses.
- Anger is a God-given emotion intended to protect and provide energy for developing solutions to life's inevitable problems.
- Anger is the emotional response of our cognitive appraisal and interpretation of an interaction or event.
- Anger—the ability to understand it and appropriately express it—is a sign of emotional and spiritual maturity.

- Anger can serve as a self-protective shield to help us guard against potentially painful events.
- Anger can provide a false sense of protection and control. It can distance us from normal and healthy yet painful emotional responses connected to past or present pains and fears of the future.

Another valuable way of understanding anger is to look at what God's Word has to say about it. When I began to study the emotion of anger I started by looking in the Bible. I was surprised to find that the Word of God has a lot to say about anger and uses a number of different words to describe the various types of anger.

In the Old Testament, the word for anger actually meant "nostril" or "nose." In ancient Hebrew psychology, the nose was thought to be the seat of anger. The phrase "slow to anger" literally means "long of nose." Sometimes people's nostrils can flare as the intensity of their feelings causes physiological changes.

Numerous synonyms for anger are used in the Old Testament. Anger is described as ill-humor and rage (see Esther 1:12), overflowing rage and fury (see Amos 1:11), and indignation (see Jeremiah 15:17). Anger is implied in the Old Testament through such terms as *revenge, cursing, jealousy, snorting, trembling, shouting, raving,* and *grinding the teeth.*

Several words are used for anger in the New Testament. It is critical to understand the distinction between these words. I have had many people remark that the Scripture appears to contradict itself because one verse teaches us not to be angry and another admonishes us to "be angry and sin not." Which is the correct interpretation, and which should we follow?

In the Greek text of the New Testament the most common word for anger is *orge.* It is used forty-five times and means a settled and long-lasting attitude of anger that is slow in its onset but enduring. This kind of anger is similar to coals on a barbecue slowly warming up to red and then white hot and holding that temperature until the cooking is done. But it often includes revenge.

In two places in the New Testament where the term *anger* is used revenge is not included in the meaning. In Ephesians 4:26 we are taught, "Be angry, and yet do not sin; do not let the sun go down on your anger" (NASB). In the Greek, the term used for anger in the first part of this verse (*orge*) is different from the term used for anger in the second half (*parorgismos*), where we are told not to let the sun go down on our anger.

In Mark 3:5 Jesus looks upon the Pharisees "with anger." In this passage and in Ephesians 4:26, the word *anger* refers to an abiding habit of the mind that is aroused under certain conditions against evil and injustice. This is the type of anger Christians are encouraged to have—an anger that does not include revenge or rage.

Another frequently used Greek term for anger in the New Testament is *thumas*. *Thumas* is anger as a turbulent commotion or boiling agitation of feelings. This type of anger blazes up into a sudden explosion, whereas in *orge* there is an occasional element of deliberate thought. *Thumas* is an outburst from inner indignation and is similar to a match that quickly ignites into a blaze but then burns out rapidly. This type of anger is mentioned eighteen times (see, for example, Ephesians 4:31 and Galatians 5:20). This is the type of anger we are called upon to control.

A type of anger mentioned only three times in the New Testament, and never in a positive sense, is *parorgismos*. *Parorgismos* is a stronger form of *orge* and refers to anger that has been provoked. It is characterized by irritation, exasperation, or embitterment. "Do not ever let your wrath—your exasperation, your fury or indignation—last until the sun goes down" (Ephesians 4:26b AMP).

IMPORTANT CHARACTERISTICS OF ANGER

Let's move on to a little different way of looking at anger. What are some of the characteristics of this emotion that are important for us to understand? What do we need to know about anger to help it work for us rather than against us?

- *Anger is a God-given emotion.*

When God made us in His image He gave us a mind, a will, and a bunch of different emotions. No human being— nobody, male or female—is immune from experiencing the full range of human emotions. One of the occupational hazards of being human is that we experience emotions, *all* the emotions, including the basic human emotion of anger. From the nursery to the nursing home the emotion of anger is a universal experience.

The Bible has a good deal to say about the emotion of anger. The first mention of anger occurs in Genesis 4:5, the last in Revelation 19:15. In the Old Testament alone anger is mentioned 455 times, with 375 of those references dealing with God's anger.

The Old Testament reports numerous instances in which God expresses anger or is described as being angry. God is described as being angry with the people of Israel for their unfaithfulness, disobedience, stubbornness, and rebellion. His anger came out of His love for them. It resulted in acts of love, including loving discipline, designed to restore Israel's broken relationship with Him. God's anger revealed how much God really cared. It revealed His compassion. It revealed His patience. It revealed Himself.

- *Anger is a secondary emotion.*

Anger is an almost automatic response to any kind of pain. It is the emotion most people feel shortly after they have been hurt. When you trip and fall or stub your toe, it hurts, and you may experience mild anger. When your spouse forgets a birthday or anniversary, it hurts. When a good friend says she will meet you for lunch and then doesn't show up, it hurts, and you may experience anger.

When your teenaged son or daughter is out two hours past his or her 11:00 P.M. curfew and hasn't called, you may experience concern and fear. When he or she waltzes in the door and calmly announces, "Sorry, Mom, I forgot to call," you may experience anger.

Anger is often the first emotion we see. Sometimes it's the only emotion that we are aware of. However, it is rarely the only one we have experienced. Just below the surface are almost always other, deeper emotions that need to be identified and acknowledged. Hidden deep underneath surface anger are fear, hurt, frustration, disappointment, vulnerability, and longing for connection.

At a very early age many of us learned that anger can help us divert attention from those more painful emotions. Anger is safer. It provides a sense of protection for the frightened and vulnerable self. It can provide a temporary sense of distance from our seeming helplessness. *If I get angry I can avoid or at least minimize my pain. Perhaps I can even influence or change the source of my anger,* we reason.

It doesn't take long to learn that it is easier to feel anger than it is to feel pain. Anger provides an increase of energy. It can decrease our sense of vulnerability and thus increase our sense of security. That security is often a false security, but it is still security of some kind.

- *Anger is a powerful emotion.*

"It's beginning to seem as if anger is our national emotion," writes Barbara Ehrenreich in an article in *Life* magazine. She continues, "You can feel it crackling along our highways, where obedience to the speed limit can get you an obscene gesture, and an obscene gesture can get you shot. It smolders in our cities, where rich and poor, often meaning white and black, face off across a gulf almost as large as the one dividing Serbs from Croats."[2]

In our experience, when most people think about anger they associate it with the most painful and violent expression of anger they have seen or heard. Anger is often associated with (and confused with) hostility, rage, aggression, violence, and destruction. And it is true that when anger gets out of control it can be expressed in horrible ways. But the problem isn't the anger. The problem is that people haven't learned how to understand and value their anger, listen to their anger, or hear the warnings their anger provides.

Anger involves power. When you are angry you feel "charged up" and ready for action. Physiologically, anger triggers an outpouring of adrenaline and other stress hormones to your central and peripheral nervous systems with noticeable physical consequences. Your voice changes to a higher pitch. The rate and depth of your breathing increases. Your perspiration increases. Your heart beats faster and harder. The muscles of your arms and legs may tighten up. The digestive process slows down. You may feel as though a war is being waged in your head and stomach.

Anger involves passion. Anger causes many people to feel alive and gives them a sense of safety and power. It makes them feel they can do something. Many women have discovered that moving from a position of passivity, vulnerability, helplessness, and frustration to anger produces a wonderful sense of security, safety, and power.

> I remember times when my anger felt nothing short of sublime. It gave me a heady sense of power. It made leaving easier. It motivated me to make healthy changes in my life. It drove me to prove to everyone (especially myself) that I was competent and that I could do anything I wanted to do in life. Anger insidiously, but mercifully, masked the fear and pain and poison within.[3]

- *Anger would win the prize as the emotion "most likely to be mislabeled."*

When people are asked, "When is the last time you remember experiencing anger?" they frequently have a difficulty remembering a specific time. Why? Since many people view anger only in it's out-of-control form, they are unaware of the various ways the emotion of anger can be experienced and expressed in everyday life.

In my counseling practice I have spent many hours with people who are confused, frustrated, and stuck in their efforts to grow and live effectively. Much of this is due to their failure or inability to acknowledge, understand, and constructively deal with anger. Because there are taboos on anger in many evangelical circles, Christians can be particularly blind to the value of this emotion. Instead of identifying the emotion and facing it squarely as a fact of life, they either try to shut their anger out or allow it to dominate their lives.

A person who is worried usually looks and acts worried. A person who is depressed usually looks and acts depressed. A person who is overcome by fear usually looks and acts afraid. But a person who is angry may or may not look and act angry. He may appear instead to be worried, depressed, or afraid, or he may not give any external indication of his anger.

> Of all the emotions, anger is the one most likely to be labeled as something else. Of all the emotions, anger is the one most likely to be identified as dangerous. What are some of the most common disguises anger can take? When we begrudge, scorn, insult, and disdain others; or when we are annoyed, offended, bitter, fed up, repulsed, irritated, infuriated, incensed, mad, sarcastic, up tight, cross; or when we experience frustration, indignation, exasperation, fury, wrath or rage, we are probably experiencing some form of anger. Anger can also manifest itself as criticism, silence, intimidation, hypochondria, numerous petty complaints, depression, gossip, sarcasm, blame, [and] passive-aggressive behaviors such as stubbornness, half-hearted efforts, forgetfulness, and laziness.[4]

An important part of learning how to make our anger work for us is to be able to identify the many masks or disguises of anger.

- *Anger is the emotion "most likely to be blamed" for the effects of other emotions.*

Think about it. Is there any other emotion people are encouraged to avoid as much as anger? Is there any other emotion more likely to be labeled a sin? Is there any other emotion people are more uncomfortable talking (or reading) about? This God-given emotion has a bad reputation.

I've heard many pastors and counselors talk about anger, the problems it causes, how to deal with it, and how to avoid it. I've heard few people talk about how to distinguish anger from ire, rage, fury, indignation, hostility, aggression, or chronic resentment. Let's take a look at some of the many different faces of anger.

Ire suggests greater intensity than anger, often with a clear physical display of feeling such as flushed cheeks or dilated pupils. *Rage* suggests loss of self-control leading to violence. *Fury* is a controlling and destructive rage that borders on madness. *Indignation* suggests a healthy anger at what one considers unfair, mean, or shameful behavior. We will look more closely at these types of anger in chapter 5, which deals with anger styles.

When we don't deal with our anger we are more likely to dwell on the causes. The more we focus on how we were wronged the easier it is for the anger to turn into hostility. We want to punish, hurt, or in some way repay the person who caused us pain. Over time it is easy for our hostile thoughts to become aggression.

Healthy anger lets others know exactly how you feel and why. It is honest and clear. Hostility is neither honest nor clear. You know you are in trouble, but you're not sure why. You know you have done something wrong, but you're not clear what. And you have little idea what you can do to change it.

Rage is much more than mere anger. It is anger under a pressure that seems to demand immediate action. There's no time to think about your anger. Rage demands to be acted upon. Anger influences, but rage controls. If anger is a stream, then rage is a roaring river that's flooding over its banks.

The actions we take under the influence of rage are almost always overreactions. The rageaholic shouts, yells, screams, hits, hurls painful words and half-truths—and sometimes objects. He damages and destroys and then waltzes off into the sunset with no sense of guilt or remorse. Why? Because "they deserved it."

Anger is often confused with hate. It is true that anger and hate are both emotions. But they are different emotions. Anger is not hate. Hate is not anger. Hate is the antonym of love. Anger is the antonym of apathy.

> With men and women, anger often arises out of bitterness and hatred. In fact, the association is so strong in some people's minds that the two are often seen as synonymous. Anger becomes a sign of hatred. This error can make it difficult to understand God's anger. There are some Bible teachers who have never clearly seen the distinction between anger and hate. They seem to teach that God is a primarily punitive God who acts out of His hate for certain people. This thinking implies a very small and insecure God—one who gets upset at every offense to His pride. God turns quickly, then, from love to hate, depending on His mood at the moment.[5]

A careful study of the Bible reveals that there is a big difference between anger and hate. Psalm 106 provides a good example. In verse 40 we read that "the Lord was angry with his people." It is clear that the rebellion of His people caused the anger. But further reading shows this not to be the emotion of hate. The response is not of punishment, but of discipline and correction. Yes, the Lord did hand the Israelites over to their enemies. But in addition, "many times he delivered them [and] took note of their distress; . . . he remembered his covenant and out of his great love he relented" (vv. 43-45 NIV).

These are not acts of a raging and out-of-control God. Instead, God's anger arose out of His love. It was the means whereby God communicated His character. His painful discipline had its foundations in His love.

It's unfortunate that many people confuse the emotion of anger with the way some people choose to express or act out that emotion. This confusion has caused anger to take the blame for some other emotions. Anger is not an evil emotion. The emotion of anger has never caused the breakup of a marriage, although inappropriate expressions of anger may have. Anger is not necessarily a dangerous or destructive emotion, nor is it always a deadly sin. The problem lies in how we choose to express it.

- *Anger is learned.*

One woman wrote, "As a child the anger I knew was the stand-on-the-chair, yell-at-someone-and-throw-things kind of anger." Another woman wrote, "When I hear the word anger I think of coldness, sarcasm, contorted faces, slammed doors, extended silences, sobbing in back bedrooms, cold eyes, and dark moods that kept everyone in the house on edge for days or weeks."

As men and women who are made in God's image we are designed by our Creator to express ourselves. Given the fact that we are "born to communicate" it's surprising that clear communication is so difficult for so many people. I think there are two reasons for this: original sin and our upbringing. I have a three-year-old son. For the most part little Andrew has had few reservations about and little difficulty in expressing his feelings. He does it naturally. But all parents teach their children what is acceptable to express and what is not acceptable. By the time children become adults they have learned which emotions and expressions of emotion are acceptable.

Children don't learn those emotional dos and don'ts just by what we say. As a part of their learning process children often imitate and then adopt the behavior patterns they see demonstrated in the adults around them. There are also external influences that contribute to their sense of what is appropriate behavior. Those influences include friendships and role models picked up from television, movies, and books.

A good example of this is the myth that it's more acceptable for women to express emotions than men. This concept is conveyed to children at an early age, when they learn that it's OK for little girls to cry, but that a boy needs to "be a man." (And we all know that being a "real man" involves having affective bypass surgery, that noninvasive procedure by which men initially aware of their feelings learn to keep quiet about them.) After a while the child has suppressed his emotions for so long he not only no longer recognizes them but isn't even aware of them. By the time many boys become men they have lost the ability to express themselves. They have learned all too well that expressing emotions is not masculine and is thus unacceptable.

Unexpressed emotions don't just magically disappear. They become internalized and usually lead to an inability to understand oneself and/or to relate to and be intimate with others. Learning how to open up isn't always easy, but it is vital. In later chapters we will discuss ways to open up.[6]

- *Mismanaged anger can be hazardous to your health.*

What is mismanaged anger? It is anger that is not identified or understood and not dealt with in healthy kinds of ways. It is anger that is stuffed, repressed, suppressed, denied, or ignored. It is out-of-control anger that keeps us from knowing what we are really feeling—and it does damage to ourselves and others.

Gilda Carle, a corporate communications specialist based in Yonkers, New York, warns:

> Anger that isn't accepted and confronted openly can be lethal. It leads to stress, burnout and physical illness. Recent studies of workers under stress, for example, show they have higher cholesterol levels than colleagues who are less pressured. And a recent study of some 700 men and women conducted at the University of Michigan found that people who suppressed their anger were three times more likely to die prematurely than those who vented their frustration.[7]

Dr. Marianne Legato, a professor of cardiology at the Columbia University College of Physicians and Surgeons in New York, has published research showing that internalized anger may be a major cause of heart-related illness in women. When compared with calmer women, those who deal with anger in unhealthy kinds of ways are more likely to suffer and eventually die of heart disease.

Legato and her colleagues report that due to women's expanding roles in the work force, heavy family responsibilities, and unequal pay and power compared to men, the number of angry, frustrated women in this country is rising. These findings are especially problematic because women with heart disease are less likely to report symptoms and are less likely to be treated aggressively. Even when they are treated, research indicates that women are less likely than men to survive heart disease.

According to the 1992 edition of *Heart and Stroke Facts,* an annual publication of the American Heart Association, in 1988 more women (503,542) died of heart and blood vessel diseases than men (476,246). The report adds that women are twice as likely to die during coronary bypass surgery, and that women who survive one heart attack are twice as likely to die of heart disease before they suffer a second heart attack.[8]

If we bury our anger it is possible that, in time, our anger will bury us. Dr. Leo Madow, professor and chairman of the department of psychiatry and neurology at the Medical College of Pennsylvania at Philadelphia, explains what happens when we "blow our top." In discussing the effects of repressed anger he states:

> Hemorrhage of the brain is usually caused by a combination of hypertension and cerebral arteriosclerosis. It is sometimes called apoplexy or stroke and may have a strong emotional component, as is shown by such expressions as "apoplectic with rage" and "don't get so mad, you'll burst a blood vessel!" Anger can produce the hypertension which explodes the diseased cerebral artery, and a stroke results.

Not only does repressed anger produce physical symptoms from headaches to hemorrhoids, but it can also seriously aggravate already existing physical illnesses. Even if illness is organic, anger can play an important role in how we respond to it. If we get angry at having a physical sickness and being disabled, unable to work with added financial burdens, the anger can prolong both illness and convalescence.[9]

WHAT'S SO GREAT ABOUT ANGER?

Since we wrote our first book on anger we have received numerous comments along the line of "I didn't realize that anger has such great potential for good" and "I never thought I would see the day when I'd view the emotion of anger as something positive." It's no wonder why.

In our survey of more than 3,000 women we asked the question: "When you hear the word 'anger,' do you tend to have a positive or a negative response to that word?" In a random sample of more than 500 of the surveys 77 percent of the respondents said "negative." When we asked, "From your point of view, is anger primarily a positive or a negative emotion?" out of a random sample of 850 surveys 78 percent of the respondents said "negative."

Yet as we have already mentioned, this oftentimes renegade emotion was designed by God as a gift and has tremendous potential for good. Let's take a look at some of the specific ways healthy anger can help us.

- *Anger is a signal.*

Anger is to our lives as a smoke detector is to a house, a dash warning light to a car, a flashing yellow light to a driver. Each serves as a warning to stop, look, and listen. It says, "Take caution, something might be wrong." In *The Dance of Anger* Harriet Goldhor Lerner observes:

Anger is a signal and one worth listening to. Our anger may be a message that we are being hurt, that our rights are being violated, that our needs or wants are not being adequately met, or simply that something isn't right. Our anger may tell us that we are not addressing an important emotional issue in our lives, or that too much of our self—our beliefs, values, desires or ambitions—is being compromised in a relationship. Our anger may be a signal that we are doing more and giving more than we can comfortably do or give. Or our anger may warn us that others are doing too much for us, at the expense of our own competence and growth. Just as physical pain tells us to take our hand off the hot stove, the pain of our anger preserves the very integrity of our self. Our anger can motivate us to say "no" to the ways in which we are defined by others and "yes" to the dictates of our inner self.[10]

People who don't know how to listen to their anger are missing out on one of anger's greatest functions. As we learn to acknowledge anger's warning signs we are more likely to be able to recognize and deal with an issue while it is still manageable.

When we don't recognize a problem issue or choose to ignore the warnings of anger, we are more likely to face bigger issues and greater problems down the road. When we ignore the warning lights of our emotions, what we might have been able to deal with fairly simply at an early stage will in time become a major problem.

- *Anger can provide a powerful source of motivation and energy to move us to positive action and change.*

Everyone wants to be different, but nobody wants to change. Change is frustrating. Change is threatening. Change produces insecurity and increases our vulnerability to anxiety and fear. Change is one of the most difficult things in the world for most of us to accomplish. Yet change is what keeps us out of ruts. Without change there is no growth. Without growth there is psychological, spiritual, or relational stagnation.

Anger can be a prime catalyst for change. Anger is merely an emotion that alerts us to the fact that something may be wrong. Anger itself doesn't hurt or destroy. Anger that is wisely directed can provide valuable energy for moving on. I've worked with many women who have confronted their anger. They tell me that once they understood and were able to mobilize their anger it provided a powerful source of motivation for change. The following story illustrates the point.

For twenty-five years Frances Conley has been engaged in the practice of neurosurgery. In 1977 she was only the fifth woman in the country to be certified as a brain surgeon, and she was Stanford University's first female faculty member in neurosurgery. It wasn't easy being in her position. Even though she was a respected neurosurgon, she was insulted, humiliated, and demeaned by male colleagues at the hospital.

She ignored their suggestive remarks and dirty jokes, silently endured being addressed as "honey" in front of her patients, and fended off sexual innuendos and advances. On the outside she appeared not to be objecting, but on the inside she was smoldering.

Finally she decided that enough was enough. "I was known as a good sport," she says, "but I came to see that, unfortunately, being a good sport for a woman can be degrading and demoralizing."

When one of the physicians who had been most offensive was chosen to be the permanent chairman of the department, she was outraged. She decided to go public with her complaints. In June of 1991 she wrote about her experiences in a local newspaper editorial. She gave details but didn't mention any names. That article produced an avalanche of local and national media attention.

The attention the problem received got results. Stanford officials decided that, due to his "troubling insensitivity, especially toward gender issues, and frequently displayed demeaning behavior in his words and actions toward women," the offending doctor would be removed as permanent chairman of the department.[11]

- *Managed anger can contribute to more intimate relationships.*

What do you think of when you hear the word *intimate?* Do any particular people come to your mind? What is it about them and your relationship with them that you would characterize as intimate?

When most people hear the word *intimate* they think of safety, trust, transparency, security; of dealing with "someone who really knows me." They think of such people as a spouse or a best friend or bosom buddy. Webster's defines *intimate* as "belonging to or characterizing one's deepest and most private nature." It is marked by very close association.

True intimacy doesn't occur overnight. It takes time, a lot of it. Intimacy involves getting to know someone. It involves not only sharing the ways in which you are similar, but also sharing and working through your differences. It is through our differences that we reveal ourselves to one another as the unique persons God has made us to be. It is in working through our differences that we learn to understand and trust one another.

The emotion of anger is one of the most important ways we become aware of differences. Anger tells us that something is bothering us about something another person said or did. When this happens we can choose to move toward a surface and cosmetic harmony and pretend that everything is fine, or we can risk discomfort and awkwardness by speaking the truth in love, understanding and resolving the issue, and in the process increasing the depth of the relationship.

Being open about what is bothering us can lead to an increased risk of being misunderstood and being hurt. After that happens a few times we will be much less likely to take a similar chance again. But the cost of not communicating, expressing ourselves, of letting someone we love know what we are struggling with is equally negative: isolation, loneliness, a lack of understanding, shallowness, and superficiality.

The road from not understanding to understanding often goes through the town of misunderstanding. Rarely are we able to communicate everything clearly the first time or understand someone else the first time, especially if it involves something as complex as emotions, particularly when we don't always understand them ourselves. (And sometimes it is only in the process of trying to communicate our feelings to someone else that we ourselves understand them.)

The emotion of anger doesn't strengthen or weaken relationships. What strengthens or weakens relationships is how we choose to express that emotion. If you choose to sit on your anger, the relationship is likely to remain shallow at best and, at worst, die a slow death. That is why a woman can come into my office and say, "I've been married to this man for thirty-five years, and I have no idea who he is."

As we risk expressing and then moving beyond the secondary emotion of anger to its root causes, such as fear, hurt, or frustration, we will be able to identify and grow beyond the differences that divide. We will learn that it is not only safe to disagree but is essential for meaningful growth to identify and express the differences that inevitably follow.

When we allow God to teach us how to use our anger-energy to get unstuck in our closest relationships, we will be free to move with greater confidence, certainty, clarity, and calm in every relationship we are in.

- *Anger can help us set boundaries and clarify who God has created us to be and to become.*

One of the most important yet difficult tasks in the process of becoming an adult is what psychologists call *individuation.* Individuation is the process by which we become distinct individuals, related to, yet at the same time distinct from, those who have come before us and those who will follow us. Individuation involves the subtle yet significant shift by which a person comes to see herself as separate and distinct from the relational context from which she came. It involves an increasing delineation of an "I" within a "we."[12] An important part of the process of individuation is the establishment of personal boundaries.

Webster's defines *boundary* as "the mark of a limit or border." A personal boundary is part of what defines and distinguishes an individual. A personal boundary is where I leave off and you begin. Boundaries provide a sense of knowing that God has made me an individual with unique needs, wants, feelings, desires, and dreams. Boundaries define appropriate behavior and expression of feelings. They let a person know when she is being violated or abused. They identify what is acceptable and unacceptable, appropriate and inappropriate.

Anger can be a warning that a personal boundary has been crossed, that you are being violated, abused, or taken advantage of. It can give you the power to say no. Yet our surveys have shown that many women find it almost impossible to say no. Because they are not clear about who they are and who God created them to become, they direct most of their energy toward taking care of others and making them feel comfortable.

Not being able to say no makes a woman more vulnerable to becoming overresponsible. If a problem develops, she assumes it must be her fault. She spends much of her time apologizing for something she should have done, information she should have known, or something she did but didn't do quite right. She has trained herself to take care of others, be mindlessly submissive, and follow everyone else's instructions, not only sacrificing her own needs but becoming substantially unaware of them so that she can more effectively cater to the needs of others.

One woman wrote: "I feel like my job is to function as the emotional thermostat for everyone else in the family." When that happens you don't have any way to measure your own emotional climate. You deny your God-given talents and gifts. You are unaware of God's plan and purpose for your life.

Christ never asked us to exchange our backbone for a wishbone. Being a godly women doesn't mean not having your own ideas and opinions. A bumper sticker put it well: "Jesus died to take away our sins, not our brains." That means that we are not to be conformed to what our family-of-origin, our spouse, or our friends say we should be. As believers, we have the mind of Christ, and it is to Him that we are to be conformed.

CONCLUSION

Anger is an emotion God may use to get our attention and make us more aware of opportunities to learn, grow, deepen, mature, and change significantly for the good. Anger, like love, has tremendous potential for both good and evil. That is why it is so important for us to understand it. Carol Tavris has written:

> I have watched people use anger, in the name of emotional liberation, to erode affection and trust, whittle away their spirits in bitterness and revenge, diminish their dignity in years of spiteful hatred. And I watch with admiration those who use anger to probe for truth, who challenge and change the complacent injustices of life, who take an unpopular position center stage while others say "shhhh" from the wings.[13]

TAKE ACTION

Dr. Redford Williams of Duke University has developed three questions that will help you identify if you are the kind of person whose hostility places her at risk of health problems down the road.[14] Answer the following questions by circling the answer that best describes you.

1. When friends or even strangers do things that hold me up or keep me from accomplishing a task I often think they are selfish, mean, and inconsiderate.

   Never   Sometimes   Often   Always

2. When someone does something that seems incompetent, messy, selfish, or inconsiderate, I quickly feel frustration, irritation, anger, or even rage. At the same time I often am aware of uncomfortable physical sensations, such as my

heart racing, difficulty in getting my breath, and sweating palms.

Never   Sometimes   Often   Always

3. Whenever I have those kinds of thoughts, feelings, or bodily sensations, I am more likely to communicate my feelings to the person I see as the cause of my discomfort with words, gestures, a change in my tone of voice, or negative facial expressions.

Never   Sometimes   Often   Always

Dr. Williams's research has shown that if you answer "Often" or "Always" to two of the three survey items, it is probable that your level of hostility places you in a high-risk group for health problems. You may have what Dr. Williams calls a hostile heart.

NOTES

1. Adapted by permission from an unpublished manuscript by an author who wishes to remain anonymous.
2. Barbara Ehrenreich, "Cauldron of Anger," *Life*, January 1992, 62–68.
3. Susan Jeffers, *Opening Our Hearts to Men* (New York: Fawcett Columbine, 1989), 35.
4. Adapted from Gary Jackson Oliver and H. Norman Wright, *When Anger Hits Home: Taking Care of Your Anger Without Taking It Out on Your Family* (Chicago: Moody, 1992), 216–17.
5. Ibid., 46–47.
6. Adapted from "Getting All Emotional: The New Beauty Tools; a Kiss . . . a Laugh . . . a Fit of Anger," *Mademoiselle*, June 1990, 192–95.
7. Nancy Marx Better, "He vs. She," *Self*, June 1992, n.p.
8. Deborah Rissing Baurac in *The Chicago Tribune*, "Anger Blamed for Fueling Heart Disease in Women," reprinted in *The Denver Post*, 16 February 16 1992.
9. Leo Madow, *Anger: How to Recognize and Cope with It* (New York: Scribner, 1972), 85.
10. Harriet Goldhor Lerner, *The Dance of Anger: A Woman's Guide to Changing Patterns in Intimate Relationships* (New York: Harper & Row, 1985), 1.
11. Adapted from Marianne Jacobbi, "Just Call Me Doctor" *Good Housekeeping*, August 1992, n.p.

12. For more information see M. Karpel (1976), "Individuation: From Fusion to Dialogue," *Family Process* 15, no. 1 (1976):65–82.
13. Carol Tavris, *The Mismeasure of Woman* (New York: Simon & Schuster, 1992), 23.
14. Adapted from chapter 10 of Redford Williams, *The Trusting Heart: Great News About Type A Behavior* (New York: Times Books, 1989), 165–75.

CHAPTER FIVE

Why Do Women Get Angry?

Karen woke up exhausted and weary. She had been in bed for seven hours but had tossed and turned most of the night. Her legs and back still ached from helping her best friend move a week earlier.

She got out of the house a little later than usual, and the freeway traffic was at a standstill due to an accident. Because she had an important presentation to make at 10:00 A.M., she had wanted to get to work early to have more time to prepare. She had worked at this accounting firm for several years. She was a hard worker who consistently earned excellent reviews. Yet male colleagues with less experience and less time with the company continued to be promoted ahead of her. She was hoping that this presentation would help her get a much deserved promotion.

When she finally arrived at work her boss happened to walk by and, noticing she was late, reminded her of the important presentation she had to make and also mentioned how disappointed he was that she hadn't come in earlier.

In the afternoon she received a call from her son's principal saying that he had been involved in a fight at school and would have to stay after school. That meant he would miss the bus. She would have to pick him up before going home to prepare a dinner she hadn't had time to even think about. At six o'clock, just as she was putting the food on the table, her husband called to tell her a meeting had gone longer than expected and that he would be an hour late.

Put yourself in Karen's shoes. You've just hung up the phone after talking to your husband. What are you thinking? What are you feeling? What do you feel like saying to him? What do you feel like saying to the world? What would you like to do?

You're probably asking, "What did Karen do? How did she react?" Well, up to this point she had done a great job of "holding it in." "I thought I was managing to ignore my fears and frustrations," Karen told me with a hint of pride. "But when Tom called that was the last straw." With a pause she looked down, shook her head, and said in a subdued tone of voice, "I lost it!"

Each of us has our own way of "losing it." We can get quieter or louder, can withdraw or can attack, can blame others or blame ourselves, can throw words or throw objects. Karen reacted by getting louder. She verbally attacked her husband and then her son. She blamed the traffic, her boss, her son, her husband. And then she blamed life. "How did you feel after getting all that stuff out of your system?" I asked. "Did it accomplish anything positive?"

"I wish it had," she replied. "To be honest it felt great while I was dumping. But after it was over, and especially after seeing the look on my son's face, I felt even worse than I did before I let it fly."

Can you remember a day in your life when it seemed as though nothing went right? When you encountered back-to-back pressures, demands, discouragements, and criticism? How long ago was it? By the end of the day what were some of your thoughts? Can you recall some of the emotions you felt? When the last straw hit what was your immediate response? How do you wish you had responded? Do you remember why you were angry?

Why was Karen angry? Was it the achy body from helping her friend move, the lousy night's sleep, leaving home later than she had expected, the traffic jam, the pressure of her presentation, her boss's critical remark, frustration with gender bias at work, her son's getting into trouble, having to change her schedule to pick him up, having to prepare dinner while being exhausted after a draining day, her husband's phone call —or was it a combination of all of these?

One of the things that makes anger a difficult emotion to deal with is that when we experience it there is rarely only one source or "cause." From our research and from our own experience it is obvious that there are any number of situations that can trigger an anger response.

In *When Anger Hits Home* we identified the ten major causes of anger in men and women, including childhood experiences, physiological factors, accumulated stress from normal everyday events, injustice, low self-esteem, worry, conflict, fear, hurt, and frustration.[1]

At anger workshops and in our interviews and surveys we have asked women, "What are some of the specific factors that increase your vulnerability to getting angry? What situations or circumstances make it more likely for you to experience anger?" In a group of close to a hundred women we received over two hundred different responses. Some of the most frequently mentioned responses included the following:

When I'm not taken care of	Abandonment
When I sin	Unrealistic expectations
Dealing with children	Stress
Unfair comparison	Disrespect

Discrimination because I'm a woman	Not dealing with previous anger
Overcommitment	Being a people-pleaser
Lack of affection from spouse	Feeling insecure around people
Selfish demands	Entitlement of men
Getting older	PMS
When I see I've gained weight	Not enough quiet time for myself
Tired and worn out	Feeling sorry for myself
People talking behind my back	When I've been embarrassed or laughed at
Teenagers and in-laws	Having to wait
When I've been used or betrayed	Not having my feelings valued

When we looked at all of the factors listed by the women we were able to identify several factors that can contribute to or are likely to trigger an anger response. Notice that I said "contribute to" rather than "cause." That is an important distinction. The same event can happen to five different people, and each might have a different emotional reaction to it. There are a number of situations that can increase the probability that a person will experience anger.

But as you already know by now, anger itself isn't the main problem. It is only a symptom. The real problem is the difficulty we have in identifying and understanding our anger and thereby choosing healthy ways to express it. The first step in anger management is to identify and understand the root causes of that anger. If we can't do that it will be almost impossible for us to make our anger work for us.

A MORE HOSTILE PLAYING FIELD

Why do women get angry? Women get angry for many of the same general reasons that men get angry: injuries, attacks, injustice, intrusions, disappointments, threats, innuendos, misunderstandings, fear, hurt, and frustration. However, although men and women's anger often have similar causes, there are several social and cultural conditions that in a unique way contribute to women's ability or inability to experience this valuable emotion.

One woman wrote that "the anger felt by Christian women over years of hurt, isolation, and being ignored is like magma just below the surface of a long dormant volcano that is about to erupt. These women want to keep their values, belief systems, and marriages, but can barely contain their anger any longer. Society's seeming openness to women's issues is calling forth emotions that Christian women have eschewed for centuries."[2]

Few would debate the fact that for many years women have been discriminated against. Why? Merely for being women. This sometimes subtle and at other times blatant discrimination has created an environment that is more hostile to women than it is to men. It puts women in situations in which they have more reason than men to be afraid, more likelihood of being hurt, and more likelihood of experiencing frustration. All of these emotions—fear, hurt, and frustration—can be root causes of and lead to the emotion of anger.

A DOUBLE STANDARD

On the day of the 1992 vice presidential debates a front page article discussed the similarities and differences between the two contenders, Dan Quayle and Albert Gore. At one point the reporter noted, "Both have strong-willed wives and attractive children."[3] Something about that sentence struck me, so I went back and reread it. Suddenly I saw what bothered me. Many of the women we interviewed for this book had talked about it, but this was one of the first times I had noticed it on my own.

What had I noticed? It was the expression used to describe Marilyn Quayle and Tipper Gore. They were described as "strong-willed" women, an expression rarely used in our culture as a compliment. When I talked about the article with several other men and women and asked their opinion about it, they all had the same response as I.

What was it about the two women that made them "strong-willed"? They both were educated, verbal, and able to clearly communicate their opinions. They both were not afraid to take a stand. They both communicated their convictions with clarity and passion. A male with all those attributes would be described as "an assertive and strong leader." But when the wives of the two vice presidential candidates possessed those attributes they were labeled "strong-willed." That appeared to me to be a double standard.

The double standard of our culture displays itself in many ways. We are quick to view a woman who expresses anger as a sick, troubled, disturbed, or irrational person. Men have "clear convictions," but women are "opinionated." A woman's healthy expression of anger, criticalness, or competitiveness directed toward a man is often interpreted as an unhealthy display of aggression or an attempt to control. I've heard terms such as "hostile," "domineering" or "controlling" used to describe a woman's expression of anger when a similar expression by the man was termed "strong" or "confident." For many years what has been acceptable for a man has for a woman often been viewed as at best inappropriate and at worst pathological. In the face of such a double standard a woman's main options are to stuff, repress, suppress, or deny the emotion or anger—and that, of course, will only decrease her sense of value and worth and increase her sense of powerlessness.

INJUSTICE

This double standard has placed women in a one-down position and has led to many injustices. Webster's defines *injustice* as a violation of another's rights or of what is right. The definition presupposes that there exists a sense of fairness and equality that ought to apply. An injustice involves an injury, a wrong, a disservice. It is the instance of something inequitable and unfair.

People who consistently suffer from inequality respond to it in two ways. They may become hypersensitive to anything unjust or unfair, or they may cease to exist as unique individuals. They may see themselves as not as good, important, valuable, or significant as others, and in turn may come to see themselves as not good, important, valuable, or significant *at all.*

Charles Dickens's novel *Great Expectations* contains a classic illustration of this pattern. One day after the central figure of the novel, Pip, has been humiliated by his cruel older sister he bitterly reflects:

> My sister's bringing up had made me sensitive. In the little world in which children have their existence, whosoever brings them up, there is nothing so finely perceived and so finely felt as injustice. It may be only small injustice that the child can be exposed to; but the child is small, and its world is small, and its rocking-horse stands as many hands high, according to scale, as a big-boned Irish hunter. Within myself I had sustained, from my babyhood, a perpetual conflict with injustice. I had known, from the time when I could speak, that my sister, in her capricious and violent coercion, was unjust to me. Through all my punishments, disgraces, fasts and vigils, and other penitential performances, I had nursed this assurance.[4]

GENDER BIAS

Recent research suggests that women feel much less comfortable with their status in life and to a much greater extent than men believe that they suffer from gender bias. In a poll conducted by the Gallup Organization in February of 1992 women were asked, "Do you ever resent the expectations society places on you?" Forty-eight percent of the married women said yes, whereas only 13 percent of the married men said yes.

When asked "What are the greatest pressures American women/men face today?" 85 percent of the married men listed "financial worries," with job/career concerns a distant second at 33 percent. When asked the same question, the two top responses of women were "job/career" at 59 percent and "family concerns/single parenting" at 55 percent. Those responses are another indication that women, much more than men, see themselves as bearing a double burden.[5]

The median annual salary of women ages forty to forty-four is now $20,000 for full-time work. According to the Institute for Women's Policy Research, that is about the same salary a twenty-five- to twenty-nine-year-old man earns as he is just starting his career. "A woman with a four-year college degree now earns about the same as a man with a high-school diploma," says Pamela Hughes of the American Association of University Women.[6]

In academia most tenured professors are men. Women in business may hold management positions, but they earn about 71 cents on the dollar compared to men. Prior to the 1992 elections there were only two women in the US Senate, and only 6 percent of seats in the House of Representatives were held by women. Just three states had female governors. Only one Supreme Court justice—ever—has known what it means to bear a child.[7]

Several women indicated that they feel as though they live in a constant double bind. "Either I do something too much or not enough. Enough is never enough." Carol Tavris has captured the feeling expressed by many of the women in our survey. Most of the books written about women today, she says,

> imply that women aren't doing anything right. Women are irrational and moody because of their hormones. They cry too much. The love too much. They talk too much. They think differently. They are too dependent on unworthy men, but if they leave the men to fend for themselves, they are too independent, and if they stay with the men they are codependent. They are too emotional, except when the emotion in question is anger, in which case they aren't emotional enough. They don't have correct orgasms, the correct way, with the correct frequency. They pay too much attention to their children, or not enough, or the wrong kind. They are forever subject to syndromes: the Super-

woman Syndrome causes the Stress Syndrome, which is exacerbated by the Pre-menstrual Syndrome, which is followed by a Menopausal Deficiency Syndrome.[8]

Women are tired of being the object of comedian's humor. Remember some of the "dumb blond" jokes that recently circulated around the country? Well, one day I found in my mailbox at work a list of "dumb men" jokes that a woman in one of our women's groups had given to the leader. Here is a sample:

Do you know why all dumb blond jokes are one-liners?
So men can understand them.

What is the difference between government bonds and men?
Government bonds mature.

What's the difference between a man and E.T.?
E.T. phoned home.

Why is psychoanalysis a lot quicker for men than for women?
When it's time to go back to his childhood, he's already there.

How do men define a 50/50 relationship?
We cook/they eat; we clean/they dirty; we iron/they wrinkle.

How do men exercise at the beach?
By sucking in their stomachs every time they see a bikini.

How are men like noodles?
They are always in hot water, they lack taste, and they need dough.

Why is it good that there are female astronauts?
When the crew gets lost in space, at least the women will ask for directions.

INEQUALITY

Women are born into a socially subordinate position. Dr. Jean Baker Miller, a professor of psychiatry at the Boston University School of Medicine, says that simply being born into a subordinate position can generate anger. The dominant group doesn't allow the expression of that anger, so it gets repressed. Eventually the anger can develop into a much larger sense of undirected rage. Because that feeling of anger and frustration is sometimes falsely referred to as a "bottomless well," many women may be afraid to tap into it.[9]

A contributor to *Women's Ways of Knowing: The Development of Self, Mind, and Voice* observes:

> With the Western Tradition of dividing human nature into dual but parallel streams, attributes traditionally associated with the masculine are valued, studied and articulated, while those associated with the feminine tend to be ignored. Nowhere is the pattern of using male experience to define human experience seen more clearly than in models of intellectual development.[10]

A recent poll indicated that the second most mentioned complaint of women is that they are frustrated with the division of the work load at home. Women work an average of fifteen hours more than men per week—including household chores. By any standard that isn't fair, and it is a major source of resentment in many women. One woman told me, "I wasn't even aware of it at first. I just thought that's the way it is. That's what women do. But after ten years I started resenting Bob. I became more negative and critical, and I wasn't sure why."

It took her close to a year to realize that the real source of her frustration and anger wasn't because her husband was a bad person. It was because of the unidentified and unacknowledged hurt and resentment that had accumulated over years of living under this double standard.

Another study found that 39 percent of women—as compared to 26 percent of men—mentioned "neglect of home or children" as a major cause of divorce. It was the second most common reason women cited for divorce—behind "mental cruelty" but ahead of financial problems, physical abuse, drinking, or even infidelity.[11]

UNREWARDING WORK

In my counseling I have observed that another major source of anger in contemporary life is the unrewarding work many people are engaged in. Today many people are engaged in work where they play an intermediary role. They know that what they do is dispensable. Their work is a series of intermediate and repetitive tasks whose fruits are rarely evident. Very few workers today have a part in the end result of their work with which they can identify and feel pride over.

Whatever diminishes our sense of value, worth, and significance increases our sense of powerlessness. That can either increase our desire for approval and thus increase our vulnerability to being taken advantage of, or it can contribute to an "I could care less" spirit in which people give up trying or respond by attacking the system.

According to our interviews and survey this principle is especially applicable in the lives of some mothers and homemakers. Many women have told us that being a homemaker is a lonely and often thankless role. "When I decided to stay home with my children I didn't expect to feel isolated and underappreciated by the community."

Many women feel they are victims of a double-edged sword. If they stay at home they feel unappreciated and unrewarded. If they go out of the home into the workplace they face bias and discrimination.

Connie is a friend of our family and has a delightful sense of humor. In a recent conversation she captured well the frustration that many women feel. She told us that in the past week her husband Bob had come home and excitedly talked about the major deal he had closed and the fact that he would probably get a $5,000 bonus. He was especially excited that his boss made a point of congratulating him in front of other senior management.

Now on the one hand I was truly delighted for him and for the family. He has worked long and hard on this contract, and we can use the money. But on the other hand it frustrates and angers me. When he comes home what do I have to share with him? That I cleaned the house and picked up our two preschoolers' toys seven times, that I changed eleven damp and soiled diapers and prepared a meal that will be downed in fifteen minutes to be followed by the joy of dishes? And then when the kids are in bed I can anticipate another thrilling day of doing exactly the same thing. Well, not exactly the same. The number of dirty diapers can vary.

Where's my compliment and what's my bonus? Can't you just see Bob coming up to me saying, "Honey, I want you to know that you really have a gift with baby wipes. I know other women who would take at least two or three of them to clean up what you are able to clean up with just one. I sure don't deserve a gifted, hard-working wife like you. I can't tell you how much it means for me to know that our babies bottoms are in such good hands."

Now in fairness to Connie, she loves being able to be a full-time mom. She doesn't have to be. She chose to be. Both she and Bob share the belief that what she is doing is, in the long run, a significant investment of her life and their resources. On several occasions I've heard Bob say (and I know that he means it) that what Connie does is much more important and valuable than what he does.

Yet at the same time it is clearly more routine, more mundane, less challenging, less stimulating, and less rewarding in the sense of short-term, tangible rewards. "I can tell myself that it doesn't matter, that it shouldn't matter, that if I were a bit more spiritual it wouldn't matter," Connie said, "but the reality is that sometimes it does matter."

(For more information and different perspectives on the gender issue see the list of resources at the end of this chapter.)

SHAME ON ME

The cultural conditions and social demands of our society make many women especially vulnerable to the ravages of unhealthy shame. One woman wrote, "I think my parents should have named me Avis because I have lived my life believing that I've always got to try harder." Her humor served as a thin veil to much deeper layers of guilt and shame.

God designed the emotion of shame to lead us to Himself. Healthy shame says, "God loves me. I have been made in His image. I have value and worth. But I am also a sinner. I am not perfect. I have made and will make mistakes. I need God." Healthy shame leads us to acknowledge that we are image-bearers as well as sinners, and that reality drives us to the cross.

When shame becomes the basis for our identity, the shame that God intended for good can become unhealthy. A shame-based person is one who focuses on her shame to the exclusion of Christ's completed work for her on the cross. At this point shame becomes toxic and hazardous to our emotional and spiritual health.

John Bradshaw, in *Healing the Shame That Binds You*, speaks to this point:

> Perhaps the most damaging consequence of being shame-based is that we don't know how depressed and angry we really are. We don't actually feel our unresolved grief. Our false self and ego defenses keep us from experiencing it. Paradoxically, the very defenses which allowed us to survive our childhood trauma have now become barriers to our growth.[12]

Women who are shame-based either ignore or are functionally unaware of the reality of who they are in Christ and of what He accomplished on their behalf at the cross. They are unaware of their legitimate needs as well as God's promise and plan for their lives. They have little sense of their value and worth, have given up on the possibility of experiencing the abundant life, and, because of the undercurrent of hopelessness and helplessness, often have abandoned the opportunity to grow and to become all that God would have them to be.

At first they ignore and then become numb to their own feelings and needs. Like Connie, they tell themselves that what they feel doesn't matter, isn't valid, isn't important, is a sign of developmental or spiritual immaturity, or is just plain sinful.

They set aside appropriate personal goals to achieve the relational goal of harmony. After all, aren't women supposed to be the great peacemakers? The price for that peace is often their own God-given uniqueness, individuality, and identity. While ignoring their own happiness they are more vulnerable to assuming responsibility for the happiness of others. At times they will even go so far as to take the blame for something they haven't even done.

Their unhealthy shame leads them down the path of perfectionism and into the welcoming arms of a performance-based life. That is the kind of life where your value and worth is determined by what you do and how well you do it, rather than who you are or, to put it more precisely, who God has declared that you are.

Over time, this unrewarding and unfulfilling lifestyle leads to an attempt to numb the pain of meaninglessness through increased busyness, even higher standards, greater guilt and shame, or the adrenaline rush that comes from losing one's temper. We become more negative and critical of others because it is always easier to focus on the faults and weaknesses of others. If my focus is on what is wrong with everyone else I don't have time to be aware of my own stuff.

David Seamonds writes:

> I have yet to counsel a performance-based and perfectionistic Christian who was not at heart an angry person. This doesn't mean such persons are always aware of or express it openly. They often impress us a being extremely controlled or very loving. But when we get to know them better, and they open up to share their inner selves, we inevitably discover a core of anger deep within their personalities.[13]

We've taken a look at some of the social and cultural variables that affect women and increase their general vulnerability to anger. Now, let us take a look at what the women in our survey told us are the two major sources of their anger.

HURT

Hurt is one of those emotions we all experience but don't like to talk about. When we talk about hurt we often relive the experience, reexperience the pain, and become retraumatized. Over time it is easy for hurt to turn into boiling resentment.

Hurt is another one of those uncomfortable emotions that can lead to anger. Where there is anger there is almost always some kind of pain. Where there is pain something is usually broken and needs to be fixed.

When we're hurt we are vulnerable, weak, drained, and feel hopeless and helpless. When the pain of hurt is denied and stuffed into the unconscious we may not think about it, but that doesn't mean it has magically disappeared. Out of mind does not mean out of memory.

Anger puts up a wall to protect us from hurt. The short-term effect is that we don't hurt. The long-term effect is that the problems we have been avoiding and trying to run from get worse, and the hurt that is experienced then is always greater than it would have been if we had used our anger-energy to address the problem in the first place.

The following poem illustrates ways in which anger can temporarily block the pain that comes from hurt:

Walls of Anger, Walls of Pain

Escaping the daggers of pain that pierce my heart,
I build walls of anger to protect myself from the hurt.
No one can do this to me I claim,
so I shut them all out to avoid the pain.
Lonely, empty, bitter and without joy I live,
no one can come near me, I have nothing to give.

But God has said these walls cannot stand,
and so with a loving and all-knowing hand

117

He pushes away the bricks one by one,
until there is no protection and no place to run.

A flood rushes in and breaks over my soul,
a hurtful, healing flood that makes me whole,
for instead of a life destroyed by anger and sin
He enables me to love, hurt and feel joy again.

Walls of Anger, Walls of Pain,
O Lord, Let me never build such walls again.[14]

Eventually the layers of hurt, confusion, and misunderstanding make it more difficult to access the facts and interpretations that caused the initial trouble. Unfortunately, the pain of repressed hurt can simmer for years. Like smoke rising out of a campfire, anger can rise up out of the embers of hurt. If hurt is not dealt with it can suddenly boil to the surface, moving past the potentially positive emotion of anger to the damaging emotion of rage.

Hurt is emotionally draining. Anger can give us energy to throw up walls to protect ourselves. At first the walls can keep people out and thus keep the hurt out. Anger can veil the hurt, fear, pain, and sense of loss that comes from real or perceived rejection. *If no one gets close to me, then no one can hurt me,* we think.

Many people are surprised to learn that hurt and anger go hand in hand. It is not uncommon to assume that the angry person is so insensitive he must be incapable of being hurt. That's just the point. Frequently the obnoxious person is precisely the one who has experienced deep hurt, often in childhood. It is a fact that we are more likely to be hurt by people who are important to us. Therefore, we are more likely to feel anger toward people who mean a great deal to us.

It is important to learn how to distinguish between hurt and anger. Paul Welter has written that for the most part hurt is the first emotion to be felt but the one that is least accessible to memory. Anger is the second emotion we experience and the one we are most aware of.[15] If we ignore the warning sign of anger it can easily turn into resentment and a desire for revenge. If we allow resentment to have it's way, it will keep us imprisoned in our past, will poison our present, and ravage our future.

FRUSTRATION

There are numerous sources of frustration in a woman's life. The majority of frustrations fall under the categories of blocked goals and desires and unmet needs and expectations. Frustrations are those seemingly little things that, if they occur with enough frequency or at the wrong time, can become big things. For example:

- You have just spent close to an hour scrubbing and cleaning the tile floors. As you stand back and look with a degree of pride at the good job you have done, mixed with relief at the fact that it is done, one of your children opens the patio door—and in rushes your dog, who has been digging out in the snow-covered yard. In a matter of seconds not only does your tile floor look a mess but in trying to catch your dog he (it must be a he, because a female dog would be more sensitive) runs through the living room, and now it is a mess too. Your children were trying to help, and your dog thought everyone wanted to play with him, but now you have twice as much work to do. At this moment what is your view of dogs, children, housework, and your source of meaning and purpose in life? What are some of the emotions you are feeling? What did you have to keep yourself from saying? How loud would your voice have been if you had said it?
- Your two precious little preschool aged boys have had their usual active morning. They've wrestled, played tag, pretended they were Ninja turtles, and built forts. In the process of being normal, delightful, and healthy kids

they have trashed much of the house. All day long you've looked forward with eager anticipation to their nap time so that you can get the house ready for your evening guests and maybe, if you are really lucky, sit down for a few minutes and relax. You finally get them down for a nap, have taken the phone off the hook, and are on a roll with your housework when . . . the doorbell rings. *I knew I forgot something,* you say to yourself as you go to answer the door. When you get to the door you hear the kids making noise upstairs and are told by the person at the door that they have gotten the wrong house. What thoughts are running through your mind at this moment? What emotions are you feeling? What are you saying to yourself about doorbells, life, the person at the front door, and your ability to ever have a normal life again?

- You are late for an appointment, but finally the traffic in the lane next to you seems to be moving. You put your turn signal on, change lanes, and are starting to make good time. You breathe a sigh of relief and say to yourself, *If this keeps up I won't be late after all.* Suddenly a car pulls in front of you going ten miles an hour slower than the rest of traffic. What are you thinking now? What are you feeling? What would you like to say to that driver?

In addition to the myriad of things that happen to us on a daily basis, the women in our research indicated they are frustrated by not being appreciated for what they do, by feeling as though they are not good enough as a wife/mother/daughter/friend/career person, by excessive demands and unreal expectations, by feelings of powerlessness, and by "being expected to look like the women in magazines and on billboards who work part-time, have personal fitness trainers, have had surgeons work on their face, legs, and other body parts, and have people who cook their meals and clean their homes."

An increasing number of women are frustrated by their need to choose between wanting to be a full-time vocational mom and yet having to work outside the home. In 1960, 20 percent of mothers with children under six years old were in the labor force; by 1991 that number had swelled to 58 percent, with most of the mothers working full-time.

Cindy is a thirty-eight-year-old mother of three whose shift can run twelve hours a day during the busy summer season at her factory:

> "I never feel like I'm a full-time mom," she said. "I bake cookies, make their lunch and the home-made costumes for Halloween. I volunteer for everything I can to make up to them for not being there.
>
> "By the time I do all of that I'm so worn out that my kids end up with an exhausted and crabby mom. And then I feel more guilt and shame because I'm cheating them in a different way. I'm frustrated and discouraged by the fact that no matter what I do it's never enough."

It is not that there aren't any solutions to these frustrations. It is just that most of the time those solutions don't come easily.

Another source of frustration is the gender bias we discussed earlier in this chapter. Companies may say they treat women equally, but the actual results suggest that the proverbial "glass ceiling" blocking a woman's ability to rise to the upper levels of the corporate world does exist. Women face unequal access to credit, exclusion from government contracts, and, at times, blatant discrimination. It's not fair, and that's frustrating.

> When Adela Cepeda realized that her employer would probably never allow her to become a managing partner she was faced with a choice. She could stay where she was and continue to feel hurt, frustrated and angry. She could turn the anger inward and tell herself that the men were right and she didn't deserve anything better. She could dump her anger on

everyone around her. She could whine, criticize, complain, threaten and in subtle ways sabotage the company.

Or, rather than spend her anger-energy in self-defeating kinds of ways she could choose to invest her anger-energy in pursuing other options, options with greater risks but also with greater potential. The Harvard-educated mother of three decided to leave her job at a Wall Street investment firm and, with two women partners, started her own investment company.

It wasn't easy. At almost every turn she found her best efforts frustrated. When she tried to obtain financing she was turned down. She was frustrated by the bank officials who suggested she ask her family for the money. She was frustrated by the fact that in spite of her exemplary track record male clients seemed hesitant to trust their investments to a woman. While she had experienced a "glass ceiling" on the inside she was faced with a "brick wall" on the outside. She didn't give up.

Today Cepeda's company, Abacus Financial Group, has $40 million in assets and is outperforming the bond-index average. She is one of a growing number of women who have decided that enough is enough. As many as 7 million women now run their own businesses that generate as much as $500 billion in annual revenues. That's up from $98 billion 10 years ago.[16]

Women are frustrated with being told that they are not strong enough, not smart enough, not tough enough, not fast enough, not this or that enough. Several women got together and decided to communicate their frustration in a creative and humorous kind of way. They put together a series of seminars they believe all men need to take. Here are some of the offerings:

Seminars for Men

Once again the female staff of the university will be offering courses to men regardless of their marital status. Please note that the name of some of the courses have recently been changed. Attendance in at least seven of the following courses is mandatory. The seminars are in great demand, so please register early.

1. Combating Stupidity
2. You Too Can Do Housework
3. PMS—Learning When to Keep Your Mouth Shut
4. How to Fill an Ice Tray
5. Why We Do Not Want Sleazy Underthings for Christmas
6. Wonderful Laundry Techniques (Formerly: Don't Wash My Silk)
7. Parenting—No It Does Not End with Conception
8. How Not to Act Like a Jerk When You're Obviously Wrong
9. Spelling—You Can Get It Right
10. You—Understanding the Weaker Sex
11. Understanding Your Financial Incompetence
12. How to Stay Awake After Sex
13. Garbage—Getting It to the Curb
14. 101: You Can Fall Asleep Without It—If You Really Try
15. 201: The Morning Dilemma—If It's Awake, Take a Shower
16. How to Put the Toilet Seat Down
17. The Weekend and Sports Are Not Synonymous
18. How to Go Shopping with a Woman Without Getting Lost
19. The Remote Control—Overcoming Your Dependency
20. Romanticism—Other Ideas Besides Sex
21. Helpful Posture Hints for Couch Potatoes
22. How Not to Act Younger Than Your Children
23. Honest, You Don't Look Like Mel Gibson—Especially When You're Naked
24. The Attainable Goal—Omitting #(&$! from Your Vocabulary
25. Why Fluffing the Blankets After Eating Burritos Is *Not* Necessary
26. Male Bonding—Leaving Your Friends at Their Homes

TAKE ACTION

SOME QUESTIONS REGARDING HURT

1. When was the last time you experienced a significant hurt?

2. How and when were you hurt? Who hurt you?

3. Have you ever experienced a similar kind of hurt in the past?

4. How did you deal with it then? What did you learn from it?

5. Is there any way you could have prevented the hurt?

6. If so, how? Why didn't you? If not, why not?

7. What part of you experienced the injury?

> Your sense of self-worth?
> Your trust?
> Your pride?
> Your competence?

8. Could you be hanging onto your hurt as a way to control others?

9. Does holding onto a grudge justify your staying angry?

HOW TO IDENTIFY YOUR ANGER PATTERN

For the next thirty days maintain an Anger Log. Whenever you become aware of anger, grab your Anger Log and record the following information:

1. The date and time of day.
2. The intensity of your anger on a rating from 1–10, with 1 meaning that your anger is barely noticeable and 10 meaning that you have gone beyond anger into rage. (In fact a 10 means that you are totally out of control.)
3. The identity (where possible) of the primary emotion or emotions that led to the secondary emotion of anger.
4. The issue that led to your anger. (You will not always be able to identify the issue.)
5. Your self-talk about the situation. Does your self-talk reflect passive or aggressive reactions or an assertive response?

Here is a sample for for an entry into the anger log:

Date: _____ Time: _____

Intensity 1   2   3   4   5   6   7   8   9   10

Primary Emotion: (a) Hurt (b) Frustration (c) Fear (d) Other

Issue: _____

Self-Talk: _____

_____

_____

_____

_____

_____

RESOURCES ON THE GENDER ISSUE

Cook, Kaye, and Lance Lee. *Man and Woman: Alone and To-gether.* Wheaton: BridgePoint, 1992. See especially chapters 4 and 5.

Gilligan, Carol. *In a Different Voice: Psychological Theory and Women's Development.* Cambridge: Harvard Univ. Press, 1982.

Piper, John, and Wayne Grudem, eds. *Recovering Biblical Manhood and Womanhood.* Wheaton: Crossway, 1991.

Tavris, Carol. *The Mismeasure of Woman.* New York: Simon & Schuster, 1992.

Tanenbaum, Joe. *Male and Female Realities: Understanding the Opposite Sex.* Incline Village, Nev.: Robert Erdmann, 1990.

Van Leeuwen, Mary Stewart. *Gender and Grace.* Downers Grove, Ill.: InterVarsity, 1990.

NOTES

1. Gary Jackson Oliver and H. Norman Wright, *When Anger Hits Home: Taking Care of Your Anger Without Taking It Out on Your Family* (Chicago: Moody, 1992), 91–124.

2. Lanell Schilling, in a personal conversation with Gary J. Oliver.

3. Guy Gugliotta, "Quayle-Gore Face-Off a Baby Boomer Clash," *Denver Post*, 13 October 1992, 1A.

4. Charles Dickens, *Great Expectations*, 2d ed. (New York: Holt & Rhinehart, 1972), 59.

5. Cited in Nancy Marx Better, "He vs. She," *Self*, June 1992, n.p.

6. Michelle Morris, "The Wage War Against Women," *Working Mother*, June 1992, 61–63.

7. Adapted from Jon Tevlin, "Why Women Are Mad As Hell," *Glamour*, March 1992, 207–8.

8. Carol Tavris, *The Mismeasure of Woman* (New York: Simon & Schuster, 1992), 16.

9. Tevlin, 208.

10. Mary F. Belenky, et al., *Women's Ways of Knowing: The Development of Self, Mind, and Voice* (New York: Basic, 1986), 6.

11. Tevlin, 209.

12. John Bradshaw, *Healing the Shame That Binds You* (Deerfield Beach, Fla.: Health Communications, 1988), 137.

13. David Seamonds, *Healing Grace* (Wheaton, Ill.: Victor, 1988), 168.

14. Source unknown.

15. Paul Welter, *Family Problems and Predicaments* (Wheaton, Ill.: Tyndale, 1977), 130.

16. Adapted from Anneta Miller, Karen Springen, and Dody Tsiantar, "Now: The Brick Wall," *Newsweek*, 24 August 1992, 54–56.

CHAPTER SIX

Controllers—
Peacekeepers and Anger

I've been married for fifteen years," June, a thirty-five-year-old wife told me. "I'm exhausted and tired of trying to please my husband. He tries to dictate every part of my life. He's overbearing and tells me and everyone else what to do. He's got an opinion for everything and everyone, whether he knows anything about it or not. And I guess I play along. I can't stand his anger, so I go overboard trying to keep everything just right. But I'm starting to seethe inside. I've even thought of some ways to get even with him."

Kay was in her twenties, single, and struggling with being an adult daughter of an overprotective, worrisome mother. "My mother has the market cornered on worry. She thinks up things to worry about and calls me every day. I swear she goes over the same things each time, but she has to check up on me to see if I listened to her the day before. I think she creates a checklist of questions to ask. I've told her I'm twenty-seven years old and have been on my own for years, but it doesn't register. She was born a checker-upper, and I guess she'll always be one. I used to work for a person like that, but in time I said, 'Enough of this,' and I quit. But I can't quit being her daughter, and I don't want her upset with me either. I want her to be happy with me, but try as hard as I do I can't seem to really please her. I don't want her angry at me, but I'm getting more and more angry with her!"

Does this sound familiar? We all struggle sometime or another with controllers. They're bound to get their own way one way or another. They pressure, get angry, persistently remind, intimidate, manipulate, pout, sulk. Nothing seems to stop them. If you have to interact with a controller, life feels like an ongoing contest. You're constantly on guard, trying to protect and please. Life wasn't meant to be lived like this. It's denying you the right to be who you really are.[1] It's a pressure point in your life, and it will feed your anger. And too many women end up having to contend with this source of stress and anger in their lives.

We all want control over our lives. We want to be independent. And this is where the issue of control becomes a spiritual issue, because a full life is not the independent life, it's being dependent upon God and Jesus Christ. By so doing we can experience a full and healthy freedom, as well as gain the strength to deal with those who seek to dominate our lives.

You may be struggling with what we call a control addict, a person who has to control no matter what. They go to extremes, and many times they know they're this way but see no need to change. Others control just as much but are subtle about it. You could be accommodating such individuals without even being aware of it.

Who really controls other people—a controller or a peacekeeper? That's an interesting question. We'll get to the answer later. Consider the two roles—peacekeeping and controlling —as we listen to some responses from women in counseling.

Bobbie Reed calls control addicts "me only" people. They only want to please themselves all the time and at the expense of others. They demand, fight for themselves, choose for others because they think they know what is best, and are highly critical, but they are oblivious to the criticism of others.[2]

They convey their underlying anger through control. It's a great way for them to hide their insecurities. You end up viewing your husband, your parent, or your employer as a villain because you have fallen into the trap of accommodating them. It seems to you that they are the ones making your life miserable, and that angers you. It seems to you that they have taken away your freedom of choice, and that angers you. It seems to you that because of what they do you can't really reflect who you are or do your job the way you want, and that angers you. You see them as the villains. Before your life can improve, they must change![3]

Do you know what the word *accommodator* refers to? If you have a controller in your life, it could be you. Most of us actually accommodate controllers in some way or another, and we're not even aware of it. There could even be someone shaping your life in some way at this time, but you're not aware of it. Accommodating tends to be automatic. When we accommodate someone, we don't usually think about what we're doing.

There are different ways to respond to a controller. The most obvious is to just give in and be compliant. But does this satisfy a controller? Not usually, for it encourages him or her to control you even more. You end up internalizing your frustration into worry, stress, anxiety, hypertension, and ulcers. Another way to respond to a controller is to anticipate his or her attempts and react immediately to establish your boundaries and the fact that you will not be controlled. All too often this ends up being an overreaction. If the controller has not made any apparent move he will end up looking like the good person and you the villain. That, too, can frustrate and anger you, and the reality remains—the controller has still controlled your reaction.

Some people have learned the victim role so well that no matter where they are or what situation they're in they tend to collect controllers like a flame draws moths. The question arises: Who is actually creating the problem? Who is creating the stress and the anger? Is it the controller's action and response that contributes the most to the problem, or is it the accommodator's compliance? It's something to consider.

If you're a peacekeeper, you have little tolerance for other people's anger or dissent. You probably feel uncomfortable in the presence of an argument or are bothered when people disagree with you. You've worked hard to keep the peace, not realizing the cost to yourself. You are constantly watching your step and anticipating and outguessing other people's probable responses. You act as a censor on yourself to make sure you don't say or do the wrong thing. You live in fear that others might abandon you if you do something wrong.

It is difficult to relax and be at ease under those conditions. If the other person ever sulks, pouts, or withdraws from you in any way you either try to guess what's wrong or chase after the person by pampering or coaxing or trying to draw him out. I like the way Reed describes what she calls "people pleasers." Do you identify with any of these characteristics?

- People pleasers are addicted to approval and will do almost anything to gain it. If approval is out of the question, they will settle for acceptance or just attention.
- People pleasers generally have low self-esteem in that they do not consider themselves worthy of being pleased. Adults who have grown up with a desperate need for approval have usually failed to develop either a healthy sense of who they are or a strong sense of self-worth. They have an idea that they probably deserve respect, but they are unable to stand up, speak out, or reach for the love and affection they want.
- People pleasers don't believe they will be accepted by others unless they are actively working at winning approval, so they go to extraordinary lengths to win applause. They dress to please. They act to please. They say what they think others want to hear—or they keep their mouths shut, except to compliment others. They

spend their hard-earned money on gifts for others. They give more of their time and energy than they can afford to give. They are great self-sacrificers. They live as performers rather than as themselves.

- People pleasers work twice as hard as other people in their relationships. They are usually prompt (not wanting to keep anyone else waiting), gentle listeners (not venturing to express a conflicting opinion), and eager servants ("Please, let *me* do that!"). People pleasers are not pushy, except when smothering others with gifts, favors, and helpfulness.[4]

The way in which pleasers get back at controllers generates stress and pressure, because it's covert. It's an underground, indirect response. Often sulking, pouting, or using the silent treatment is employed. Other retaliatory tactics include withholding sex, talking behind the controller's back, spreading rumors in the office, going above the boss's head, bungling tasks, making messes, or accidentally losing materials or purposely being late on deadlines. The anger is expressed in this way, but it is stressful because the fear of being confronted over these behaviors is ever-present.

If you respond to a controller by rebelling against him, you fall into a different trap, that of becoming just like him. The rebellion is usually an overreaction to the extreme. The anger you feel can be seen by anyone who happens to be in the way. You visibly resist him and totally refuse to listen to him or validate what he says. You disregard any contribution he might want to make, even if it might be a good suggestion.

You express your irritation and frustration through criticism, barbs, and even character assassination. Your tactics are obvious, and nothing can dissuade you because you believe the controller deserves everything you dish out. It seems as though you are there every second, ready to pounce on what he does or what you believe he intends to do. Some people rebel only in their mind and imagination; others let it all out. Guess who ends up looking like the villain!

What's your style of reacting to the controllers in your life?[5]

RECOGNIZING YOUR ACCOMMODATION STYLES

What is your most typical response to a controller? Do you try to please, get even, or keep the peace? The test below can help you begin to see the patterns you slip into automatically when you are dealing with people who try to control you.

Rate each of the statements using the following scale:

$$1 = \text{strongly disagree}$$
$$2 = \text{moderately disagree}$$
$$3 = \text{slightly agree}$$
$$4 = \text{moderately agree}$$
$$5 = \text{strongly agree}$$

PEACEKEEPING

1. I'd rather give up what I want than have someone upset with me. _____
2. It's easier to get what I want if I make the other person think it's her/his idea. _____
3. I try to figure out what someone else wants and do it before she/he can become upset with me. _____
4. When someone I care about is angry with me, I'll do almost anything to get her/him to calm down. _____

   Total: _____

PEOPLE-PLEASING

5. I hate the "silent-treatment" and will do almost anything to get someone to stop doing it. _____
6. What others think of me is very important. _____
7. I respond to criticism by trying to change whatever is "wrong." _____
8. When I think I might have offended someone, I bend over backward to make it up to her/him. _____

   Total: _____

SELF-SACRIFICE

9. I do everything I can to avoid hurting other people. _____
10. I often get overloaded because I can't say no when I think someone needs my help. _____
11. When someone I care about asks me to do lots of things for her/him, I believe it only shows how much she/he needs me. _____
12. If someone at work seems overwhelmed, helpless, or incompetent, I'll do her/his task myself—even if I'm already overloaded. _____

Total: _____

Total of items 1–12: _____

PASSIVE RESISTANCE

13. When I'm upset with someone, I don't say anything but she/he gets the idea. _____
14. When someone is yelling at me, I won't give her/him the satisfaction of responding or even listening. _____
15. I often pretend I don't understand or know how to do something so a controller will stop asking me to do it. _____
16. When someone makes an unreasonable demand, I don't say no, but I take my own sweet time about doing it. _____

Total: _____

RETALIATION

17. I get back at people who try to take advantage of me by giving them the silent treatment. _____
18. Sometimes I "forget" to do something just to see someone sweat it out her/himself at the last minute. _____
19. I tend to be more clumsy (spill or break things) around people who have a lot of power over me. _____

20. When I'm in a situation where I'm forced to do what someone else wants, I can usually find a way to get even. ____

Total: ____

REBELLION

21. When someone tries to make me do something, I refuse to do it—even if it's a good idea. ____
22. I lose my temper when someone tries to bully me, and often say or do things I regret later. ____
23. Even though I stand up to a controller, I find myself fighting the same battles over and over. ____
24. I would rather stand up to a controller than be a wimp—even if I have to pay for it later. ____

Total: ____

Total of items 13–24: ____

YOUR SCORES

A total possible score for each scale is 20. A score of 14 or more on any scale indicates that you probably rely on that pattern when responding to a controller. Comparing the total score for items 1–12 with your total score for items 13–24 will show you whether you typically use giving in or fighting back responses. If the scores are relatively even, you probably use both kinds of automatic responses, depending on the situation. Pay special attention to any single item rated 4 or 5.[6]

Too often the person on the receiving end of the controller is so busy pleasing, sacrificing, or resisting he never stops to realize what drives the controller. Most of the controllers I've met have just as many insecurities as the pleasers, only they cover them up better by their offensive moves. They remind me of many of the small breeds of dogs who are aggressive yappers. If a large dog wanders into their territory they go ballistic with their barking and getting into the face of the large dog to "defend their territory." But inside they're quivering, and sometimes it shows with the puddles on the pavement!

Controllers soon discover that their "yapping" tactics meet their needs (at your expense) in tangible and intangible ways, which in turn reinforces that pattern of behavior. Sometimes the respect, power, or emotional rush they receive is what they're really after.

Think about it for a moment. If you're accommodating a controller, what needs are you helping him or her meet? Can you identify the tangible or intangible results he or she is after? If you are able to identify those needs and results, does that impact your feelings toward the controller? How does it affect your anger, fear, and compassion? How does it affect his or her power over you? Does it increase it or lessen it?

People use control to protect themselves from real or imagined concerns. Their use of control is part of their survival system. They believe "the best defense is control." Their greatest fear is imagining the disastrous results and consequences of not being in control. They fear rejection, abandonment, hurt, disappointment, and losing control itself. What about *your* controller? Is he defending himself against some concern? If so, do you know what it is? How does knowing what concerns him affect your feelings toward him? How does it affect his power over you?

I have worked with numerous controllers in counseling whose controlling tendency is an integral part of their personality. Some have told me, "I know I control. But why not? I have a lot to offer and I know what I'm talking about. Why waste time? I want to see things happen—fast and efficient. And I can do that!"

Can you think of personality types that reflect this control habit? How about the perfectionist who believes that satisfaction comes from having everything the way it should be? There are severe disorders that reflect a drive to control. The obsessive-compulsive has a compelling drive for order. The narcissist controls to make sure that the behavior of others will reflect positively upon him. The "Type A personality" is driven by anger and time.[7]

Does your controller reflect any of these patterns? Do his responses fit "who he is"? How does knowing the basis of his typical behavior affect your feelings toward him?

Both my wife, Joyce, and I (Norman Wright) enjoy fishing. Over the years we've collected a vast array of different hooks, including single barb, double barb, triple barb, and barbless. Controllers are people who have learned to use hooks well— emotional hooks that definitely are not barbless.

Controllers use *indebtedness*. They let you know that you owe them something by pushing your guilt button. "If it weren't for the good words I put in for you, you'd still be stuck in that pathetic job."

Controllers use *sarcasm*. You feel the bite of it, and often the tone and nonverbals (which make up 93 percent of the message in face-to-face conversation) are the vehicles used to transport their intended control. A statement like, "Oh sure, you remembered the party tonight. Then how come you arrived here an hour late and looking so sloppy? Sure you remembered." This emotional hook not only drags you in, but you can feel the irritation beginning to build. Usually the more you explain, the greater the degree of sarcasm and disbelief on their part. It is irritating to be labeled a liar.

One of the hooks that is a real set-up is what is sometimes described as an *assumed agreement* with an underlying threat of being criticized. "June, now stop and think about this for a minute. If you'd stop to think you'd see I'm right and it's best to go along with this. An alert person could see this right away." You end up feeling trapped.

One hook that really makes you feel trapped is being made the victim of a *forced choice*. "Jane, tell me which day you're coming over this week. I'd like to know now." You feel the pressure beginning to build. Later you probably feel anger toward him, but you are also angry with yourself for getting pulled in.

Another hook is one in which the controller *pretends to be talking about himself at the same time making clear he's talk-*

ing about you. He says such things as "I should have known better. Loaning you that camera was a mistake. It's my fault for letting you use it, and now it's gone forever." Guilt and anger eventually rise to this clever blame attack.

"You really shouldn't let your mother run your life like that, you know. At thirty-three-years-old you need to be your own person by this time in your life." Well, that's easy for him to say. *Judgment statements* are made to let you know the controller knows what's best for your life, more so than you.

Every now and then I read or hear a disclaimer made by an organization or radio station: "The views expressed by this speaker are not necessarily the views of the management of this station." Controllers voice similar *disclaimers* when they say "I don't mean to be critical but . . . ," or, "I don't mean to be telling you how to run your life, but . . ." Yes, they do want to run your life! They know it, and you know it, but you struggle with knowing what to do about it.

Sometimes their criticism is hidden so deep in a statement it's difficult to confront it directly. *Imbedded criticism* is like that. It's usually expressed in the form of a question delivered in a surprised or amazed tone of voice. "You aren't actually going to wear that to church are you?" You know what they're saying even if they deny it. They don't like it, and you should know better.

Controllers use *absolutes* such as "always" and "never" when they make statements to you. They fail to give you the benefit of the doubt or see exceptions in a person's life.

The phrases "If it weren't for you . . . ," or "Because of you I . . ." are *blame and shame* statements. Blame for whatever has gone wrong in the controller's life is thrust onto your shoulders, whether true or not. And the more defensive you become the greater their level of deafness.

Controllers often use *blame-shifting* to get their point across without having to shoulder any of the responsibility. "It doesn't bother me that you're not going to attend, but I think it is going to bother management" (or your mother or your father or your friends). They just can't seem to come out straight and truthful. It's maddening when you try to confront them by saying "Are you saying you're bothered too?" because they will deny it forever. I've heard wives use this approach with their husbands. "Some wives would be upset if their husband took the entire weekend off to go fishing," they say, and then when their husbands ask if *they* would be offended they quickly respond, "Oh, no. Not me. But some wives I know would be."

Double implied messages are characteristic of controllers. Their message contains a denial of what they're saying, but you know it's still true. "Oh, go on. Why should I mind that you can't call your old mother every day?" (or come to see her every Sunday).[8]

Do you realize what is happening when you cooperate with a controller? You have the same problem that Kuwait had with Iraq. Kuwait's borders were overrun, and there was a terrible conflict until US troops came in and put the Iraqis in their place. You don't need US troops for the repulsion of the invader in your life. You can do it yourself. The question you're probably asking right now is, "How?"

Several choices are available to you. It all begins in your thought life and the attitude you have toward yourself. Attitude has been defined as a manner of acting, feeling, or thinking that shows one's disposition, opinion, or mental set. In this case it's your attitude toward yourself that could be crippling your response to the controller. There are many resources available to assist you with questions of self-esteem, boundaries, and codependency, and these are listed at the conclusion of the chapter. But for now, know that it is important that this root issue be addressed, for that will make it much easier for you to put into place the suggestions that follow.

- *You could give in.*

Before you react and say that's been the problem all along, let me clarify. There are different ways of giving in. Some giving in is automatic, unconscious, a conditioned reflex. But if you make a conscious choice to go along with the controller, who is really in charge? Sometimes not giving in could put you in a precarious position with regard to your family or your job. Choosing to give in with a pleasant, strong attitude could convey a message to the controller and possibly lead to some sort of compromise. Giving in at one point in time doesn't mean that is your life pattern. It may lead to a stronger position when you really want something that's highly important to you. Besides, if you are in the wrong about something, why not take the initiative and admit it right out? That will often diffuse the controller, who may be hoping you'll resist. It's also a scriptural way of responding:

> A man who refuses to admit his mistakes can never be successful. But if he confesses and forsakes them, he gets another chance. (Proverbs 28:13 TLB)

> It is a badge of honor to accept valid criticism. (Proverbs 25:12, TLB)

There is another reason for giving in. If you know that losing is inevitable, it may help to give in early because that may prevent the difficulty from escalating.

If I were talking with you right now, I can just imagine your asking, "Isn't giving in to my boss (husband, parent, whomever) just going to reinforce his tendency to control me and keep my anger alive?" No. Because you choose to give in, your anger will be lessened, and if you let the person know this is your choice, you will give him something to think about.

I've heard people say, "Well, I've got several choices, but this time I'm deciding that I'll go along with you." Or, "I think that doing what you are requesting is my best choice." Or, "I'm going to do what you've asked this time. In the future I would appreciate it if you would give me a few minutes to think over your request as well as some of the reasons for doing it. I'm sure that will work to your advantage as well."

- *You can refuse his/her request.*

This may be the best alternative for you. In order to have a life of your own you do need to set some limits. If you never say no, you reinforce a controller and continue to feed your anger. You may believe it's easier to live with yourself when you continue to say yes, but it isn't. Be willing to accept the reaction of the controller when you say no. In fact, as you prepare in advance to refuse (which is essential), anticipate how you think he will react. In your heart and mind give him permission to respond in this way. I've seen many successful refusals. Here are steps you can take to make it work.

Identify exactly what you want to say. Keep it short, don't apologize, and above all do not give any reasons. He may ask, but you don't need to give any. Your reasons are your own business.

In your mind and then out loud, standing in front of a mirror, rehearse what you're going to say until it becomes comfortable. Do it again and again. One of my clients formulated a strong response to a person at church who was always forcing people into jobs and tasks they were not gifted for. She said, "I've thought over what you've asked me to do, and I've decided not to do it. In the future I would appreciate your not asking me to do anything, and I will let you know when I do want to take on any responsibilities. Thank you for your cooperation."

The man responded exactly as she had predicted. He asked her "why" she couldn't. She responded by using the broken record technique and repeating what she had previously said word for word. He gave up. Sometimes you have to repeat your statement several times, but it can be very effective.

- *You can let the controller know that you know how is he going to respond, and that's all right, but you won't change your mind.*

This tactic can be effective. Since you are the one to suggest how he will respond and have noted that it's no big surprise to you, the person's response loses its significance and effectiveness as a control base. Before you say this tactic won't work, experiment with it and use it in several settings. Work together with another woman, plan it out, and pray about it together.

- *You can "unplug."*

I don't have an answering machine at home. When I don't want to be bothered I simply unplug the phone. It works well. Sometimes you need to unplug yourself from the controller literally so that you're not overwhelmed. How can you do that? It's quite simple. You can leave the situation by leaving the room or hanging up the phone. This could mean leaving a poor employment situation. In a marriage with a controlling partner, it could mean saying, "You have a choice. You can back up and approach me with sensitivity and courtesy, and we will discuss what you want. If not, and you continue in the same way, I will leave the room. If you pursue me, I will go next door to the neighbors. Then when you want to change your approach, I will be willing to talk with you."

- *You can limit your contact with the controller and not be dissuaded by manipulative tactics.*

You have other options as well. Some comments can be ignored and overlooked. You may want to limit your time with those who attempt to control you. I've made this choice with people who have invited me to activities I would ordinarily have enjoyed except for the fact that they were either overbearing controllers or overtalkers. If the controller in your life attempts to make you feel bad by pouting or looking depressed, let him be. Don't go running after him. Identify his tactics and discover a new way of responding. If he uses the ploy, "I'm just offering you a suggestion," thank him and respond with, "I'm glad that was a suggestion, since suggestions give us the free choice of saying yes or no."

- *You can cut him off.*

There are times, if you know fairly well what he is going to say or do, you can interrupt and say, "Please tell me the point

141

of this discussion." I don't care for phone solicitors, and I usually can tell when they're selling something. Instead of listening to their canned presentation, which is usually being read, I simply and nicely interrupt and say, "Thank you anyway. I'm not interested." If they persist, I repeat myself and then hang up. Years ago I felt I needed to listen to every last word, but I've learned.

Sometimes when I receive calls from an organization asking for donations, they use the tactic of saying, "We want to thank you for your gift from last year and . . ." At that point I interrupt and say, "Excuse me. Exactly what did I give last year? I keep very close track of all donations, and I don't have you on my list." Usually they disconnect immediately.

- *You can ask for clarification.*

When emotional hooks are being used on you, you could say, "Can you clarify that for me," or, "I don't seem to recall that. Could you be more specific?" or, "If I understand what you're saying it's . . ." The best way I've discovered to handle unsolicited phone callers is to have my golden retriever answer the phone and bring me the receiver. When they hear all the commotion and him panting it really throws them.

Please remember that your attitude, nonverbals, and tone of voice make all the difference in the acceptability of what you say.

- *You can level with him.*

Another option available to you is leveling. This can take many forms. The purpose is to convey information to the controller, not change him. It is vital that you plan your statement in advance when you're calm and rehearse it again and again, even tape recording it and listening to yourself. When you level with a person, you do several things. You tell him what you want or don't want from him, what you think about what he is asking you to do, how you feel about his behavior, and finally, what you are willing or unwilling to do. You can probably see the value of rehearsing your statement in advance. It is a clear form of "speaking the truth in love" (Ephesians 4:15).

And when you do see the controller begin to adopt a different response in relation to you, affirm him. Let him know you appreciate his hearing you.[9]

I realize this may not be a simple task, and you may struggle with it, but consider the alternative—being controlled and angry.

- *You can decide to please God.*

As you shift your position, you will find your anger diminishing as well as feeling better about yourself. That doesn't mean that you should never accommodate and please others. We all do accommodate and please others—but should be doing it out of a position of strength and choice. I like the alternative shared by Bobbie Reed:

> A second alternative to a people-pleasing lifestyle is to decide to seek to please God. If we can't please people, if we shouldn't live to please people, and we can't succeed by just pleasing ourselves, then what do we do? Paul says it best when he writes in Galatians 1:10, "For do I now persuade men, or God? or do I seek to please men? for if I yet pleased men, I should not be the servant of Christ" (see also 1 Thessalonians 2:4). Peter and the apostles refused to follow the high priest and the Sadduccees, stating that "We ought to obey God rather than men" (Acts 5:29).
>
> To live in a way that is pleasing to God and fair to ourselves, we must:
>
> —Choose to live by God's standards (John 15:10–11).
>
> —Recognize that we won't be approved of by others all of the time, even if we are approved of by God. The world doesn't really want us to live just for the approval of God. There are plenty of people—even some friends, even some Christians—who want us to break God's laws (John 17:14–17).
>
> —Live intentionally, consciously, and deliberately in accordance with those standards and goals, and experience the abundant life Jesus came to give us (John 10:10).

—Live peaceably with all men, as much as lieth within us (Romans 12:18).

To accomplish this, we have to rethink our choices. We have to redefine satisfaction, rebuild our self-concepts, deepen our awareness of and relationship to God, and set goals. We must also develop inner strength, abandon our neediness, develop balance in our lives, and regain our personal power. We do this all so we can learn to do for others out of love rather than out of a desperate need for approval.

In the process, we will learn to abandon the bondage we have chosen. In Galatians, Paul tells us to stand fast in the freedom Christ has given us. When we live as people pleasers, we choose to put ourselves in bondage to others. We are trying to serve the wrong masters. Other people aren't to set the standards for us, but God and His Word. We are like Peter, who took his eyes off of the Lord and started to sink in the sea. When we look away from Him for our direction, we can only sink.

It is a tall order. The process will not always be easy or satisfying. But in the long haul, it will be worth it. Life will become exciting, abundant, and free.[10]

NOTES

1. Adapted from Gerald W. Piaget, *Control Freaks: Who They Are and How to Stop Them from Running Your Life* (New York: Doubleday, 1991), 1–25.
2. Adapted from Bobbie Reed, *When Pleasing You Is Destroying Me* (Dallas, Tex.: Word, 1992).
3. Adapted from Piaget, 13–14.
4. Reed, 14–15.
5. Adapted from Piaget, 50–61.
6. Piaget, 60–63.
7. Adapted from Piaget, 86–88.
8. Adapted from Piaget, 154–55.
9. Adapted from Piaget, 102–5.
10. Reed, 56–57.

CHAPTER SEVEN

Stress and Anger

Let's become introspective for a moment. It's time to reflect upon you.

Do you ever find yourself struggling with making decisions? I don't mean just the major ones, but the little ones as well. You're either unsure of what to do, or it seems like such a chore.

Do you ever have fleeting thoughts, which are now becoming more common, such as *Oh, I'd like to get away from all of this. I want to get away from my kids, my husband, my job—everything. I need a break!*

Do you find yourself increasing your use of any kind of substance as a stimulant, such as alcohol, cigarettes, coffee, Cokes®, tranquilizers, or diet pills to keep you going?

Do you find your mind taking a vacation on you in the sense of finding your thoughts trailing off when you are speaking to someone or writing? Do you catch yourself saying, "Now, what was I talking about?" and then wonder what's wrong with you? Why is this happening?

Do you worry excessively? You know what worry is. You go over and over a real or imagined situation in your mind. You focus on the future, asking the question "What if . . . ?" and answer it not just once but again and again. You begin to take on the worries of others as well as your own.

Do you find yourself snapping and exploding at others more than usual? Your anger is riding just under the surface, and it doesn't take much for it to explode.

Do you find yourself having difficulty trusting others? Your suspicion index is starting to climb even with close friends as well as family members.

Are you beginning to forget appointments, dates, and deadlines, and this is not usually your pattern? Your image of being responsible is starting to shatter.

Do you find yourself brooding over events and issues, and not just major ones either? Little things become the catalyst for sitting and vegetating. More and more you have feelings of inadequacy with no apparent basis.

Are people beginning to say about you, "She just doesn't seem quite herself anymore." They're aware that your typical behavior is changing.[1]

All of the items above are symptoms of stress overload. Is this you? If so, consider the relationship of anger to each of those characteristics.

Stress is a simple, common word. It has been used as a catchall to explain a physical and emotional response when no other explanation can be found. But it's real. There is a direct correlation between stress and anger. Stress can generate anger, and anger can generate stress. In our national survey, stress was identified as the second leading factor that increases women's vulnerability to anger.

DEFINING STRESS

We've looked at the characteristics of being stressed. But

what contributes to stress in a woman's life? And what exactly is stress? It is any situation or condition that chronically irritates or upsets you. Because of it you are thrown out of balance physically and psychologically.

Stress is the feeling of being drawn tight like a rubber band when it is stretched taut and stays in that position. When the pressure is released, the rubber band returns to normal. But if it stays in that position too long, the rubber begins to lose its elastic qualities, becomes brittle, develops cracks, and eventually breaks. Under stress you're also the victim of a flood—of adrenaline.

What is stressful to one woman is not to another. Your background, life experience, how you learned to handle the upsets of life, and your neurological structure will affect your response.

Not all stress is bad. It can motivate and activate us. It brings a feeling of exhilaration. It's good because it doesn't last long.

One woman therapist searched through a decade of therapy notes with her female clients and looked for the stresses that women could call their own.

- There are the stresses associated with physiology: breast development, menstruation, pregnancy, and menopause.
- There are the stresses connected to life changes: becoming a wife or a mother, enduring a divorce or economic collapse, moving into the forties in a youth-oriented society, having adult children return home, and widowhood.
- There are the psychological stresses experienced by the lonely single woman and the homemaker coping with the pressure to break out of the routine and go back to school or develop a career. There are the stresses experienced by the career woman who is being pressured to give it up, go back home, and be a family member, or the stress endured by an exhausted working woman constantly short on sleep and money.

- There are the not-so-apparent stressors that tend to not only distract a woman but over time deplete her resources, leading to a feeling of distress. Those stressors include the pressure of commuting, being isolated with young children, crime and the threat of being attacked because of being a woman, fighting the chauvinism of others, and sexist comments as well as harassment.
- Finally, there are the life crises that unfortunately tend to be handled more by women than by men. Those can include caring for a sick or dying parent or child, parenting a handicapped child, and handling the aftermath of her own or her child's divorce.[2]

The '90s also ushered in what is referred to as "the era of the new woman." Many more women work than ever before, either out of choice or necessity. The jobs that women hold today are more of the stressful, pressure-laden ones. In 1988 women made up 39 percent of all those holding managerial, executive, and administrative positions, a 13 percent jump from ten years before. Many more women today see their work as a career rather than just a job, which means they have a greater personal investment in it.

BARRIERS, CONTRADICTORY FEELINGS, AND CHANGING EXPECTATIONS

In *Beyond Chaos: Stress Relief for the Working Woman,* Sheila West talks about "the glass ceiling" (mentioned earlier in this book) and what West calls "the reeling effect." The glass ceiling is a perceived barrier that allows women to glimpse, but prevents them from obtaining, positions farther up the corporate ladder. It is a barrier that still exists in society as well as in the mind-set of some women themselves. It's a fact in some settings, whereas in other settings it exists only in the eyes of the beholder. Either way, the glass ceiling creates pressure if it's allowed to hinder progress.

The reeling effect is difficult to overcome, since its ingredients are change plus apprehension, equaling uncertainty. Many women experience this. Constant change along with apprehension about their work leaves them feeling as though they just stepped out of a tornado.[3] It's the mixture of opposing feelings. "Oh, I really want to work," vs. "When am I going to be able to quit?" "Is it always going to be like this?" Or, "This is so challenging and informative," vs. "How will I survive all these deadlines? Help!" When Sheila West described the contradictory feelings that create the sense of uncertainty in women she had this to say:

> For many women, indecisiveness arises when they simply occupy a job slot instead of effectively creating a career path. A job is accepting a task that has to be done. A career is the pursuit of results that have a long-term significance, even if that pursuit is on a short-term basis.

> If I go to work just because I have a job, it confines my perspective to a narrow slice of reality. The phrase "just a job" conjures up unpleasant associations: mundane assignments, boring routines, something to be endured. In this kind of environment, our feelings are bound to fluctuate with daily activities in an aimless moodiness. All too soon we start asking, "What now?" When we're not sure what we're accomplishing or what the ground rules are for doing it, and we receive a meager paycheck to boot, we'll continue to question whether we made the right choice.

> But women who are trapped in entry-level jobs are not the only ones suffering from the clash of expectations and reality. Even women on a career track are often caught off-guard with what they find in the marketplace. There doesn't seem to be much security or continuity in many fields.

> Women often find that staying on the competitive edge means treacherous climbing rather than sustaining accomplishments. The thrill of a new challenge gives way to the agony of moving too fast to be adequately prepared. We thought we knew what we wanted, but once we get it we're not sure it's what we had in mind.

The Reeling Effect keeps us frustrated over the constant effort to prove ourselves, the energy required to avoid unnecessary confrontations with others, and the enduring stress of having to maintain high-quality performance. The stress can reach the point where even if we do love work, we want out anyway. The pleasure of accomplishment is just not worth the struggle for survival.[4]

SINGLE IN A MARRIED WORLD

The new woman is more likely to experience a divorce. Estimates say that one-half to two-thirds of women who married in the '80s will end up divorced. More of them will never marry, and more of them who are married won't ever have a child. More of them are less dependent on men. In 1990 only 31 percent of women believed that to be really happy, you needed a man. In 1970, 66 percent believed that.[5]

Nevertheless, if you're single, you'll experience stress, especially if you're getting older and want to get married. If you're over thirty-four you have a problem, as the pool of eligible men is very small. The stress of "I must find a man" that propels many women in their thirties and forties keeps them from living a full life. There is another stress as well. How does our society view single women? Is it positive or negative? The stereotype is that they are unhappy and perhaps defective in some way.[6]

NEW FREEDOMS BUT FEWER OPTIONS

What generates so much stress and anger is that few women end up having the life they thought they were going to get when they were growing up. Yes, there are new freedoms and changes, but there are also fewer options. A permanent marriage, children, and handling work and home are not sure things. Life is more unpredictable. We used to hear that women could have everything they ever wanted. Many have become disenchanted with that idea because it is not only not working out, but what accompanies the new options and lifestyle is enormous stress, much more than ever before.

The doors have opened more for work for women, but that has added much more stress to women's lives. Working wives and mothers have discovered that when they work they are still expected to run the home and fulfill the same duties they did when they were just at home. Husbands do not help out that much, partly because they are let off the hook too easily. Naturally, that causes stress and anger and eventually resentment.

GUILT OVER WORKING

Many working wives, and especially mothers, struggle with guilt over working. To make up for it, they put forth a double effort at home to show they are adequate mothers and can handle both work and homemaking. Soon they're stressed, running on an empty tank, and a candidate for burnout.[7]

BEING A HOUSEWIFE IN A TROUBLED MARRIAGE

Many times I've heard people say that in the end the most fulfilled women will be the ones who stayed at home ("where they belong" is usually implied) and raised their children. If you're among those who agree with that statement, you may be surprised at the findings of the 1990 report from the American Psychological Association National Task Force on Women and Depression.

The report cites a study that ranked women from least depressed to most depressed, starting with the least depressed. Here is that ranking, with least depressed women listed first:

1. Employed wives with a combination of low marital strain and low job strain.
2. Employed wives with low marital strain but high job strain.
3. Unmarried women with low job strain.
4. Nonemployed wives with low marital strain.
5. Employed unmarried women with high job strain.
6. Employed wives with high marital strain and low job strain.
7. Nonmarried, nonemployed women.
8. Employed wives with high marital strain and high job strain.
9. Nonemployed wives with high marital strain.

The happiest women are those who are pleased with both their jobs and their marriages. The least happy women—they have five and a half times the risk of depression as the first—*are housewives with troubled marriages* (italics added).[8]

TOO MUCH TO DO IN TOO LITTLE TIME

Time is one of the stress inducers for many women. Even with economic problems, two out of three say they would prefer more time rather than money.[9]

Taking on too much or attempting to accomplish too much in a limited time span will add pressure to your life. Some questions for you: "Why do you do all that you do? Why must it be completed in the time schedule you have given yourself? Who has determined your schedule? Others or yourself?"

There are times when we need to make a list of all of our activities and evaluate them to see which are really that important. Some women continually take on new activities but never give up any. Every woman needs time for herself each day to be alone and do something she enjoys. You might say, "But it's impossible with my schedule and demands. There's never enough time." It may help to evaluate what you are doing.

BOREDOM

Boredom—or lack of meaning in what you do—can cause stress. This may come as a surprise to some of you, but continually doing the same routine or being bored can become a stressor. Homemakers and those in routine jobs may struggle with this. Sometimes a woman may have to work at discovering the meaning in what she is involved in doing. She may need to become creative and develop some new ways of responding to a monotonous environment.

UNREALISTIC EXPECTATIONS

Unrealistic expectations will keep you stressed. We all have expectations for ourselves and for others. But can they all be attained? Where did they come from? Perfectionists are people with excessively unobtainable expectations. They are great candidates for stress. There is a difference between living a life of perfectionism (or attempting to, since no one has ever been successful at it yet) and a life of excellence. The dictionary states that to be perfect is to be "complete and flawless in all respects." Excellence is defined as something "outstandingly good or of exceptional merit." Perfection is defined by absolutes. Excellence, on the other hand, means you do things to the best of your ability, and you make mistakes.

Perfection is an end state, whereas excellence leaves room for growth. Aiming for excellence allows for forgiveness. A perfectionist may be 98 percent successful in something but allows the 2 percent to white out all the success. She focuses on the flaw and doesn't see the value in progress. Remember that if you are striving to be a perfectionist, you are still living by works and have not yet learned to live by the grace of God. If perfectionism is a struggle for you, perhaps you would benefit from reading *Hope for the Perfectionist* by David Stoop (Nashville: Thomas Nelson, 1987) and *How to Stop Living for the Applause: Help for Women Who Need to Be Perfect,* by Holly G. Miller and Dennis Hensley (Ann Arbor, Mich.: Servant, 1990).

ROLE CONFLICTS

Role conflicts will contribute to your stress. If you are in a job ill-suited to you, it may be stressful. If you are a housewife and would rather be following a career, you may experience stress, and feeling stuck will build your anger.

A RELATIONSHIP LACKING OPEN COMMUNICATION

If you are dating or married and open communication is blocked, stress will build. Relationships are built upon communication. When a spouse or parent refuses to talk or puts pressure upon others to be quiet, there will be damaging results. In a marriage relationship, when one partner is either overly quiet or pulls the silent treatment, very little intimacy can develop. This is one of the major causes of marital disruption and destruction.

THE UNIQUE PRESSURES OF THE WORKPLACE

Today more women than ever have entered the work force. It is estimated that 90 percent of the women in this country have worked or will work for pay at some time during their lives. Most women work because they have to, but many have said they would work even if they didn't have to. They've assessed the benefits of being employed.

As more and more women have gone to work they have discovered that work not only brings in money but can generate stress. Sometimes the stress overrides the benefits. Many factors contribute to that stress:

- Having a great deal of responsibility, but little authority or control
- Having an abundance of work, but insufficient time to complete it
- Having a strong desire to advance in your job, but the chances are limited
- Discovering you are more competent than your boss, but are still being ignored
- Being underpaid for what you do, or discovering that men in the same position are paid more
- Having a lot to do, but constantly being interrupted
- Doing work that is not exciting, challenging, or stimulating, but is instead boring and redundant
- Experiencing sexual harassment or discrimination on the job
- Those in clerical jobs tend to experience these situations the most[10]

BEING A TYPE A

It used to be believed that the "Type A syndrome" described by cardiologists Meyer Friedman and Ray Rosenman was a condition of achievement-oriented males. But article after article is now discussing this condition as a definite potential for women in high-pressure jobs. The most dangerous factors connected with this problem are time urgency and chronic anger. Much of the anger stems from insufficient time and too much to do, unrealistic expectations, and guilt.

A Type A woman experiences *free-floating hostility,* a sense of lasting, indwelling anger. This hostility increases in frequency, demonstrating itself even in the most minor frustrations. A Type A woman may be clever at hiding this tendency or finding excuses and reasons for her irritation. But she becomes upset too frequently and well out of proportion. She is overly and outwardly critical and belittles and demeans others.

A Type A person's *sense of time urgency* manifests itself in two ways. First, she speeds up her activities. The way she thinks, plans, and carries out tasks is accelerated. She talks faster and forces others to do the same. It is difficult to relax around her. Everything must be done faster, and she looks for ways to increase the speed. Second, she has many different thoughts and activities on the burner at the same time. Leisure time doesn't reduce the tension. She overschedules activities even during leisure time. She attempts to find more time and tries to do two or three things at once. She overextends herself in a multitude of activities and projects, and often some go undone.

In time your body will tell you if your behavior is Type A. A true Type A person's body experiences more noradrenaline, which constricts the blood vessels and pushes up blood pressure.

CUMULATIVE STRESS

In the 1970s two medical doctors named T. H. Holmes and R. H. Rahe developed the Holmes-Rahe stress test, which has been widely used but until recently, when it was updated for women, had not been updated or revised. The Holmes-Rahe test was based upon a series of life events, with each event receiving a numeric score for its stress potential or value. In the original sample the researchers discovered that those with scores of over 300 points for the past year had an 80 percent chance of experiencing an illness or depression within the next two years because of the amount of stress. The results showed the correlation between life change stress and physical and emotional stress.

In the updated survey 2300 women in twenty states were surveyed to see how they were affected by the same events listed in the original survey. The top ten stressors with their original ranking and new ranking are listed below. The numbers in parenthesis are the point values for each.

Top Ten Stressors

New Rank	Stressor	Old Rank
1	Death of spouse (99)	1
2	Divorce (91)	2
3	Marriage (85)	7
4	Death of close family member (89)	5
5	Fired at work (83)	8
6	Marital separation (78)	3
7	Pregnancy (78)	12
8	Jail term (72)	4
9	Death of a close friend (68)	17
10	Retirement (68)	10[11]

The respondents were given the opportunity to add new stressors to this list. Below are listed the top thirteen with the percentage of the sample mentioning the item (keep in mind that the sample was made up of 2,300 women).

New Stressors

Stressor	Percentage of Sample Mentioning the Item
Parent's illness	59
Husband's stopping work	58

New Stressors (continued)

Stressor	*Percentage of Sample Mentioning the Item*
Child's illness	58
Spouse's illness	55
Chemical dependency	31
Remarriage	29
Commuting	27
Crime victimization	26
Depression	23
Raising teens	22
Husband's retirement	22
Infertility	19
Single parenting	18

It was enlightening to note the stress ratings for these and other new items. They are given below.

Stress Ratings for the New Stressors

Stressor	*Points*
Disabled child	97
Single parenting	96
Remarriage	89
Depression	89
Abortion	89
Child's illness	87
Infertility	87
Spouse illness	85
Crime victimization	84
Husband's retirement	82
Parenting parents	81
Raising teens	80
Chemical dependency	80
Parent's illness	78
Singlehood	77[12]

The changes in stress are quite apparent. Where do you fit in all of this? Would you rate these the same as other women? What are the five major stressors in your life at the present time? What are the effects in your life because of each one? Which of these evokes anger or brings out your anger more?

STRESS THAT HAS REACHED THE BURNOUT STAGE

I've talked with many women who have said they used to feel they were stressed and were quite angry over their situation, but now they just don't have the energy to be angry. It's as though they don't care anymore. That isn't stress. It's burnout. There is overall burnout, parental burnout, job burnout, and marital burnout.

A simple, overall definition of burnout is: "To wear oneself out by excessively striving to reach some unrealistic expectation imposed by one's self or by the values of society."

Someone who is burned-out is "in a state of fatigue or frustration brought about by devotion to a cause, way of life, or relationship that failed to produce the expected reward."

Stated another way, trouble is on the way whenever the expectation level is dramatically opposed to reality but the person persists in trying to reach that expectation level anyway.

Burnout is a complex process that involves all five major areas of our lives: physical, intellectual, emotional, social, and spiritual. The physical aspect refers to the amount of energy available to do what you need to do and want to do. Burnout's first symptom is an all-around feeling of fatigue.

The intellectual aspect refers to the sharpness with which you think and solve problems. In burnout, this ability diminishes.

The emotional aspect refers to whether your emotional life is basically positive or negative. Are you optimistic or pessimistic about what is occurring in your life?

The social aspect of burnout refers to feelings of isolation compared to feelings of involvement. What kind of support system do you have? Do you feel free to share your feelings of frustration, anger, fatigue, or disillusionment?

The spiritual aspect refers to the degree of meaning you have in your life.

Perhaps you're wondering whether you're simply stressed or have hit burnout. Consider the differences:

- Burnout is a defense characterized by disengagement
  Stress is characterized by overengagement

- In burnout the emotions become blunted
  In stress the emotions become overreactive

- In burnout the emotional damage is primary
  In stress the physical damage is primary

- The exhaustion of burnout affects motivation and drive
  The exhaustion of stress affects physical energy

- Burnout produces demoralization
  Stress produces disintegration

- Burnout can best be understood as a loss of fuel and energy

- The depression of burnout is caused by the grief engendered by the loss of ideals and hope
  The depression of stress is produced by the body's need to protect itself and conserve energy

- Burnout produces a sense of helplessness and hopelessness

OVERCOMING STRESS

What's the answer? How do you lessen the stress in your life and make yourself less prone to anger? There are several steps to consider. You could try to change your environment, whether it be working conditions, home schedule, travel, or moving. Some things, however, are difficult to change.

You can work on changing your response to the stressful elements in your life. Some of the steps mentioned in this chapter will help you reduce your reactions. Relaxation techniques do help. Tranquilizers are sometimes prescribed for stress, but it should be remembered that some people become overly dependent on tranquilizers.

Perhaps the best approach after you take all the corrective action possible is to change your thoughts and perspective on what is taking place in your life, for that is where much of our stress comes from.

At the heart of most of the stress of life is our attitude—our belief system. If you are stuck on the freeway and have an appointment in twenty minutes for which you will now be late, what do you say to yourself? Many sit there and begin to fuss and make statements such as "I can't be late! Who's holding us up? How dare they? I've got to get out of this lane!" You begin to lean on the horn and glare at others. That's why you are getting upset—it's your statement.

I know it's inconvenient to be stuck, to be late, to have a boss pile on work at the last minute, to miss the bus, to break a nail just before church, but the key factor that moves you from feeling like a victim to becoming an overcomer is taking control of your circumstances by giving yourself permission to be in the situation you're in: to have your plans disrupted, or to be given too much work, or what ever it may be. That will put you back in control, and you'll feel there is some hope.

It works. I've seen it work. And it can work for you. It's learning to put Philippians 4:13 into practice: "I can do all things through Christ who strengthens me" (NKJV). Proverbs 15:15 applies also: "And all the days of the desponding afflicted are made evil [by anxious thoughts and foreboding], but he who has a glad heart has a continual feast [regardless of circumstances]" (AMP; brackets in AMP).

Here are a number of suggestions for reducing the stress in your life that have worked for others. It may take you a while to see a change. Making these changes may be uncomfortable at first because you are giving up a way of life that is comfortable, even though it is also potentially destructive. But it is worth the effort to reduce the stress in your life.

- Each day think about the causes of your time urgency and the reasons you feel stressed. Write down one of the consequences.
- As part of your new program read *When I Relax I Feel Guilty* by Tim Hansel (Elgin, Ill.: Cook, 1979) in a leisurely fashion.
- Reduce your tendency to think and talk rapidly by making a conscious effort to listen to others. Become "a ready listener" (James 1:19 AMP). Ask questions to encourage others to continue talking. If you have something to say, ask yourself, *Who really wants to hear this? Is this the best time to share it?*
- Begin each day by asking God to help you prioritize those items that need to be done first. Then do only those items you really have time for. If you feel you can accomplish five items during the day, do only four. Write them down and then check them off.
- If you begin to feel pressured about completing your tasks, ask yourself these questions: *Will completing this task matter three to five years from now? Must it be done now? If so, why? Could someone else do it? If not, why?*
- Try to accomplish only one thing at a time. If you are going to the bathroom, don't brush your teeth at the same time. If you are waiting for someone on the phone, don't attempt to look through the mail or a magazine. Instead, look at a restful picture, or do some relaxation exercises. When someone is talking to you, put down your newspaper, magazine, or work and give the person your full attention.
- Make it a point to relax without feeling guilty. Give yourself permission to relax and enjoy yourself. Tell yourself it is all right, because indeed it is.
- Reevaluate your need for recognition. Instead of looking for the approval of others, tell yourself in a realistic way, "I did a good job and I can feel all right about it."

- Begin to look at the Type A behavior of others. Ask yourself, *Do I really like that person's behavior and the way he or she responds to people? Do I want to be that way?*
- If you have a tendency to think in numbers, such as "How much?" and "How many?" change the way you evaluate others or situations. Express your feelings in adjectives and not numbers.
- Begin to read magazines and books that have nothing to do with your vocation. Go to the library and check out novels or books on different topics. Become adventuresome, but don't see how many different books you can read—or brag to others about this "accomplishment."
- Play some soft background music at home or at the office to give a soothing atmosphere.
- Attempt to plan your schedule so that you drive or commute when traffic is light. Drive in the slow lane of the highway or freeway. Try to reduce your tendency to drive faster than others or just as fast.
- Pick days to leave your watch at home. Keep track of how often you find yourself looking at your wrist that day.
- Tape record one of your own phone or dinner conversations and play it back. Note whether you talk most, ask questions, or listen to answers. Do you look for something else to do while you're on the phone? Do you try to speed up your conversation by supplying the endings of sentences for your partner? Do you interrupt or change the topic to fit your needs?
- Don't evaluate your life in terms of how much you have accomplished or how many material things you have acquired. Recall your past enjoyable experiences for a few minutes each day. Take time to daydream about pleasurable experiences as a child.
- Make your noon hour a rest time away from work. Go shopping, browse through stores, read, or have lunch with a friend. After a meal with a friend make notes of the concerns that person shared with you. Use your notes as a prayer guide. Follow up later to see how the

person is doing. You may want to call a different person each week. Let them know you have been praying for them and want to know how they are doing.

- Begin your day fifteen minutes early and do something you enjoy. If you tend to skip breakfast or eat standing up, sit down and take your time eating. Look around the house or outside and fix your interest upon something pleasant you have been overlooking, such as flowers in bloom or a beautiful painting.

- Begin to recognize what your values are. Where did they come from, and how do they fit into the teaching of Scripture?

- When you arrive home, announce to others (even if it's just the cat) that the first ten minutes belong to you. When you come home from the office de-stress yourself before you deal with home. Or read while you have a cup of tea in a restaurant for ten minutes. Stop at church for five minutes for prayer in the quiet of the sanctuary. Ask your husband to watch the children while you take a fifteen-minute bath or shower before you start dinner. Make this a regular part of your day.

- This one will sound crazy, but get in the longest supermarket line to practice waiting without getting upset. Give yourself permission to be in a long line. Discover how you can make time pass pleasantly. Speculate upon the lives of those around you. Talk to them about positive things, not about how long the line is. Review pleasant memories.

- As you play games or engage in sports, whether it be racquetball, skiing, or cards, do it for enjoyment and not for competition. Begin to look for the enjoyment of a good run, an outstanding rally, and the good feelings that come with the recreation you have been overlooking.

- If you have a tendency to worry, begin to follow the suggestions given in my (H. Norman Wright's) book *Afraid No More!* (Wheaton, Ill.: Tyndale, 1992).

- Allow yourself more time than you need for your work. Schedule ahead of time and for longer intervals. If you usually take a half hour for a task, allow forty-five minutes. You will see an increase in the quality of your work.

- Evaluate what you do and why you do it. Lloyd Ogilvie offers some insights on our motivations and the pressures we create:

> We say, "Look, God, how busy I am!" We equate exhaustion with an effective, full life. Having uncertain purposes, we redouble our efforts in an identity crisis of meaning. We tack up performance statistics in the hope that we are counting for something in our generation. But for what or for whom?
>
> Many of us become frustrated and beg for time to just be, but do our decisions about our involvements affirm that plea? A Christian is free to stop running away from life in overinvolvement.[13]

In one of Ogilvie's sermons he raised two interesting questions that relate to what we are doing and how we are doing it: "What are you doing with your life that you couldn't do without the power of God?" and "Are you living life out of your own adequacy or out of the abundance of the riches of Christ?" Both questions deserve an honest answer.

- The real answer to stress is found in applying God's word to your life. What I have done with many counselees is to suggest they read the following passages out loud several times a day. You may want to do the same.

> Now to Him Who is able to strengthen you in the faith which is in accordance with my Gospel and the preaching of (concerning) Jesus Christ, the Messiah, according to the revelation—the unveiling—of the mystery of the plan of redemption which was kept in silence and secret for long ages. (Romans 16:25 AMP)
>
> Then [Ezra] told them, Go your way, eat the fat, drink the sweet, and send portions to him for whom nothing is prepared; for this day is holy to our Lord; and be not grieved and depressed, for the joy of the Lord is your

strength and stronghold. (Nehemiah 8:10 AMP; brackets in AMP)

And He shall be the stability of your times, a wealth of salvation, wisdom, and knowledge; the fear of the Lord is His treasure. (Isaiah 33:6 NASB)

You will guard him and keep him in perfect and constant peace whose mind [both its inclination and its character] is stayed on You, because he commits himself to You, leans on You and hopes confidently in You. (Isaiah 26:3 AMP; brackets in AMP)

Do not fret or have any anxiety about anything, but in every circumstance and in everything by prayer and petition [definite requests] with thanksgiving continue to make your wants known to God. (Philippians 4:6–9 AMP)

Fret not yourself because of evildoers, neither be envious against those who work unrighteousness—that which is not upright, nor in right standing with God. (Psalms 37:1 AMP)

NOTES

1. Adapted from Keith W. Sehnert, *Stress/Unstress* (Minneapolis: Augsburg, 1981), 74–75.
2. Adapted from Georgia Witkin-Lanoil, *The Female Stress Syndrome: How to Recognize and Live with It*, 2d ed. (New York: Newmarket, 1991), 16–17.
3. Adapted from Sheila West, *Beyond Chaos: Stress Relief for the Working Woman* (Colorado Springs: NavPress, 1992), 104.
4. Ibid., 106–7.
5. Adapted from Witkin-Lanoil, 118–19.
6. Adapted from Witkin-Lanoil, 125–26.
7. Ibid., 118–21.
8. American Psychological Association National Task Force on Women and Depression, "Women and Depression: Risk Factor and Treatment Issues" (Washington, D.C.: The American Psychological Association, 1990); as cited in: Witkin-Lanoil, 122.
9. Keri Report, "The State of American Women Today" (Bristol-Meyer, 1991).
10. Ibid., 132–33. Adapted.
11. Ibid., 91.
12. Ibid., 102.
13. Lloyd Ogilvie, *God's Best for Today* (Eugene, Oreg.: Harvest, 1981).

CHAPTER EIGHT

Harassed and Abused— You Need to Be Angry!

A phrase in the book of Ecclesiastes says, "There is a time to speak and a time to be silent." Whenever abuse of any variety occurs, or any form of sexual harassment, it is a time to speak. What has been tolerated and accepted for decades by women is no longer acceptable. It's been the reason for a contained anger that in some cases simmers for years but with no outward expression. This is a time for righteous anger to be put into action to counter the violation of God's creation. Too often a woman unwittingly cooperates with the pattern of abuse or harassment for numerous reasons. But that does not have to continue. Whether the abuse and harassment occurring today is more than occurred in previous decades is not certain, but the message is: "No longer will this be tolerated."

Do you know what it's like to be abused? Have you ever talked with a victim of abuse? Do you know what abuse is?

DEFINING ABUSE

Susan Forward and Joan Torres, in *Men Who Hate Women and the Women Who Love Them,* define abuse this way:

> *Abuse* is any behavior that is designed to control and/or subjugate another person through the use of fear, humiliation, and verbal or physical assaults. In a sense, it is the systematic persecution of one family member by another.[1]

Fists and feet are the weapons of physical abuse, whereas words and looks are the weapons of emotional abuse.

Physical abuse is some form of purposeful brutal physical contact rather than accidental. It can include any behavior that either intends to inflict or actually does inflict physical harm. The varieties include pushing, grabbing, shoving, slapping, kicking, biting, choking, punching, hitting with an object, or attacking with a knife or a gun. I will never forget the first abuse victim I saw. Her husband had beat her head against the bathroom floor and pulled out patches of her hair.

Emotional abuse has a multitude of expressions. Scare tactics, insults, yelling, temper tantrums, name calling, and continuous criticism fall into this classification. Threatened violence is a form of emotional abuse, too. Holding up a weapon, swinging a fist near your face, destroying property, or kicking your cat falls into this category. Withholding privileges or affection or constantly blaming you for the family's difficulties is abuse.

I've heard some people defend their shouting pattern as normal. They say, "That's just the way we did it in our family. Everyone shouted, and we accepted it. That isn't abuse!" But in their new marriage it may become abuse because of the sensitivity of their spouse. Shouting can become terrifying and overwhelming if it is constant, intense, and loud.

WHO ABUSES—AND WHY?

Is there a person in your life who abuses you? It could be a father, husband, or boyfriend. Do you know why they do what they do?

Men who come from homes in which they experienced a violent and abusive childhood are more likely to abuse their spouse or girl friend. Abusers typically were abused personally, or they witnessed the abuse of their mother or father. When verbal or physical abuse is the pattern for settling disputes and conflict within a family, the children are limited in their opportunity to learn alternative ways of expressing their anger. Why shouldn't they continue the pattern? It's what they know best.

Even if your abuser was not personally subjected to abuse as a child, if someone else in his family was, he was victimized by it. If he was the victim, the greater the frequency of abuse within his home, the greater the possibility he will repeat this pattern as an adult.

Another characteristic of men who abuse is difficulty in expressing their feelings with words. Much is said about the inexpressive male in our society. It is a common problem. Men who abuse often have difficulty not only in expressing their feelings but in identifying and dealing with them when they occur. All too often, whether the feeling is fear, frustration, or anxiety, the only way they can let it out is through anger. Often they have difficulty expressing affection, and it too ends up being expressed through abuse.

In some families a man may use his inexpressiveness as a power tool to dominate others. When he's silent, who knows what he is thinking? Who's willing to shatter the calm by rocking the boat? So the family members go along with what he wants rather than risk unleashing what may be inside of him. Then if his inexpressiveness isn't working, he can use actual physical abuse to vent his inner rage and control others in that way.

Many studies indicate that abusive men are usually nonassertive away from home and struggle with low self-esteem. Their behavior within the home reflects this. In feeling poorly about themselves and not living up to our society's portrayal of what a man should be, they exceed what is normal behavior and become abusive.[2]

It is unfortunate for both the abuser and the abused person that the abuse seems to work. The abuser then has no reason to give it up and learn healthy ways of relating. Nor does he see any need to come to grips with his own insecurities. The person he is abusing is cooperating with him and letting him get away with it.

The inflexibility of abusive men is seen in their rigid beliefs about the role and responsibility of husbands and wives. They want to dominate every area of their spouse's life. Often a wife becomes socially isolated and then has to become dependent upon her abusive husband for emotional support.

The abuser has a belief system about what a husband should be—the absolute, autocratic leader in the home. Unfortunately, I have encountered Christian men who misinterpret and misuse Scripture to substantiate this belief. This view of a man's role also includes the view that he should never appear to be weak; should never ask others for help; should be the one to make all family decisions; should be "honored and respected" in all ways by his family; and should always be in control of his emotions. He expects his wife to be both submissive and inferior in all areas.[3] In other words, he has a distorted view of what a man is and what Scripture teaches.

One last characteristic is not surprising. Many abusers have difficulty with substance and alcohol abuse, especially the latter.[4]

WHO TOLERATES ABUSE—AND WHY?

What are the women like who tolerate abuse? Is there a pattern? Those who are abused have many characteristics in common, but of course there are exceptions to what is stated here. Many women will not tolerate this behavior and either intervene in a successful way or immediately terminate the relationship.

Like the abuser, an abused woman often comes from an abusive family background and has a poor self-image. Actually, some women accept abuse as normal behavior because they were raised in an abusive home. Unfortunately, many women tend to blame themselves for the abuse they experience, thinking, *If only I had responded differently he wouldn't have been physically abusive.*

A woman who is abused tends to have low self-esteem, and this feeling makes her easy prey to her husband's abuse. The emotional abuse of threats, ridicule, put-downs, and criticism is devastating and feeds her feelings of low self-esteem. If you hear a negative, repetitive tirade over a period of time you begin to believe the statements. Many women end up believing that they don't deserve anything better. They become "pleasers," attempting to meet the needs of everyone in the family except themselves.

If you are being abused, you're probably holding on to an unrealistic hope. You believe that in time if you're patient and faithful your abusing man will change. You accept every promise he gives, and since the times when abuse is absent are good, you do have a taste of what you have always hoped for.

One of my clients, Judy, had been coming to counseling for several weeks. One day she arrived and said, "I'm not sure that I need to come for counseling anymore. Jim has done such a dramatic turnaround and seems to be living up to his promise of not abusing me anymore. I think he really means it this time. And when he isn't abusive the relationship is so wonderful."

My reply was a twofold question. "Judy, how long has it been since he was abusive toward you, and how many other times has he said he wouldn't do it again?" I already knew the answer from our previous discussions, and when I asked, the smile left her face as she too remembered the litany of broken promises. It had been only ten days since the last abuse occurred.

If you're abused, you tend to isolate yourself over the months and years. You begin to isolate yourself socially because you are afraid that others will discover your situation and

171

because your husband prefers that you be available at all times. In time, you either are or will be so cut off that you're unaware you have any other alternative. Then you become more enmeshed in the abusive pattern.

Dependency, both emotional and economic, tends to keep you locked into this relationship. If you have little education or few work skills you're probably afraid of being left without anything. If you are working, who controls your money? The chances are, your husband.

One of the tragedies in this situation is the loss of healthy boundaries. Abused women lose the sense of objectivity to make the determination that they're in any danger. The abuse becomes so common that even blood, bruises, and pain don't signal that their personal boundaries have been invaded.

One of the most difficult problems may be in clinging to a traditional role in marriage. This is not wrong in itself. But you may allow your husband to remain at home, even if he is a threat to you and the children, in order to save your marriage. You're unwilling to consider separation for your own safety. Or you may believe wives should be tolerant of such transgressions in order to be patient, loving, submissive, and giving. If your marriage isn't working, you may believe that it's your task to fix it. And if your self-worth is tied up in the success of your marriage, it is easy to see why you're under so much bondage to fix it.

To you, divorce would be a sign of failure, and that, coupled with cultural, Christian values and perhaps your coming from a divorced home, keeps you where you are.[5] Sometimes, though, a temporary separation of residence is needed to convince your partner that he is harming both the marriage and his family.

WHAT CAN YOU DO IF YOU ARE BEING ABUSED?

What can you do now? What if you find yourself in this situation or you know someone who is? You could use the following suggestions for yourself, or give them to a friend.

- *Assess the potential or level of abuse that exists in your relationship at the present time.*

One way of doing this is by using the assessment tool given below.

CSR Abuse Index

Are You in an Abusive Situation?

This questionnaire is designed to help you decide if you are living in an abusive situation. There are different forms of abuse, and not every woman experiences all of them. Below are various questions about your relationship with a man. As you can see, each possible answer has points assigned to it. By answering each question and then totaling these points as directed, you can compare your score with our Abuse Index. You will know if you are living in a potentially violent situation. And if you are abused, you will have some estimate of how really dangerous that abuse is.

Directions: Circle the response to each question that best describes your relationship.

Frequently	Sometimes	Rarely	Never	
3	2	1	0	1. Does he continually monitor your time and make you account for every minute (when you run errands, visit friends, commute to work, etc.)?
3	2	1	0	2. Does he ever accuse you of having affairs with other men or act suspicious that you are?
3	2	1	0	3. Is he ever rude to your friends?
3	2	1	0	4. Does he ever discourage you from starting friendships with other women?

Frequently	Sometimes	Rarely	Never	
3	2	1	0	5. Do you ever feel isolated and alone, as if there was nobody close to you to confide in?
3	2	1	0	6. Is he overly critical of daily things, such as your cooking, your clothes, or your appearance?
3	2	1	0	7. Does he demand a strict account of how you spend money?
3	2	1	0	8. Do his moods change radically, from very calm to very angry, or vice versa?
3	2	1	0	9. Is he disturbed by your working or by the thought of your working?
3	2	1	0	10. Does he become angry more easily if he drinks?
3	2	1	0	11. Does he pressure you for sex much more often than you'd like?
3	2	1	0	12. Does he become angry if you don't want to go along with his requests for sex?
3	2	1	0	13. Do you quarrel much over financial matters?
3	2	1	0	14. Do you quarrel much about having children or raising them?
3	2	1	0	15. Does he ever strike you with his hands or feet (slap, punch, kick)?
3	2	1	0	16. Does he ever strike you with an object?
3	2	1	0	17. Does he ever threaten you with an object or weapon?

Frequently	Sometimes	Rarely	Never	
3	2	1	0	18. Has he ever threatened to kill either himself or you?
3	2	1	0	19. Does he ever give you visible injuries (such as welts, bruises, cuts, lumps on head)?
3	2	1	0	20. Have you ever had to treat any injuries from his violence with first aid?
3	2	1	0	21. Have you ever had to seek professional aid for an injury at a medical clinic, doctor's office, or hospital emergency room?
3	2	1	0	22. Does he ever hurt you sexually or make you have intercourse against your will?
3	2	1	0	23. Is he ever violent toward children?
3	2	1	0	24. Is he ever violent toward other people outside your home and family?
3	2	1	0	25. Does he ever throw objects or break things when he is angry?
3	2	1	0	26. Has he ever been in trouble with the police?
3	2	1	0	27. Have you ever called the police or tried to call them because you felt you or other members of your family were in danger?

To score your responses simply add up the points following each question. This sum is your Abuse Index Score. To get some idea of how abusive your relationship is, compare your score with the following:

120–94	Dangerously abusive
93–37	Seriously abusive
36–15	Moderately abusive
14–0	Nonabusive[6]

According to the authors, 0–14 lives in a nonabusive relationship. A woman with a score in the 15–36 range lives in a home where she has experienced some violence at least once in a while. The thing to watch out for here is the possibility of escalation.

Women with scores in the 37–93 range are in a seriously abusive situation that can become most dangerous if outside pressures impact the family. There is the likelihood the woman has experienced injury already, and the prospect of serious injury is high. The woman needs to enter into counseling and try to involve her husband in counseling. Perhaps she should leave the home for a while and work through her options. She needs help.

Women with scores in the top range of 94–120 are in serious jeopardy. They need to consider carefully at least a temporary separation or other outside interventions. The violence will not miraculously disappear. The chances are that the woman's life is very much at risk and perhaps the lives of her children as well.[7]

- *If you are currently being physically abused (or any family member by your spouse), take the necessary steps to **remove yourself from the setting where you are being victimized.***

This last point is assuming that you have tried on your own through proper confrontation or even using a family and friend's intervention program and nothing has changed. Remember that you are a valuable, chosen person, and your body is a temple of the Holy Spirit. Don't let others mistreat you; no one deserves abuse. If you are in a church that tells you to stay in an abusive environment, find another church.

Go immediately for professional help. The person or agency can assist you with the following steps. (1) Find out what the laws are about abuse and what legal steps you can take. You need to know your legal status and options, spouse abuse or child abuse laws, police procedures, and victim options. (2) Devise a safety plan for you or the other abused person(s). This should include a safe environment—one that is accepting, non-threatening, and protective. Develop a plan to get to the safe environment, including the best timing, transportation, money, clothes, and so on. (3) Develop a network of other people to rely on and who can support you.[8]

After removing yourself from the threat, focus on changing your life so that your being a victim does not occur again. This will take courage, but change in our lives happens when we allow the Holy Spirit to give us strength and courage.[9]

- *Get in touch with all of the feelings you have about being abused.*

Write them out. If you don't feel any anger, something is amiss. Focus on what has been done to you and how wrong it is and the injustice of it all. You didn't deserve to be abused. No one does!

- *Fourth, if you are the victim of verbal or emotional abuse, decide and define what you want from the abuser rather than what you are now receiving.*

You might decide that you want to be listened to, spoken to with courtesy and kindness, respected, to be understood, and your opinion respected.

Then decide what you want to stop permitting to occur in your relationship. It is important that you become quite specific at this time. You might say:

— I won't permit him to swear at me.
— I won't permit him to insult me.
— I won't permit him to yell at me.

177

— I won't permit him to berate me in public.
— I won't permit him to tear down my self-esteem.
— I won't permit him to try to control me.

Then you decide the statements that you are going to make to him. As you think of those statements you may also begin to experience fear and panic just over the thought of saying them. You can get over the panic and fear, however. Some of the new assertive statements you can make are the following:

— "It's not acceptable for you to speak to me in this way. The way you can talk to me is . . ."
— "It's not acceptable for you to treat me like this. The way you can treat me is . . ."
— "Yelling is not going to be effective anymore. What will work best for us is . . ."
— "This will not intimidate me now or ever. When you want to get my cooperation you could . . ."
— "This may have worked before. Now it won't, but here is something that will . . ."
— "I will not discuss this when you are like this. I will when you are like this . . ."[10]

Notice that each phrase concluded by pointing out what would be acceptable.

Pick out one of the statements and sit facing an empty chair. Practice saying each statement out loud to the empty chair and imagine your abuser reacting to your statement. This will create a number of emotional responses on your part, but the more you practice, the more confident you will become and the more your emotional stress will lessen. Remember that when you do respond with your assertive responses you don't have to give him any reasons why you are saying this. As he asks different questions of you, use the broken record technique and simply repeat what you said the first time. Stay away from debates or arguments. We have found that it has also been helpful to practice or rehearse your response with a trusted friend.

One thought to keep in mind whenever you're on the receiving end of any kind of abuse. In place of thinking (as so many do), *What is wrong with me that he treats me like this?* think, *What's wrong with him that he's treating me in this way?* Whenever you see the behavior you want, reinforce it with thank-yous and praise. Such phrases might include "I really appreciate that," or, "Thank you for your consideration," or, "That really draws me to you when you talk to me like this!"[11]

SEXUAL HARASSMENT

The phrase *sexual harassment* is explosive today. You hear about it weekly if not daily in some form of the media. Even if you have never yet experienced it, it's happened to someone you know. It could have happened to you and perhaps you weren't even aware that it occurred. It can happen anywhere. Now that I understand it better, I remember incidents in high school when it occurred between male teachers and girls in our class. It's rampant in the work arena.

In October of 1991 the results of a poll by the National Association of Female Executives was released. Seventy-seven percent of all those polled stated that sexual harassment was a problem in the workplace, and 55 percent said it had happened to them. However, 64 percent did not report it, and of those who did, most felt the issue was not addressed satisfactorily. They were forced either to resign, quit, or transfer to a position they did not want.[12]

Most cases of sexual harassment are not reported because the woman feels so degraded, is too uncertain of her rights and options, or lives in fear of retaliation.

What exactly is sexual harassment? Sexual harassment refers to a wide range of behavior, and all of it is illegal. It is deliberate or continuous behavior of a sexual or sex-based nature that is unwelcome, not asked for, and not returned. It is deliberate and repeated and can be verbal, nonverbal, or physical. It can include sexual comments, jokes, suggestions, or innuendos. Nonverbal harassment is quite common and includes suggestive looks, leering or ogling, blocking the woman's path, or acting as though he's going to grab her.

Actual physical harassment can include "accidental" as well as "deliberate" action. Accidentally brushing up against a woman or deliberate "friendly" pats, squeezes, or pinches are considered minor deliberate steps. But the harassment can become very serious. It can range from direct fondling and rubbing to a boss or employer forcing a woman employee to sleep with him in order to keep her job.

As with other problem areas a number of myths have been developed (probably by men) to explain away the problem.

MYTHS ABOUT SEXUAL HARASSMENT

MYTH: Some women ask to be sexually harassed.

REALITY: Being subjected to sexual harassment is a painful and difficult experience. Defenses such as "she wore provocative clothes" and "she enjoyed it" are neither acceptable nor accurate.

MYTH: If a woman really wanted to discourage sexual harassment, she could.

REALITY: Often, the harasser is in a position to punish the woman by withholding a promotion or giving a bad evaluation. In this society, men often rationalize their behavior by claiming that a woman's "no" actually means "yes."

MYTH: Most charges of sexual harassment are false.

REALITY: Women have little to gain from filing false charges. It is exceedingly difficult to file sexual harassment charges, and confronting the harasser can be both physically and financially draining.

MYTH: Sexual harassment is inevitable when men and women are working together.

REALITY: Although interaction between the sexes might be inevitable, uninvited sexual overtures are not.

MYTH: If you ignore sexual harassment, it will go away.

REALITY: Only 29 percent of the women recently surveyed who said they tried to ignore the behavior said that it "made things better." Over 61 percent said that telling the person to stop made things better.[13]

Why is it so difficult for some women to speak up? There are numerous reasons. Guilt, shame, embarrassment, or the fear of being labeled by others as an overreactor or an agitator or as being too sensitive or hysterical could all be factors. The woman's upbringing may make the very subject too painful or upsetting for her to face. Some women may even think that sexual harassment is just part of life and women have to learn to handle it. Some women have said they don't think it will do any good to report someone, or they're unclear about or don't trust the procedures to follow in doing so.

But perhaps there are deeper and more significant reasons tied into tradition and culture. Women have long been considered the ones responsible for controlling the level of sexual involvement. They are looked to for setting the boundaries, so when harassment happens often a woman wonders, *What have I done wrong?*

Sexual harassment that occurs at work is more than just a desire for sex of some kind. It's usually an abuse of power to keep a woman in her place. It's used to force her out or for advancement. It's a tactic to make a woman vulnerable.[14]

STOPPING SEXUAL HARASSMENT

If sexual harassment is occurring in your life, your goal is to get it stopped immediately. If it's happening at work, your goal is to get it stopped *and* keep your job as well as your potential for advancement. Here are some steps you can take.

- Be sure you admit that a problem exists; don't deny it to yourself. You may choose, as a tactic, to ignore it and see if it goes away. Choosing to ignore it is quite different from denying that it's happening to you.

- Recognize sexual harassment for what it is—deliberate or repeated sexual behavior and control that's unwelcomed by you. You may want to consider if the behavior is sexual or directed at you because of your gender. Is it happening on purpose or is it accidental? Is it repeated over and over? Does he know it's unwelcome? Have you said or indicated that you don't like it? Exactly what have you said? Do you participate in or initiate the behavior, such as telling off-color jokes yourself or smiling when you're saying no to his advances?

- Remember that no matter what the behavior is or how infrequently it occurs, it's a problem that usually won't just go away.

- No matter what kind of harassment it is, it's very costly to everybody. You pay a cost with a higher stress level, and your job efficiency and effectiveness are mostly likely affected too. It's degrading and damaging to you, personally and professionally. It needs to be stopped immediately.

- It's important to remember that your company has an investment and an interest in stopping harassment at work. Sexual harassment damages a company or business in terms of absenteeism, loss of productivity, and lowered morale and motivation.

- Accept responsibility for taking part in solving the problem. You can do something to take control of the situation that you're caught up in. Deal with the harassment as soon as it occurs.

- Calmly, and in private, speak up and tell the person you don't like his behavior. Keep the conversation brief.

Aim for a relaxed, confident stance. Do not hunch or strut. Take time to adjust your position so that you're looking neither up at him nor down at him. The tone of your voice should be even and firm. Look him in the eye. If standing, stand at a distance that feels comfortable—not too close, not so far that you have to raise your voice unnaturally. Make only appropriate gestures. Do not wring your hands, look down, stare, move in toward the person, or shake your finger under his nose. This poise and restraint in your gestures usually works best, especially if it's the first time you've said something about the offense and if it's a less serious behavior.

- Use an "I" statement, saying, for example: "When you call me 'honey' (touch me/tell me jokes)"—describing the behavior you don't like—"I feel very upset (embarrassed/angry/offended)"—saying what your feelings are —"because I want to be taken seriously (want to be treated as an equal/want respect)"—saying why it bothers you. Don't smile, touch the person, or give any mixed messages. Don't use humor.

    Sometimes it helps to write out your "I" statements and rehearse them ahead of time.

- Use the broken-record technique by acknowledging the person's response and then repeating your statement. If the offending employee responds by saying that he didn't mean to hurt your feelings, or you're too sensitive, you can say, "I understand that you didn't mean to hurt my feelings; however, when you (stating the offense) I felt (stating your feelings) because (stating your rationale)." You do not need to change your original "I" statement.

HOW TO SAY NO—AND BE HEARD

A professional therapist who works with harassed women suggests the following:

> If you are being pestered by a male coworker or supervisor for a lunch date you don't want, I recommend starting out with a rather benign statement the first time you speak to him. You might say: "I am comfortable with our business relationship, but I'm not comfortable carrying it any further—even for lunch."[15]

Other steps you might want to take to end harassment:

- Request what you do or don't want by saying "Please always call me by my name (don't touch me/don't tell me those jokes)." Be specific.

  If he persists in the unwanted behavior, make an escalated assertion, something like: "I've told you three times that I am not interested in any other relationship. I would like you to stop asking me."
- Try this mini-plan once or twice. If you don't get results from the offending employee, you'll have to do more.
- Ask a coworker for support and even help in talking with the offender. Sometimes the offender can hear a message more clearly from another person or when there is more than one person present.

  If the harassment persists, write the person a letter, spelling out what behavior you object to and why. Be sure to specify what you want to happen next. If you feel the situation is serious or bound to escalate, let him know that you will take action against the harassment if it doesn't stop at once. If your company has a written policy against harassment, you may want to attach a copy of it to your letter.[16]

  If the harassment continues, collect evidence, which can include saving any offensive notes, letters, or photographs you receive. Make copies of offensive cartoons or jokes posted at work and note the dates and any reaction when you asked to have them taken down.

  Keep a journal documenting events that occur at work, school, or home. This can include person-to-person situations or telephone incidents. Indicate what is done and said to you and the frequency.
- Go to a supervisor, manager, or owner to get additional help if the behavior does not stop. If the problem is the employer, get legal advice to see what your options are.
- Don't assume the harassment will stop if you ignore it. Seventy-five percent of the time, sexual harassment

problems intensify and get worse when ignored. The person is getting away with it, so why should he stop?

- Don't try to deal with severe harassment alone, even the first time. Let your friends and family know. In serious cases, let someone in the company know about it immediately.
- If a simple plan doesn't work, or if the problem is more complex or serious, a more thorough plan might be called for. In that case, it's important to find and maintain your balance and perspective by looking at all the elements of the problem.
- Make your plans specific with regard to time, place, and actions. Think through all the consequences of each plan. Keep in mind that you have two simultaneous goals at this point: to get the behavior stopped and to maintain your effectiveness in your job.
- Include other people in your plans. If this problem is happening to several, a group approach can be effective. You may think you are the only one and it's embarrassing to tell others. They may be thinking the very same thing! Don't handle it all alone, especially with harassers who seem to be insensitive or malicious. Call on those friends, supervisors, or managers who you think can be of help.
- Keep your plans flexible. The response of the harasser or of the manager or company representative may change your plans or timetable.[17]

What has been suggested here is a plan for you or any woman to use in taking positive action against harassment. It is a constructive way to use your anger to correct a malignancy in our society. Respect by each gender for one another is what God wants for us. Be careful of falling into the trap of thinking that all men are abusers or harassers. They're not. And those that are need to hear the message that it will no longer be tolerated. Perhaps that will shock them and encourage them to deal with their own problem areas and the confused set of values that feeds this behavior.

Remember that God created you with value, worth, and dignity. If a man invades your boundaries, you have every right to stop him. In doing so you will be stopping abuse and harassment not only for yourself but for other women as well.

NOTES

1. Susan Forward and Joan Torres, *Men Who Hate Women and the Women Who Love Them* (New York: Bantam, 1986), 43.
2. Howard J. Parad and Libbie G. Parad, eds., *Crisis Intervention, Book 2: The Practitioner's Scourcebook for Brief Therapy* (Milwaukee: Family Service America, 1990), 161.
3. Kathleen H. Hofeller, *Battered Women, Shattered Lives* (Palo Alto, Calif.: R & E Research Associates, 1983). n.p.
4. Grant L. Martin, *Counseling for Family Violence and Abuse* (Dallas: Word, 1987), 36.
5. Adapted from Parad and Parad, 163.
6. William A. Stacy and Anson Shupe, *The Family Secret: Domestic Violence in America* (Boston: Beacon, 1983), 122–27.
7. Martin, 58.
8. Parad and Parad, 167.
9. Adapted from Gary Jackson Oliver and H. Norman Wright, *When Anger Hits Home: Taking Care of Your Anger Without Taking It Out on Your Family* (Chicago: Moody, 1992), 209–10.
10. Adapted from Forward and Torres, 219–26.
11. Ibid., 222–29. Adapted.
12. Adapted from William Petrocelli and Barbara Kate Repa, *Sexual Harassment on the Job* (Berkeley: Nolo, 1992), 3/23.
13. Ibid., 1/6. Adapted from "Combating Sexual Harassment: A Federal Worker's Guide," a pamphlet published by Federally Employed Women, Inc., 1991.
14. Ibid., 3/5. Adapted.
15. Ibid., 3/30.
16. Ibid., 3/30.
17. Adapted from Susan Webb, *Step Forward: Sexual Harassment in the Work Place; What You Need to Know* (New York: MasterMedia, 1991), 96–101.

CHAPTER NINE

Anger
and Your Family

Have you ever wondered why you respond the way you do with your anger? You were born with the capacity to be angry, but somewhere you learned what to do with it, and that somewhere was your family. As you progressed through infancy to preschool and up through adolescence you filed information about anger into your memory bank.

Your family passed on to you a legacy of anger expression. It may have been healthy, and then again, it may not have been.

A number of women have told me they were thankful their parents showed their anger openly. They said, "It helped me accept my anger, and they demonstrated an appropriate display of what to do with that irritation." Other women have told me, "Mom didn't ever tell me not to be angry, but instead guided me to express it in healthy ways. That I appreciate." But many others don't appreciate what they saw and heard about anger. They either saw anger out of control or lived in a repressed, avoidant type of atmosphere. Some family members screamed and raged while others sulked or played the martyr role. Whatever pattern was there, it influenced you.

In our National Survey we asked the question, "As a child, the primary ways that I saw anger expressed were . . ."

Here is a sampling of the results:

- Raised voices, foot stomping, clapping of hands together (Mom), silence (Dad)
- I usually wasn't allowed to show anger
- Quiet steaming up
- Loud voices, door slamming
- "Mean" talking (rejection)
- Parents wouldn't speak to each other; my sister and I would argue
- Yelling, tears
- My father was semi-abusive, would call us names, spank us, shove us into walls; my mother would scream, hit cabinets, hit us with a brush on the bottom; my sibs (the two older hated each other) and I tried to mediate
- Loud voices; Father hit my mother; she became cold and distant
- Physical abuse, verbal abuse; in our family, feelings were not ever spoken of, everyone was always interrupting
- Shaming and sarcastic expressions
- Screaming, sometimes objects were thrown (my mother was volatile and explosive; my father was passive and very slow to anger)
- My mother would say I never saw anger as a child because she says she was never angry; I think she's wrong
- Voices were silenced, distance, sleep, work very hard, depression, illness (physical), tears, loud fast talking and blaming and then release, or sometimes we (?) or my parents (?) would talk about it and then move on

DENIAL OF ANGER

If you were fortunate to come from a healthy family you probably experienced accurate information about feeling angry and what to do with it. But many women have not had that privilege. Of all the unhealthy displays of anger in a home, the worst is no display—when anger is purposely avoided and not expressed.

Many homes give the appearance of stability and healthy interaction. From all outward appearances the parents appear calm, consistent, and balanced. But anger still exists. You find it in tight lips, piercing looks, painful punishing silence, and feeling cut off from their love. The children don't express their anger. They wouldn't dare. It's forbidden. They are taught, "Not only do you not show anger, you don't feel it either." As if that were possible!

These children are being taught a life-debilitating pattern of denial. You may have learned this pattern as a child. Or, as an adult, you may be teaching your own child this behavior. The denial of any emotion leads to an accumulation of it. Soon there is an overabundance with no proper avenue of drainage. Denying an emotion means you have turned its energy back against yourself and are slowly destroying yourself and your potential.

David Viscott, a psychologist and author, describes the consequences of pent-up anger:

> When we hold in feelings, we distort the world around us. We really do not believe what we profess to be true and so we doubt our judgment. We make villains out of the people we love and begin to lose belief in ourselves as well. We become more interested in being right than in making peace. Although we hold feelings back to stay in control, doing so makes us feel fragile and at risk of going out of control. Our anger builds. We struggle to keep from exploding. We take it out on innocent people. We are easily triggered by minor frustrations.[1]

THE ANGER-AVOIDANT FAMILY

What about you? Does this sound familiar? To help you decide, let me clarify what is meant by the term *anger avoidance.* It's a pattern of thinking, acting, and feeling in which a person tries to ignore, avoid, and suppress his anger.

Some families can be described as anger-avoidant. Either all or most of the family constantly works at minimizing their expressions of anger. Often the children carry this pattern with them and perpetuate it in their own families, or the pattern creates tremendous tension if their spouses are the opposite.

In an anger-avoidant family at least one parent models the pattern. The children are perceptive enough to see that this parent lives in fear of his own anger or is repulsed by any show of anger. They learn to see anger as bad, dangerous, or shameful —or all of these.

Why do families follow this pattern? For many, this is their way of attempting to keep the family together and functioning. When anger is expressed it threatens the stability and functioning of the family because of the possibility of family members' distancing themselves from each other or of anger's raging out of control. One or both parents may believe that anger is always going to be destructive. In some of these families the pattern is maintained because of the false belief that the other family members don't have the ability to cope with anger. They fear the worst possible consequences. Anger is infused with more power, and especially negative power, than is warranted.

MECHANISMS DEPLOYED AGAINST ANGER

In these families various mechanisms to defend against anger are employed. Family members fail to notice when others are irritated. Looks and tone of voice that carry anger are overlooked and denied. Feelings of annoyance are repressed or denied.

Conflict is bound to arise in any marriage or family relationship. But in these families conflict is not seen as normal. It threatens the stability of the family. Therefore, it must be dangerous.

If two family members were to sit and talk about their differences, that might lead to anger. So family members avoid, appease, and accommodate. They avoid anything controversial and give in to others as much as possible. Thus family members learn that any expression of anger can work to get them what they want.

Manipulation becomes a byword in these families, since direct requests and confrontations are avoided. If you ask, someone might become angry. And if your request is refused, you could become angry. So the family begets members who become well versed in hinting, playing the martyr, and especially in being a passive-aggressive. (This behavior pattern was described in chapter 1.) Family members learn to hook one another into negative behavior patterns.

A dangerous pattern evolves in these families that tends to reinforce the myths about anger already in existence. An anger avoider wears blinders concerning his own initial feelings of irritation and annoyance. To recognize them would be admitting to anger, and this is unacceptable. So the feelings are stuffed with the hope they'll do a disappearing act. But it doesn't work. When the container is filled, it spills over like an inflated underwater balloon bursting from its moorings through the surface of the water. No matter what is in the way, it collides with it and explodes. When the out-of-control anger is visible it only serves to validate the person's worst fears. As one woman said, "I've always lived in fear of my anger, that if I ever did get angry I would lose control—and I did. I was right to be afraid of anger, and especially when it was over such a small thing." That is a common statement for any anger avoider.

Often these families have a high degree of physiological complaints as well as depression, since the buried anger has to have some outlet. The resentment that soon develops from the buried anger finds an alternative channel of expression. It festers out of sight like a splinter under the skin, finally erupting in depression or a physical ailment.

Once in a while you will find a family like this that actually allows one or more members to express his anger. Perhaps they believe that fathers always get angry, or that anger is a characteristic of a hyperactive child, a drinker, an overworked mother, etc. But you can imagine how the angry person is treated when they cut loose! Being ignored does very little to reduce one's anger.[2]

EFFECT OF YOUR FAMILY'S ANGER ON YOUR LIFE TODAY

To be sure, uncontrolled anger within a family is always destructive. Words that are hurled along with angry reactions and behaviors separate family members, and in time the chasm between them expands. The potential for destruction is always there. This is seen in the life of Saul and his son Jonathan:

> Then Saul's anger was kindled against Jonathan, and he said to him, You son of a perverse, rebellious woman, do not I know that you have chosen the son of Jesse to your own shame, and to the shame of your mother who bore you?
>
> For as long as the son of Jesse lives upon the earth you shall not be established nor your kingdom. So now send and bring him to me, for he shall surely die.
>
> Jonathan answered Saul his father, Why should he be killed? What has he done?
>
> But Saul cast his spear at him to smite him, by which Jonathan knew that his father had determined to kill David.
>
> So Jonathan arose from the table in fierce anger and ate no food that second day of the month, for he grieved for David, because his father had disgraced him. (1 Samuel 20:30–34 AMP)

Does anyone like this come to mind in your family? If so, what part does their anger play in your life at the present time? Reflect for a moment on your family:

When did your father get angry?
How did he express his anger?
Toward whom did he usually express it?

How long did it last?
What were the results at that time?
What is its effect upon you today?

When did your mother get angry?
How did she express her anger?
Toward whom did she usually express it?
How long did it last?
What were the results at that time?
What is its effect upon you today?

When did a sibling get angry?
How did he/she express his/her anger?
Toward whom did he/she usually express it?
How long did it last?
What were the results at that time?
What is its effect upon you today?

You may feel as though you're the first person in your family to struggle with anger, but you're neither the first nor the last. If anger is a problem for you, it was a problem in previous generations as well. What you are struggling with is part of your family legacy that others struggled with in some way as well. That's why doing a family history on your family's emotions, especially anger, is so important. If you don't know about and understand your family's emotional history, you are more likely to repeat the patterns, regardless of their healthiness, or unconsciously react to them. If this is the case you have not determined who you are or what you want for your own identity. It is important that you answer the previous questions either from your own memories or by tapping into the memories of other family members, such as siblings, aunts, uncles, or other significant, knowledgeable individuals.

JEAN'S STORY: THE DESIGNATED "ANGRY PERSON"

Jean gave me a fascinating account of anger in her family that is all too common. "You've heard of people being appointed an ambassador to a foreign country and representing our own country?" she said. "Well, I received an appointment representing my family, but it wasn't a pleasant one. I was appointed as the 'angry family member.'

"I can recall even when I was young I was constantly being told that I was the angry one in the family—even when I wasn't! In time I just figured if that's what they wanted me to be, I'd go along with it. But over the years I discovered that I was the only one who expressed anger. At times I got the feeling they were waiting for me to get angry so they would feel better. They would provoke me until I got angry. I finally figured out they were releasing their own anger through me! I'd become the designated anger bearer! I wish they'd let their own anger out and quit using me!"

When I heard this story I couldn't help but wonder if Jean's parents were aware of Ephesians 6:4: "Fathers, do not irritate and provoke your children to anger—do not exasperate them to resentment—but rear them [tenderly] in the training and discipline and the counsel and admonition of the Lord" (AMP; brackets in AMP).

Did this happen in your family?

MICHELLE'S STORY: THE GREAT PRETENDER

Michelle came from a repressed home. At least it was repressed when it came to anger. Even when voices were raised in enthusiasm or intensity it was considered anger. Both verbal and nonverbal expressions were given the label of anger.

"I became the great pretender," Michelle said. "I should have gone into theater work. I wore this pleasant mask that fooled everyone—except my body. Stuffing all the anger over the years and learning to smile instead made me feel like a fractured personality. In time my body rebelled. I can't stuff much of anything anymore, since I lost half of my stomach. I guess my stomach kept score of all the hurts and frustrations. I don't like to smile much anymore either. It reminds me too much of living a lie, I wish my parents knew the result of their repression."

Did this happen in your family?

JANELL'S STORY: IN HER MOTHER'S IMAGE

Janell actually looked fierce when I met her. I don't usually say that about people, but there is no other way to describe her expression. It was fierce. Then I discovered why. Janell began by surprising me with, "After we've talked for five minutes, Norm, you will know all about my mother. And I won't be telling you one statement about her. I'm going to talk about me and between that and the way I respond you'll see her. She's the biggest pain in my life, her and her anger. And guess who is the spitting image of her? I'm her replica!"

She was right! In no time at all her intensity deepened and her anger became apparent. I discovered that not only did her mother rage and run over others like a bulldozer leveling a building, so did Janell. Her role model at home found a seed in Janell, and it grew and flourished. Part of the reason was self-preservation. But what she learned crippled her relationships with others. It seemed that other people were following the advice of Proverbs 22:24–25: "Make no friendships with a man given to anger, and with a wrathful man do not associate, lest you learn his ways and get yourself into a snare" (AMP).

Did this happen to anyone in your family?

FATHERS AND DAUGHTERS

What or whom are you angry with in your family of origin? Your father? Your mother?

If it's your father, why? I talk to many women who are angry because of a father's distance or overcloseness, lack of involvement or overinvolvement, passivity or past and present domination. Often the dominating father is also an angry man, and this is part of his controlling mechanism.

It's interesting how the anger a woman has toward her father can foster the continuation of the domination. I see it in women who have a firm determination to live their lives exactly the opposite of what their father believed or stood for. They think that in that way they will show him they won't be controlled. But their angry, negative reaction toward him shows they are still being controlled by him. No wonder their anger doesn't recede.

Some women feel they're in a Catch 22 situation with their fathers. Some fathers control by becoming demandingly dependent upon their daughters. They exaggerate their needs to control the daughter, and the daughter becomes increasingly angry at him. Eventually she makes herself less available to be used, but now her guilt directs the anger back against herself.

Perhaps one of the worst scenarios for many women is to be dominated by fear because of a father addicted to power and control. This type of father believes he owns those around him, and he conveys the message "I'm your father, and I'm more important than anyone else in your life. Meet my needs!"

A controller is quite skilled in using anger to control and manipulate those around him. He tends to hold high and unrealistic expectations for others and is known as a nitpicker. He creates fun at others' expense, often resorting to put-downs and sarcasm. He rarely apologizes, and is skilled at making excuses for his mistakes. He projects blame on others, and few dare to disagree with him. No matter what he does, he must come out on top. He must win. Everything in the family must be geared around him. He keeps everybody else on egg shells.

A father plays a significant role in his daughter's life. He passes on a legacy of values, beliefs, and character qualities; an attitude toward other men in his daughter's life; and a perception of emotions either good or bad. Was his anger a central thread in your relationship with your father? If so, what will you do with it, and where will you go with it now?

The anger of many of these daughters often hardens into a cold aloofness toward all other men or an attitude of defiance toward her father and every other man.

Dominated daughters look for men who are loving, warm, sensitive, patient, and accepting. But where are they? Usually they end up attracting men like their father or men who have the characteristics they are seeking but who seem weak in comparison. They react to both with angry rebellion.

MOTHERS AND DAUGHTERS

In many families the relationship between mother and daughter has the potential for a volatile, angry relationship. It's a relationship in which deep feelings of care and love exist along with intense anger. Most mother-daughter relationships are characterized by ambivalence. When you hear the word *mother*, what do you feel? Many women respond with, "Oh, I love my mother. She's the best." And yet in the next breath they move from love to blaming her for what's wrong in their lives. Have you ever felt like making these statements:

"She's never really understood me."
"She has never approved of any man I've dated."
"No matter what subject we talk about, she still tries to run my life."
"I wish she had paid more attention to me."
"I wish she had paid less attention to me."
"I wish she hadn't pushed me so hard."
"I wish she had pushed me more."

Women are possessive of their mothers and yet are angry at them. They want the the approval of their mothers, yet are angry at them.

Mothers and daughters can have a wonderful, fulfilling relationship one day and the next be at painful odds. It's difficult to have such conflicting feelings.

The anger you feel toward your mother may exist because of unfilled expectations for her that you carry, or because of the cultural idealization we have that mothers are and need to be perfect. Your anger toward your mother could be based on your need for her approval. When it isn't forthcoming or as much as you want, anger protects you but also causes you to feel worse about yourself.

In *Don't Blame Mother,* Paula Caplan says:

> Energy spent in angry blaming of our mothers (and ourselves as both daughters and mothers) blocks our growth. One of the world's biggest sources of misdirected emotional energy is tied up in millions of women's rage at their mothers. Major works of art could be created, social problems solved, and identity crises resolved if the force in this obsessive mother-blaming were more productively channeled.[3]

Perhaps part of the purpose of any anger you feel toward your mother is to protect you or help you overcome your feelings of powerlessness. Often anger is a cry of "I don't want this situation to continue. I want it to be different."

But as you know, anger is one step that must lead to another, because it doesn't usually change another person, nor does it prevent a repeat of what you didn't like. Anger increases the distance between two people. It is imperative that you move beyond the anger you feel toward your mother, because women tend to feel much more guilty about being angry than men ever do. When the guilt settles in it generates still more anger toward your mother, since she's the reason for your guilt in the first place (or so you think).

I find that many women put themselves at the mercy of their mothers by basing their self-esteem and self-approval upon them. That intensifies the daughters' need for any morsel their mothers can give, and reinforces their belief (true or false) that their mothers disapprove of them. That leads to anger, criticism of their mothers, and unfulfilling interactions with them—in short, a vicious circle.

Do you have any fears about your mother? Since fear is one of the major contributors to anger, identifying a woman's mother-fears may help heal the problem so that it's not passed on from generation to generation.

Mother-fears can be numerous, but three significant ones are (1) the fear a woman has of losing her mother's love, (2) the fear a woman has of her mother dying, and (3) the fear of becoming like her mother and doing what she has done.

The fear you have of losing your mother's love is connected to the feeling you have that you can't please her or live up to her expectations. As you live with this fear you are also afraid that she will die before you can please her. The frustration this fear incites can infuse still more anger into the relationship. The more you blame your mother for your problems, the greater your fear and suspicion that you are just like her.[4]

Caplan describes the process in this way:

> If we regard our mothers as masochistic, rejecting, critical, demanding, guilt-inducing, or just embarrassing, then we usually begin to suspect that we are, too. Most daughters try hard to avoid repeating what they consider the specific mistakes that their mothers made with them, and many daughters are determined to dress differently, to choose friends differently, to have different values from those their mothers have. At the same time, we often have an almost superstitious belief that we simply cannot avoid that repetition. We secretly fear that we are exactly like our mothers in all the ways that we dislike.
>
> Since we tend to believe that we are like our mothers, deprecation of them usually leads us also to self-deprecation. Hatred not only hurts the person who is hated; it is destructive also to the person who hates. Ultimately, hatred and blame keep us tied to the target of those feelings. They lead to our preoccupation with the target, who is always on our minds.[5]

Numerous women struggling with a mixture of feelings toward their mothers end up feeling sad because their own mothers will never match the image they have for them and because of the emotional distance that exists between the mother and the daughter. When anger and sadness become too intense, emotional numbness and even alienation can set in. You create a wall to keep your mother out, but it keeps you locked up too.

That wall also locks in your love. If your anger is not resolved, it may find its release in hostility toward a friend, your husband, or your own children, and thus the legacy is continued.

WHAT CAN YOU DO ABOUT YOUR ANGER?

What can you do if you fit this profile? Where will you go with your anger? How you feel about yourself will improve if your love and care feelings can be shared. It's possible to lower your expectations for your mother, identify her strengths, accept her faults, and even give her permission to have them, and disconnect your excessive need for her approval, all of which will lessen your anger. Let's consider how.

Refuse to dwell on regrets. Regret is common. I hear these statements constantly:

"If only Mom or Dad had been different . . ."
"If only I had learned . . ."
"If only I hadn't cut loose on her we would still . . ."
"If only I had said . . ."

By dwelling on these thoughts you remain encumbered by the past and your future is limited. If there was something you did or didn't do that was a sin, confess it once as stated in 1 John 1:9, "If we . . . admit that we have sinned and confess our sins, He is faithful and just . . . and will forgive our sins and continuously cleanse us from all unrighteousness—everything not in conformity to His will in purpose, thought and action" (AMP).

Then start living your life as though past failures are done with. After all, that's the way God looks at it. Give God your past and see who you can be in the future.

Refuse to dwell on recrimination. Harboring thoughts of recrimination is another ineffective way to deal with the past. You are restricting your future when you blame someone for what happened yesterday. We all have a past. I like the way Jack Hayford describes the effect of the past:

> Predecessors, plain people such as our parents, teachers or friends (even those disposed to our best interest) can cast shadows over our tomorrows. They may have set boundaries on our lives, limiting our view of ourselves or our potential. Or they may have been confined by boundaries of their own which found exact or mirrored images in us. But in either case, our predecessors often shape us, leaving an imprint which may be the source of our own present frustration.[6]

Refuse to bank on renunciation. Renunciation is another common response to the past. We promise to change and do things differently. But past behaviors and attitudes are simply renounced. They are not confronted and cleansed.[7] Lloyd Ogilvie puts this so well:

> We try to close the door on what has been, but all we do is suppress the dragons of memory. Every so often they rap persistently and want to come out into our consciousness for a dress rehearsal in preparation for a rerun in a new situation or circumstance. Renunciation of our memories sounds so very pious. The only thing wrong with it is that it doesn't work.[8]

Reflect on the beliefs you have concerning anger. Look back to some of your answers to the questions listed earlier in this chapter. Use those to help you identify two important concerns: how anger has hurt you in the past and how you want to be different in the future. In order to make this happen, look at the beliefs you have concerning anger—your anger, your father or mother's anger, or anyone else's—that are still impacting your life. Think about what you say to yourself now about

- Anger
- Your anger
- Your mother's anger
- Your father's anger

- Your sibling's anger
- What you are capable of doing
- How capable you are of changing

Consider the decisions you have made in the past that might be negatively affecting your life now. You know what I've discovered in counseling? Many men and women have made decisions in their life based on false beliefs, and those decisions keep them stuck right where they are and even perpetuate their problem with their own or another's anger. Perhaps it would help to ask yourself, *What decisions have I made over the years that are affecting my life in a limiting way now?* You may be surprised at what you discover.

Let people who have hurt you off the hook. The next step can best be illustrated by an activity my wife and I enjoy—trout fishing. Joyce is a capable fisherperson and has her own set of waders for river fishing and a float tube for lake fishing. We release most of the fish we catch. When a fish comes up close to us, we reach down and let it off the hook. Sometimes it takes the fish a few seconds to discover it has been released. Then it takes advantage of its freedom to dart away and move on with its life.

Well, it's the same with us if we're going to move on. We need to let other people who hurt us and ourselves off the hook. There's just no other way. We cannot make others or ourselves pay for our sins and mistakes. Blame is not to be a part of our vocabulary anymore, for when we invited Jesus Christ to take over our lives that is one of the words He purged from our personal vocabulary.

Letting someone off the hook means being able to reflect upon your past and see how it has contributed to the present. It means letting positive experiences have precedent over negative ones. Your task is to discover new meaning in your present life by evicting the contaminants of the past.

Think through what you want out of the role of anger in your life. Once you have let the persons who have hurt you off the hook, turn your focus upon what you want out of the emotion of anger in your life. Sounds strange, doesn't it, to rationally decide what to do with anger? But think about these questions for a moment:

What do you want to believe about anger?
What do you want to feel about anger?
How do you want to respond and react to the anger of others?
How do you want to be free from the anger of others?
How do you want to express your anger in a positive, constructive way?

When you have answered these questions you have established your goal and have become a future thinker. That's positive. You are developing and drawing toward a vision for your life. When that happens something dramatic will take place in your mind—you will begin to think of the impossible as possible.

Remember the explorers and the early pioneers in our country? They believed there was something better out west. If you know Jesus Christ as your Savior, you've been called to be a pioneer, to think differently, believe differently, behave differently, and see life through the lens of what can be rather than what was—even with your emotions.

When you have a goal and a vision, they function like a magnet.

I thought of this recently while watching the film *Dances with Wolves*. I was greatly intrigued with the animal scenes. During the stampede scene hundreds of buffalo thundered across the plain. At one point a buffalo appeared to be charging directly at an Indian boy. I wondered, *How did the filmmakers get that buffalo to do what they wanted?*

I later discovered in a magazine article that a great deal of time had been invested in the scene with that one buffalo. In order to get the buffalo to cooperate, they conditioned it by feeding it Oreo cookies. It wasn't long before the animal would practically jump through a hoop to get to those round, chocolate, cream-filled cookies. So for the stampede scene they placed a pile of Oreos next to the Indian boy (and out of sight of the camera), and the cookies drew the buffalo in the right direction, just like a powerful magnet.[9]

Write a letter to God concerning all these matters. The last step is not what you might expect. It's a letter, a prayer, a visionary prayer. I'd like you to write a letter to God telling Him about the next year of your life and how with His strength and guidance anger will have a different impact and a different place in your life. Take the time to do it. Read it out loud, not just once, but each week. Anger doesn't have to be the enemy. You can let it be one, or you can make it your ally. It's your choice.

NOTES

1. David Viscott, *I Love You, Let's Work It Out* (New York: Simon & Schuster, 1987), 67. Gary Jackson Oliver and H. Norman Wright, *When Anger Hits Home: Taking Care of Your Anger Without Taking It Out on Your Family* (Chicago: Moody, 1992), 41.
2. Adapted from Ronald T. Potter-Efron and Patricia S. Potter-Efron, *Anger, Alcoholism and Addiction: Treating Anger in a Chemical Dependency Setting* (New York: Norton, 1991), 51–54.
3. Paula J. Caplan, *Don't Blame Mother: Mending the Mother-Daughter Relationship* (New York: Harper & Row, 1989), 25.
4. Ibid., 22–30. Adapted.
5. Ibid., 31.
6. Jack Hayford, *Taking Hold of Tomorrow* (Ventura, Calif.: Regal, 1989), 33.
7. H. Norman Wright, *Chosen for Blessing* (Eugene, Oreg.: Harvest, 1992), 66.
8. Lloyd John Ogilvie, *Lord of the Impossible* (Nashville: Abingdon, 1984), 129–30.
9. Wright, 94.

CHAPTER TEN

Anger
in the Home

One of the joys of having young children is that it gives us adults the opportunity to read "children's" stories. For about a four month period my three-year-old son Andrew's favorite story was *Make Way for Ducklings*. One night after a long day of counseling I found myself reading the story again, and I came across a part of the story that caught my eye.

Mr. and Mrs. Mallard were looking for a place to live. But every time Mr. Mallard saw what looked like a nice place, Mrs. Mallard said it was no good. There were sure to be foxes in the woods or turtles in the water, and she was not going to raise a family where there might be foxes or turtles. So they flew on and on.[1]

So there they were: Mr. and Mrs. Mallard flying around, looking for a place to raise a family. Two different ducks that met somewhere, fell in love, and decided to start a life together. And then they discovered that they had different values, standards, and opinions. Every time Mr. Mallard found a nice place to live Mrs. Mallard rejected it.

If this story were about humans and not ducks their discussion would probably end in a fight.

"You never like what I like."

"Well, that's because you have such lousy taste."

"What do you mean by that?"

"You know exactly what I mean by that."

"Well your mother doesn't have such great taste either."

"What does my mother have to do with it?"

And on and on.

KIRK AND PAULA

What was especially interesting this night was that earlier in the day I had met with a couple experiencing serious marital problems. They hadn't been married long, and yet they were already bumping into one another's differences. Like Mr. and Mrs. Mallard, one of their differences involved trying to decide where they should move.

Kirk and Paula had been married only six months when she called my office asking for an appointment. After she was on the phone only a few minutes it became clear that she and her husband were beginning to make some of the uncomfortable discoveries all couples make the first year of marriage.

"I don't understand how he could change in such a short time," Paula exclaimed. "While we were dating Kirk talked a lot and seemed to enjoy being with friends. But since we've been married he's clammed up. He acts like he's taken a course from the Marcel Marceau school of communication." Her humor provided a thin veil for the confusion, hurt, and frustration she felt—not to mention the anger she was afraid to admit.

When they came in for the first session, Kirk, as you might guess, painted a much different picture. "I'm with people all day, and I look forward to coming home and just being with Paula." he said. "But it seems like if we're not talking all of the time Paula thinks something is drastically wrong."

206

Not only were they having serious disagreements about the quantity of their communication, they were also going head-to-head over where to live. Before they were married they had decided that after the wedding Paula would move into Kirk's apartment, and they would begin to save money to purchase a home.

However, three months into the marriage Kirk's accountant informed him that it would be financially in their best interest to purchase a home. Kirk had looked around and found several he considered to be dream homes. However, each time he showed one to Paula she invariably found several things wrong with it.

"Before we got married I never dreamed that we'd have arguments over such seemingly little things," Paula said. "It all seemed so much easier when we were just dating." I responded by saying, "That's because it *was* easier." I assured Kirk and Paula that they were not unique in the problems they were facing.

The marriage that they thought had been made in heaven had become anything but heavenly. Unmet needs, unfulfilled expectations, and unrealized dreams had increased their disappointment with the relationship. Add a few misunderstandings and some miscommunication and they had the perfect recipe for irritation, frustration, and anger.

Like many couples, anger was an emotion Kirk and Paula knew little about. They saw their disagreement as abnormal and unhealthy. What they didn't know was that they were in the process of taking one of the first steps on the road to developing an intimate relationship. All they could see was that something was wrong, it didn't feel good, and they wanted it to stop.

THE INEVITABILITY OF ANGER IN A MARRIAGE

Kirk and Paula had bought into one of the most devastating myths about marriage, one that cripples many relationships. They believed that when two people are really in love with each other they will have few disagreements and experience virtually no conflict or anger. This destructive perspective on the role of anger in marriage has been around at least since the Victorians.

> The Victorians had little tolerance for anger in marriage on the part of either sex and viewed that emotion as a threat to what they treasured most in the home. Angry people lost the ability to control themselves, and in a world perceived as already too much out of control, the Victorians could not forgive the introduction of chaos into the one retreat that remained. Angry people, both husbands and wives, existed, to be sure, but these were people of bad character. Good husbands and wives would raise good children, and in these children of proper character, anger would be almost excised.[2]

I've talked with many people who really believe that healthy couples don't have conflict or get angry. Now it is true that mannequins don't have conflict. It is also true that cadavers don't get angry. But real people in real relationships who are actively working toward figuring out what it means to become one while remaining distinct individuals—they will experience disagreement, conflict, and anger.

Disagreement, conflict, and anger are a key part of the process of becoming one. Disagreements in a relationship are inevitable and a fundamental part of achieving intimacy.

To become intimate you have to risk revealing yourself—not just your public self that has been trained how to be acceptable, but also your private self with its weaknesses, flaws, inadequacies, and fears of failure and rejection.

To become intimate you have to risk letting the other person know how much you need him and how important he is to you. As you become more vulnerable the risks increase. As the risks increase the fears increase. As the stakes rise, anger won't be far behind.

ANGER AS A PART OF THE PURIFYING PROCESS OF DISAGREEMENT

The process of achieving intimacy is similar to the way that gold was purified in Christ's time. The goldsmith started out with raw gold that contained alloys and impurities. He would put the gold in a container and heat it up. When the gold had melted and had reached just the right temperature, some of the alloys would come to the surface. The goldsmith would scoop these off.

He would continue the process six more times. At the end, if he had done his job well, he would have pure gold. Each time he would have to heat the gold to just the right temperature. If it wasn't hot enough the impurities wouldn't come to the surface. If it got too hot he would lose some of the precious metal.

Our relationships are a lot like gold. They start out in very rough form. We have a rough idea of what it means to love. We want intimacy but aren't always sure what it is and what is involved in achieving it. However, God knows all about intimacy. He allows differences, difficulties, and disagreements to enter into our relationships, and they tend to heat things up.

As our relationships get hotter, our personal alloys and impurities—such as pride, jealousy, selfishness, resentment, insecurity, and fear—are brought to the surface, identified, and removed. With each new conflict, the gold of our relationship becomes a bit purer. If we keep things in God's hands and allow the process to continue, we will end up with a relationship that's pure gold. But it's not easy and it doesn't happen overnight.

God wants to teach us how to use our anger to help bring the alloys and impurities of our lives to the surface. The healthy expression of our anger can help us clarify, understand, and appreciate our differences. When we deny our anger and run from conflict we are running from the very process God can use to heal our hurts and knit our hearts more tightly together in love.

THE LINK BETWEEN HEALTHY
EXPRESSIONS OF ANGER AND STRONG MARRIAGES

The greater our love for someone, the greater our capacity to experience a wide range of emotions in connection with that person. Those emotions include irritation, resentment, anger, and even rage. That is true whether we're dealing with our own parents, our spouse, or our children.

The people to whom we give the most time and energy and in whom we invest the greatest amount of love and other emotions are the ones we have the highest expectations of. They are also the ones with the greatest potential to trigger in us such emotions as fear, hurt, frustration, and eventually anger. The late David Mace is quoted as saying that "marriage and family living generate in normal people more anger than people experience in any other social situation."[3]

Anger is not necessarily a sign of relational immaturity or instability. Anger is an inherent component of *all* human relationships. It is especially prevalent in romantic ones. The more dependent on and vulnerable to someone you are, the more likely they'll be the object of your hostility as well as your affection.

People in healthy and unhealthy relationships argue and disagree. The difference is that in the healthy relationships those disagreements result in increased understanding, trust, and security. They reflect mutual respect.

Healthy expression of anger is a testimony to the strength of a marriage. Relationships that don't acknowledge or express anger are usually fragile, unstable, and anemic. For anger not to be expressed suggests that the couple aren't secure enough or the marriage isn't strong enough to handle disagreement. This immaturity and insecurity leads to the chameleon syndrome—the tendency to want to appear to the beholder whatever the beholder wants to see.

Given the inevitability of anger in all relationships, the question is not whether to express it, but how and when? The long-term success of a relationship depends on your willingness to find healthy ways of expressing and dealing with one another's anger.

TRIGGER POINTS FOR ANGER IN A MARRIAGE

We asked the women we surveyed to tell us what they saw as the things that sparked anger in a marriage. Some of what they said is given below.

- *The faults men have.*

When we asked women "Where does the anger in a marriage come from?" what do you suppose was the number one response they gave to this question? You guessed it—men. And not just men in general, but specific and not-so-enduring qualities of certain men. Here are some of the negative characteristics of men the women in our survey listed:

They don't listen	They are controlling
They fear intimacy	They aren't nurturing
They are selfish	They are arrogant
They don't know how to communicate	They think just being there is enough
They never apologize	They are too concrete
They engage in deception	They lack consideration
They have to be asked to do anything	They demand love-making without loving
They don't look you in the eye	They make jokes when I need to be serious
They only care about the bottom line	They take us for granted

Are there any items on this list that you yourself could have contributed? What isn't on the list you think should be added?

- *Children.*

The number two cause for anger was children. The demands and drains that children place on individuals in a relationship increase their vulnerability to experiencing anger, not only at the children but also at each other. Nancy Samalin expresses what many of the women in our survey have experienced.

For many families, home is a battleground, filled with constant bickering, shouting matches, and exhausting power struggles. Often, parent complaints appear so frivolous they hardly seem worth the effort of doing battle over. Parents are amazed that they can go from relative calm to utter frustration in a few seconds. An uneaten egg or spilled juice at breakfast can turn a calm morning into a free-for-all. In spite of parents' best intentions, bedtime becomes wartime, meals end with children in tears and food barely touched, and car rides deteriorate into stress-filled shouting matches . . . Whatever its source, we often experience parental anger as a horrifying encounter with our worst selves. I never even knew I had a temper until I had children. It was very frightening that these children I loved so much, for whom I had sacrificed so much, could arouse such intense feelings of rage in me, their mother, whose primary responsibility was to nurture and protect them.[4]

- *A lack of understanding of basic differences in personality.*

When Kirk and Paula were dating each was so taken with the uniqueness of his beloved and by dreams of what life would be like together, they didn't take time to note and understand some of their important differences. They loved what felt good, and they ignored or minimized what didn't.

If their premarital counseling had included exposure to a tool such as the Myers-Briggs Type Indicator they would have understood that Kirk was an introvert and Paula an extrovert. Although Kirk enjoyed being with people, he also valued his alone time. Too much people time drained him. He needed alone time to help recharge his battery. After working and talking all day he looked forward to coming home and just "being there" with Paula. Can you imagine how painful it was for Kirk to feel condemned and rejected by the woman he loved simply for being himself?

As an extrovert, Paula not only enjoyed being with people but was energized by them. Paula could work and talk all day, come home exhausted, and want to have a few friends over to help her get picked back up again. What was exhausting for Kirk was energizing for Paula. What was energizing for Kirk was exhausting for (and boring to) Paula.

Paula was correct in her recollection that Kirk seemed much more outgoing when they were dating. The process of dating and getting acquainted is a much more extroverted process. Paula had never seen what Kirk was like behind closed doors. She hadn't even considered the possibility that Kirk might need to "shut down."

On the other hand, Kirk never dreamed that Paula would want to talk "nonstop all of the time." He assumed that when they weren't together she would recharge her batteries the same way he did. That's a common mistake many people make. We often assume that other people are, or should be, the way we are. If they aren't like we are, they must be wrong.

Were either Kirk or Paula wrong? Of course not. They were simply different. *Different* is not a dirty word. Differences are what give depth and breadth to a relationship. Our differences can turn a black and white relationship into living color. Unfortunately, Paula and Kirk hadn't identified and didn't understand some of their most basic differences.

When we haven't identified and don't understanding our differences it is easy for them to catch us off guard. They can make us feel uncomfortable, challenge the perceived "rightness" of our perspective, and force us to reevaluate our opinions and ways of doing things.

- *A lack of understanding of gender differences and appreciation for them.*

Over the past ten years there have been tremendous efforts on the part of some to convince the public that there are no substantive differences between men and women. Any of what might appear to be differences are regarded as only superficial cosmetic differences caused by our society.

We disagree with that conclusion. Our research, our experience, and the experience of the women we have worked with impels us to conclude that though men and women are of equal intelligence, giftedness, significance, value, and worth, they are also different from one another. Being equal doesn't mean that we are the same.[5]

In terms of the marriage relationship, one of the most important ways in which men and women differ relates to their communication styles. Deborah Tannen notes in *You Just Don't Understand: Women and Men in Conversation* that many of the conflicts between men and women are caused by basic misunderstandings of the opposite sex. For example, while a woman and her husband were driving in the car the woman asked her husband, "Would you like to stop for ice cream?" Her husband thought about it for a minute and said, "No." Later on he became frustrated because he realized that his wife was annoyed. Why? Because she had wanted to stop. "If you wanted to stop why didn't you just say so?" he asked.[6]

Both had misread the other. She had incorrectly taken her husband's "No" as a nonnegotiable and irreversible "No." The husband had misconstrued his wife's question as a request for a decision rather than the beginning of a discussion about what both of them would like. Many men are more comfortable giving a one-word decision, such as "yes" or "no," rather than entering into a discussion whose direction is unclear.

Many men and women differ in their ways of coping with problems. When many women talk about problems they are seeking understanding and sympathy and not necessarily trying to find "the solution." They want to share their situation with someone they can trust. The support they get from the process of someone's interacting with them may be more meaningful than getting to the answer.

Since many men don't talk about problems unless they want advice, they often frustrate women by offering advice and by trying to solve the problem rather than taking the time to understand it. They are much more likely to move on to the bottom line. They think they are loving their wives by providing them with a solution to the problem. They are often caught off guard and surprised when their wives don't appreciate that response.

When in the course of a conversation a man discovers that a male friend has a personal problem, he is likely to change the subject out of his respect for the other's need for independence. Many men assume that the extended discussion of a problem will be awkward and make it even more serious and thus cause the other man to feel worse. Women are just the opposite. When a friend shares a problem with them, they are much more likely to show respect and concern by responding with active listening, inviting more information, and asking pertinent questions.

When it comes to giving feedback, women are more likely to look at one another directly, whereas men often fail to maintain direct eye contact. Women are more likely to ask questions when they are involved in a conversation. To show that they care about the person they are listening to and are tracking the conversation they may offer small cues, such as "uh-huh," "that's right," or "yeah." When a woman says "yeah," that suggests simply that she is following what you're saying. But when a man says "yeah," he's probably telling you he agrees with you. Overall, men give fewer signals than women and are more likely to respond with blanket statements and challenges.

Another difference that is a major source of hurt and anger to many women involves making apologies. Many women say "I'm sorry" as a way of making a connection and joining with the other person. It can be another way of saying "I'm sorry this happened to you," or "I'm sorry you feel so bad—I do too." For many men, saying "I'm sorry" means admitting that they were wrong and need to make an apology. They believe this puts them in a one-down position, something many men find unmasculine and unacceptable.

One final difference is the way in which men and women deal with conflict. A team of psychologists at the University of Washington led by Dr. John Gottman developed a procedure that has predicted with 94 percent accuracy which couples will divorce within three years. In an interview with reporter Joan DeClaire, Gottman stated that when there are problems in a marriage, women tend to see it as their responsibility to do something about it. Men tend to withdraw—they'll work harder, do things with friends instead of family. It's important for couples to understand this so they don't attribute problems to one another when the problems really have to do with gender differences. There's a danger, for example, that a woman would feel a man should be like her. And when he's not, she feels it's because he's unwilling, doesn't love her, doesn't care. And that's really a shame.[7]

STEPS FOR DEALING WITH CONFLICT

It's an established fact that an occupational hazard in being married is that we will experience anger. Anger often leads to conflict, and conflict can be a key to healthier, stronger, and more intimate relationships. Since dealing with anger and working through conflict have such potential for building trust and intimacy in a relationship, what are some specific ways we can more effectively deal with anger and conflict in marriage and make them work for us rather than against us?

- *Develop good communication skills.*

The first step is to work on decreasing unhealthy anger and unnecessary conflict. Since much of the anger and conflict in marriage is due to miscommunication, you can significantly reduce the number of unnecessary conflicts by actively working on developing good communication skills. This is actually easier than it might appear.

One of the best places to start is to read together a basic book on effective couple communication. There are many good books dealing with communication, but over the last fifteen years I (Gary) have found that my coauthor's book *Communication: Key to Your Marriage* (Ventura, Calif.: Regal, 1979) contains simple, practical, and easy-to-apply insights and skills for increasing quality communication.

As Kirk and Paula went through this book they were amazed at the difference it made in their communication. They had no idea that over half of the issues they were dealing with were pseudoissues caused by miscommunication. Both of them had been so focused on getting the other person to understand his point of view that neither one was spending much time listening. They had fallen into the trap of trying to solve problems they didn't understand and trying to understand problems they hadn't defined.

- *Keep short accounts.*

It didn't take Kirk and Paula long to learn that in marriage it is easy to collect fears and hurts and frustrations and put them in cold storage until they had a full load—and then "Pow!" When they tried to go back and figure out what caused the problem they had no idea why they were arguing or what they had been so upset about. In fact, they would often find themselves arguing about what they thought they had been arguing about.

Much of the anger in Kirk and Paula's marriage was over small issues that were either unidentified or were identified but not dealt with. Over time and with many repetitions these microissues became what appeared to be large issues that were threatening and seemed impossible to deal with.

These kinds of situations remind me of the huge hot air balloons I frequently see floating along the front range of the Rockies. From a distance they look small, but the closer you get the bigger you see they are. Yet once you remove the hot air from the balloons they become comparatively small and manageable. Many of the issues separating Kirk and Paula were long on hot air and short on substance.

When you become aware of a conflict, try to define the problem. What's the issue? How long has it been a problem? Whose problem is it? Is it really that big a deal? There are times when we need to learn how to draw a line between issues that need to be confronted and the frustrations that are a normal part of living with someone else.

● *Develop a sense of perspective.*

Much of the anger in marriage can be traced to personal idiosyncrasies, minor annoyances, or passing irritations. Cindy and Roger have been married for over twenty years. She said that for the first seven years of their marriage she would fuss and fume at him for a variety of behaviors she found frustrating.

Finally, at the encouragement of a friend, Cindy went to see a counselor "to find some ways to help Roger change." Her therapist challenged her to make, for a two-week period, a list of all of the terrible, awful, and horrible things Roger did that were a source of frustration. As she read through her list, Cindy told me, "I was amazed and a bit embarrassed at what I discovered." This was her list:

> He is cheery and talkative when he gets up in the morning. He likes his toast well done, almost burnt, and he makes a lot of noise when he bites into it. He fondles the remote control for the T.V. and likes to watch several shows at a time. He doesn't close the sliding glass closet doors after he gets dressed in the morning. Sometimes when he laughs he will snort. He makes a weird sound when he clears his throat. He refills the ice-cube trays too high and the water spills over and makes puddles of ice in the freezer. When he goes shopping for clothes he has a hard time making up his mind.

When she saw how small and insignificant these issues were she decided that, "all things considered, Roger wasn't that bad, and I was a selfish and immature first-class crab to let those little irritations bother me."

When you choose to express your anger, draw a line between differences that demand confrontation and those that are simply a part of living with someone else. Before you allow an issue to consume too much of your time ask yourself, "How important is this?" Is it a low ticket or a high ticket item? On a scale of one to ten, a low ticket item would score only a one through five. A low ticket item is something that may irritate or frustrate you, but it really isn't that big a deal. All of the things on Cindy's list were clearly low ticket items.

A high ticket item would rate a six through ten. High ticket items would include issues such as how affection is expressed, how important decisions are made, who decides where you spend your vacations, how finances are allocated, and, one of Kirk and Paula's favorite issues, where you will live.

- *Acknowledge your own contribution to the problem.*

Let's assume you've decided that the issue is one you need to address. Before you spend too much time looking at all the things your spouse needs to change, ask yourself, *What is my part of the problem?* It is much easier for us to pick up a magnifying glass than it is to pick up a mirror. It's much easier to pray, "Lord, change my husband, children, friends," than it is to pray "Lord, change me!"

In Psalm 139:23–24 David writes, "Search me, O God, and know my heart; try me and know my anxious thoughts; and see if there be any hurtful way in me, and lead me in the everlasting way" (NASB). David cries out to God and says search me, know me, try me, know my thoughts, examine me, and lead me.

- *Be clear about the source of your anger.*

Ask yourself, *Is this anger about my husband or my children, or is it a response to a combination of stuff that has grown throughout the day?* Several women have told us that at times they have a tendency to direct their global anger toward their husband. "Sometimes I'll come home incensed at how a few of the men at work have treated me," wrote Lois, "and it's almost as if I'm looking for my husband to make one wrong move so that I can pounce on him and thus in a crazy kind of way 'get back' at the other men. I know it's unfair and irrational."

Of course women aren't the only ones who tend to do this. It's human nature to suppress and hide our fears, hurts, and frustrations and then let them out on the people we care about and love the most. But though it is a common phenomena, it is still painful and destructive.

- *Practice constructive criticism.*

If the issue is a legitimate high ticket item, practice constructive criticism. The best place to start is by getting the facts. The best way to do that is to develop the skill of asking clarifying questions. Questions can decrease the intensity of the moment, broaden a person's perspective, encourage new ways of thinking, stimulate the need for gathering more facts, and help a person see the value of looking at as many options as possible.

Remember that confrontation is usually most effective when it takes the form of a rational, clearly reasoned discussion, not a loud tirade, brutal put-down, or devastating downpour of tears. Once again, let me emphasize that if you think you are on the verge of loosing control, take a brief time-out to clear your mind and regain your focus. Take a few deep breaths or step outside and go for a walk. Pray. Remind yourself of some of God's promises and the power of the indwelling presence of the Holy Spirit in your life. Remember that you're never alone.

A researcher on anger in women, T. Bernardez-Bonesatti, says that "in anger, the person establishes automatic aloneness and makes herself temporarily separate from the object of the anger." Bernardez-Bonesatti adds, "Many women are so afraid of this loss of connection that their expressions of anger are often accompanied by tears, guilt, and sorrow, which dilute or contaminate the anger. Or serve to nullify it entirely."[8]

- *Rehearse your confrontation and carry it out constructively.*

Before you begin your confrontation ask yourself if it would help you to rehearse what you are going to say. In Paula's case, she was working on developing some different and more effective ways of expressing her anger, and the idea of confrontation caused her to feel insecure and afraid. We have found that many women experience the same feelings Paula did. Rehearsing a confrontation would have been useful to Paula.

What are some good ways to rehearse your confrontation? These are a few:

— You can rehearse your confrontation with the Lord in prayer. You can first pray silently and then pray out loud.
— You can use the empty chair technique. That involves placing two chairs opposite each other. You sit in one chair and pretend the person you want to confront is in the other chair. Tell the empty chair what you are feeling and why.
— You can write a letter to the person that you will never mail. After you have read the letter out loud two or three times you may be surprised at how much more confident and clear you are about what you need to say and how you need to say it.
— You can go to the gym and work out. While you are working out, think and pray about your upcoming confrontation.

When you begin your confrontation be sure to address the person by name. Give him or her specific information about your concerns with one or two examples, if possible. Try to avoid coming across as too negative or critical. Let the person know how his or her behavior has affected you and how you feel about it.

If you are angry, explain that you are angry and give specific reasons for your anger. Then let the person know what you would like to see happen in the future. Make clear that your main concern is a stronger and healthier relationship.

At the end of the conversation thank the person for taking the time to listen and interact with you, and then, if he or she is a Christian, ask if you could pray together. Then never bring up the situation again.

Many of the women in our survey said that expressing angry feelings is an uncomfortable task. Remember that asserting yourself is not an act of aggression. It is an act of communication. It is saying "I value myself, you, and this relationship enough to speak the truth in love."

NOTES

1. Robert McCloskey, *Make Way for Ducklings* (New York: Viking, 1969), n.p.
2. Carol Zisowitz Stearns and Peter N. Stearns, *Anger: The Struggle for Emotional Control in America's History* (Chicago: Univ. of Chicago Press, 1986), 50.
3. Cited in Gayle Rosellini and Mark Worden, *Of Course You're Angry* (Center City, Minn.: Hazelden, 1985), 12.
4. Nancy Samalin, *Love and Anger: The Parental Dilemma* (New York: Penguin, Viking, 1992), 5.
5. For different Christian perspectives on this issue, see James C. Dobson, *Straight Talk to Men and Their Wives* (Waco, Tex.: Word, 1980); John Piper and Wayne Grudem, eds. *Recovering Biblical Manhood and Womanhood: A Response to Evangelical Feminism* (Wheaton, Ill.: Crossway, 1991); Mary Stewart Van Leeuwen, *Gender and Grace: Love, Work and Parenting in a Changing World* (Downers Grove, Ill: InterVarsity, 1990).
6. Interview with Deborah Tannen, *Bottom Line Personal,* 15 March 1991, 8.
7. Joan DeClaire, "The Importance of Understanding Gender Differences: Calling It Splits," *People Weekly* 38 (19 October 1992), 131–33.
8. Adapted from T. Bernardez-Bonesatti, "Women and Anger: Conflicts with Aggression in Contemporary Women," *Journal of the American Medical Women's Association* 33, no. 5 (1978): 215–19.

CHAPTER ELEVEN

How Do You "Do" Anger?

Anger is packaged in a variety of shapes and sizes. It hides behind many different masks. Each of us has developed his own unique style of dealing with anger. In the previous chapter we surveyed several common anger problems. Now we're going to focus on three major anger styles that will amplify some of those problems.

Not long ago I asked a group of women to call out some of the words they've heard people use to describe the experience and expression of anger. Before they were through I had filled two sheets of paper. Here are some of the words they came up with:

Affront	Aggravated	Agitated	Annoyed
Animosity	Aroused	Bad Blood	Begrudge
Bitter	Bristle	Burned-up	Catty
Criticize	Cool	Cranky	Cross

Despise	Disdain	Disgusted	Enraged
Exasperated	Exploded	Frustrated	Fed Up
Fume	Furious	Grieved	Grumpy
Grouchy	Gripe	Hateful	Hostile
Hot	Huffy	Hurt	Irked
Incensed	Ill-tempered	Ill-will	Irritated
Infuriated	Inflamed	Indignation	Jealous
Mad	Mean	Miffed	Moody
Out of sorts	Offended	Provoked	Rage
Rant	Rave	Repulsed	Resentment
Riled	Sarcastic	Scorned	Seethe
Slow burn	Spiteful	Steamed	Stew
Temper	Touchy	Tiff	Vexed
Vicious	Wounded	Worked-up	Wrath

Then I asked them to come up with a list of phrases some people use to describe the experience and expression of anger. Some of the the most common phrases included:

Flew into a rage	Hot under the collar	Did a slow burn
Boiling mad	Blew up	Swallow your anger
Simmer down	Storming mad	Defuse your anger
Get it off your chest	Blow off steam	Went ballistic
Fired up	Totally lost it	Raised her hackles

As children we experienced events that elicited an anger response. Over time what may have started out as a conscious reaction became, with many repetitions, an automatic and unconscious reaction. Because these reactions appear to be so natural, many people believe that they are a part of who they are. They see these styles as part of how God made them rather than styles that have been learned and thus can, with God's help, be changed.

The first and easiest step in the change process is to identify your characteristic style of experiencing and expressing anger. When it comes to dealing with anger most people tend to fall into one of three reactive styles. A person who is reactive has an automatic and seemingly unconscious response to a situation. She may not always react in the exact same way, but the majority of her responses fall within a pattern.

People who don't identify and work on their anger style are in an emotional rut and likely to stay there. They are vulnerable to becoming puppets of their past and slaves to their circumstances.

Some of the women I've worked with have given highly descriptive names to these three unhealthy anger styles. As you read about them, think of that might best describe your usual way of reacting. How do you see yourself? How do others see you? Where did you learn this style?

CREAM PUFFS

Patty walked into my office and told me in a quiet tone of voice that she wasn't sure why she was there. "If my doctors hadn't insisted I come for a few visits I never would have come on my own." Patty had gone to see her physician for stomach problems and difficulty sleeping. He couldn't find anything wrong, and so he referred her to several specialists. Finally he referred her to me, because he and several other specialists she had consulted concluded that there was no physiological cause for her problems.

As Patty told me her story, it was clear that part of her problem was her misunderstanding of the emotion of anger and her inability to deal it. At one point she turned to me and said, "I'm just a cream puff. I look great on the outside but I feel like I don't have much substance. I can't handle any pressure, and I collapse easily."

I told Patty she wasn't alone. We have all grown up in a culture that has for more than two hundred years encouraged the repression of anger, especially in regard to women.[1] Many women, and even some men, would describe themselves as "cream puffs."

Mary Kay Biaggio, program director and professor at the Oregon Graduate School of Professional Psychology, has studied anger for nearly ten years. Her research has demonstrated that although women experience anger in response to many of the same situations as men and may even experience similar levels of anger, they are more likely to suppress and internalize their anger, whereas men are more likely to externalize theirs.

There is a cost to this suppression. For many women it may be "lowered self-esteem, a sense of powerlessness and fear of responding to or of even recognizing a provoking or unfair condition that causes the anger in the first place."[2]

Patty had gone through most of her life letting everyone else make her important decisions for her. She was most comfortable following the directions of others. She had learned that being a good wife and mother meant taking care of everyone else. She felt hopeless, helpless, inhibited, and powerless. Yet at the same time she felt guilty for feeling that way.

Somewhere along the road Patty had learned that she wasn't important. God's promises really applied to everyone else. Patty feared rejection, criticism, disapproval, or making a mistake. Since she was unaware of her emotions and couldn't face her own problems she became more vulnerable to experiencing physical problems.

By now you may have picked up the fact that the main characteristic of the cream puff is passivity. Cream puffs avoid making clear statements about what they think and feel, especially when their opinion might make someone else uncomfortable. Their energy is focused on protecting others and maintaining harmonious relationships.

Harriet Goldhor Lerner has observed that although our culture dislikes and fears angry women, it isn't threatened by sick women meeting together to get well. It is her opinion that

> society is more comfortable with women who feel inadequate, self-doubting, guilty, sick, and "diseased" than with women who are angry or confronting. . . . Women are too, which is why they eat up these codependency books like popcorn. Women are so comfortable saying, "I am a recovering addict; the problem is in me." They are so uncomfortable saying that the prob-

lem is in society, in their relationships, in their financial standing. Women get much more sympathy and support when they define their problems in medical terms than in political terms.[3]

Cream puffs often fail to share their own legitimate needs and concerns, and thus those around them are unaware of their pain. Over time, they become less and less aware of their own feelings, thoughts, and needs. They can become so focused on hearing what everyone else has to say that they fail to hear what the Lord has to say. God's truths become real to everyone but them.

Cream puffs characteristically avoid any direct experience or expression of anger. In situations that in healthy people would evoke appropriate expressions of anger and protest they are likely to remain silent. They are more likely to say "I'm sorry" rather than "I'm hurt," "I'm afraid," "I'm frustrated," or "I'm angry."

Do you say "I'm sorry" rather than "I'm angry?" Do you say "I'm sorry" when you don't believe you have done anything wrong? Do you find yourself apologizing unnecessarily? Do you believe it is always your job to bring about harmony and reconcile differences? Were you conditioned to be a peacemaker?

At one point in our work together Patty said, "In twenty-two years of marriage I can count on one hand the number of times I've heard Ben say 'I'm sorry.' I've told myself that since he is a man it's hard for him to apologize and that it's unfair for me to expect him to." Yet Patty felt an apology was necessary, and so she would apologize for him.

In the short-term it is simpler and safer to apologize for something you haven't done. Inappropriate apologies tend to smooth things over, calm the waters, restore peace and tranquillity, and avoid further confrontation and conflict. But there are tremendous long-term consequences.

Inappropriate apologies let the guilty party off the hook. They reinforce the guilty party's immaturity, insensitivity, and irresponsibility. They desensitize her to problem areas in her own life. They encourage selfish behavior that causes problems in her intimate relationships and probably in her other relationships too. Inappropriate apologies hinder the growth, understanding, and maturity of those we love.

Another feature of the cream puff is that she avoids conflict like the plague. Do you remember little Laura in chapter 3? She grew up with an unconscious, powerful fear of conflict. Even the possibility of conflict produced tremendous anxiety in her. Anything that might be construed as arguing or fighting she saw as potentially dangerous and wrong.

This failure to address deep problems and the insistence on avoiding conflict can lead to several negative results. First, since we haven't done anything about the problem, it still remains. Not only does the problem remain, it usually gets worse. As the problem gets worse, our pain and fear increases. We experience even more fear, hurt, frustration, and anger.

As we allow those feelings to smolder inside we feel an even greater sense of hopelessness and helplessness. Continuing to ignore the problem only decreases our sense of value and worth and increases our sense of powerlessness. It becomes easier to focus on ourselves and fail to see the resources we have in Christ.

Finally, it is easy for the anger that early on could have been appropriately communicated to someone else to be inappropriately directed inward toward ourselves. What is the result? We become immobilized, overwhelmed with discouragement and depression, overrun with guilt and shame, and unable to do anything.

Pain and misery are inevitable when our ways of relating to others consist of giving in, giving up, and going along; when we assume responsibility for the happiness of other people; when we pretend that everything is going great when we know that it isn't; when we are so focused on everyone else that we ignore God's promises, provision, and plan for our own lives; when we sell our spiritual birthright for a relational mess of pottage.

When I was a kid I loved water fights. Squirt guns were OK, but it was especially fun when there was a long water hose close by. I would turn the water on full power, bend the hose, let the pressure build up, and then, just at the right time, straighten the hose and let the water fly. The longer the flow of water had been interrupted the greater the pressure of the water and the more damage I could do.

On the surface it looks as though the cream puff has been able to turn off her anger faucet. But underneath, she really hasn't. That's because though she can block the flow of anger for a limited time and choose not to express it, the emotion is still there. She might think the faucet is off when what has really happened is that the hose has merely been bent. When the pressure gets great enough the anger will flood out. If we don't learn how to express our anger in healthy ways it will eventually find a way to express itself, often in a way that is unhealthy and destructive.

Do cream puffs ever experience anger? Of course they do. However, when provoked they will usually say nothing. Most people think of anger as something hot, as in seething rage or an erupting volcano. But the cream puff's anger is usually subtle and cold. Her immediate, automatic response to even the slightest hint of anger is to suppress it.

What does it mean to suppress anger? To suppress something means to hold in; to put down by force; to prevent the natural, normal expression or development of something. When I suppress my anger I'm aware of it, but through a lot of practice I'm able to keep it down. Few people are even aware that I'm angry. If over a period of time I continue to suppress my anger, it is likely that my anger will become repressed. When I repress my anger it is kept from consciousness, and I'm no longer even aware of it. People who have anger they're not aware of almost always express it in ways that are destructive to themselves and others. They are almost powerless to deal with their anger because they aren't consciously aware of it and cannot identify its cause.

Cream puffs are like boats drifting aimlessly on the ocean with no motor, oars, or sails. They are forced to go wherever the wind blows them. But they are not totally without hope. The God-given emotion of anger can be a source of propulsion to move them out of the doldrums and into healthy and constructive paths.

A description of the typical cream puff includes these elements:

Anger suppressed	Anger turned inward
Apathetic	Toxic shame
Overcontrolled	Passive reactor
Guilt-prone	Avoids problems
Self-condemnation	Denial
Responsible for others	Self-pity
Conflict-avoider	Dependent

LOCOMOTIVES

The opposite of the cream puff is the locomotive. In fact one of the reasons many cream puffs lock themselves in a prison of passivity is their fear that if they ever let themselves get in touch with their anger they will become like the locomotive.

What is a locomotive? She doesn't have much time for the feelings or opinions of others. She has a sharp tongue and can be quick to criticize, put-down, and humiliate others. On the outside she appears confident, but inside she is riddled with fears and insecurities.

Because she needs so much acceptance it is difficult for her to compliment others. That would give them the attention she believes she deserves and needs for herself. She needs to be right all of the time, and when she errs it will be on the side of being tough and not tender.

Whereas the cream puff is a passive reactor, the locomotive is an aggressive reactor. Whereas the passive reactor doesn't give adequate attention to legitimate personal needs, the aggressive reactor is insensitive toward and doesn't give adequate attention to the needs and rights of others. Whereas the anger of the cream puff is usually implosive, the anger of the locomotive is most often explosive. When a locomotive gets angry everyone around him knows it, and anyone within eyesight is at risk of being yelled at and blamed.

When provoked, the locomotive, who already has a full head of steam, is likely to attack, label, put down, and humiliate others. The locomotive often communicates in ways that violate the dignity and rights of other people. In Philippians 2:3 we are exhorted to regard one another as more important than ourselves. In 1 Peter 4:15 we read, "If you suffer, it must not be as a murderer or thief or any other kind of criminal, or even as a meddler" (NIV). The locomotive consistently ignores these biblical principles or twists them as a basis for blaming others for not esteeming him (the locomotive) as most important.

People who make a habit of dumping their anger on others tend to get more angry more often, not less angry. When we choose to deal with our anger by an aggressive reaction style it is easy for the anger to turn into rage. It doesn't take much for us to reach the boiling point and become steaming mad and spew a verbal shower of acid rain.

Many locomotives came from a homes in which they suffered parental rejection, hostility, and rage. There were no models of healthy anger. What they learned was that aggression can be an effective way to keep people at a distance so they can't hurt you. It can also be a way to pay back those who have hurt you. However, if you can get past the rough exterior of a locomotive you will almost always find a good deal of hurt and fear.

Aggression is usually an act of desperation. It is often an attempt to overcome a sense of frustration and powerlessness. Although we may get a sense of immediate satisfaction or relief through aggression, that relief doesn't last long. When we react in ways that are antagonistic we are likely to breed even more antagonism. Negativity produces negativity. Attack increases the probability of counterattack. Attempts to coerce, overpower, or trample others only push them away and widen the gap between you. I heard one speaker quote Will Rogers as saying, "People that fly into a rage always have a rough landing."

What are some characteristics of the locomotive?

Hostile	Rage	Cruel teasing
Blatant sarcasm	Anger against others	Over-concern for self
Loud	Obnoxious	Quick to blame
Critical	Underresponsible	Has all the answers
Shallow	Few intimate friends	Prone to violence
Suspicious	Punitive	Combative
Overcompetitive	Driven	Power hungry

Is there any hope for the locomotive? Susan Jacoby recounts an encouraging story that says the answer is yes.

> Looking back on my childhood and early adulthood, it seems to me that I was always apologizing to someone for words spoken in the heat of anger. I exploded at people I loved and those I disliked, at family, friends, strangers, professional peers and even my bosses.
>
> Then, when I was 23, an incident at work literally changed my life. I was attached to a team of investigative reporters (my first real job), and our boss was transferred to another department of the newspaper. We knew that Bob, a man we all liked very much, had been asked to replace him, and we were extremely disappointed when Bob turned down the job. Then an older editor called me into his office and explained that I—and my reputation for responding furiously to any criticism—was the problem.
>
> "Bob told me he just didn't want to put himself in a situation in which every little professional dispute would blow up into a big fight," the editor explained. Then he said something that hurt enormously at the time but turned out to be the biggest favor anyone has ever done me. "You know," he said, "you're very talented. If you weren't you would have been fired long ago, because it's so hard to work with you. You can't take criticism without blowing up, even if the criticism is justified. And if the criticism is not justified, you have no idea of how to bring

other people around to your way of thinking without screaming and insulting them. Your anger is going to do you in if you don't learn how to express it differently."

I was wounded and humiliated and—for once—had nothing to say. I usually forgot my outbursts as soon as they were over, and it was a revelation to learn that other people didn't forget so easily.

This realization was the beginning of a lifelong effort to control my anger—to separate the trivial from the genuinely important and to express truly legitimate anger in ways that were destructive neither to myself nor to others. At age 39, I still haven't succeeded entirely—but I have come a long way.

At the end of the article she adds:

The editor who did me a favor by warning me about the consequences of my temper died recently, and I wrote his wife a condolence note explaining why her husband had been so important to me. She wrote back and said, "He did the same thing for me 45 years ago when I said 'I hate you' in the middle of a fight. Since then, I've never told anyone I hated him unless I really meant it. And, somehow, I don't mean it as much as I used to."[4]

When it comes to identifying their unhealthy anger style, the majority of people would put themselves in the cream puff or locomotive category. However, there is a third anger style that in some ways is more subtle and complicated than the first two but—just as unhealthy.

STEEL MAGNOLIAS

As I was working on this chapter I received the following letter:

Dear Dr. Oliver,

My name is Linda, and I'm looking forward to your talk at our Women's Fellowship on the subject "Women and Anger."

Could you address the issue of anger in passive-aggressive women? Most of the information I've read or heard about regarding anger deals with the person who shows anger by arguing, throwing things, and is physically abusive or has inner anger displayed by depression.

The woman whose anger is displayed by hostile looks, gestures which communicate disgust and rejection, or who use the manipulative power of silence to hurt another is rarely talked about.

Most people perceive this person as quiet, even gentle, because of their passive side. The rage is usually reserved for someone close to them.

I appreciate your taking the time to consider these questions and I hope you'll be able to in some way address them in your talk.

God bless you and your ministry!

Sincerely yours,
Linda

The military is highly structured for uniformity and compliance, and individuality is not encouraged. Some soldiers thrive in this kind of environment. Others deal with it by resisting, ignoring orders, withdrawing, or simply wanting out. The term *passive-aggressive* was first coined during World War II to describe the quiet rebellion of the latter type of soldier. We talked about this pattern in chapter 1, but it is such a common response it deserves more attention.

On the outside, the steel magnolia appears soft and tender. At times you will see the lovely, sweet-smelling magnolia blossom. But more than a casual encounter will reveal hardened steel. She is a contradiction to herself and to others. She is the master of the end run. A part of you wants to trust her, but the other part of you says that she can't be trusted.

You can trust the cream puff to yield to the desires and expectations of others in order to gain approval. You can trust the locomotive to ignore other people's desires and expectations. They are both fairly consistent. But you don't dare trust the steel magnolia. She may appear to be sensitive to the desires and expectations of others, but she will often go ahead and do whatever she wants. She may appear to be passive, but she is actually quite aggressive.

The steel magnolia appears calm on the outside, but inside a huge cauldron of bitterness and resentment boils. Scott Wetzler says, "Anger is at the core of passive-aggression, even when it is denied, submerged or called something else. But however much he may try to disguise it, his anger is never entirely concealed, since for him to fully hide his anger would be to miss the point."[5]

The steel magnolia doesn't state her needs but is instead indirect. Yet if you cross her or get in her way, you are in serious trouble. She may appear on the outside to be sensitive and tender, but don't get too comfortable, because the tough side is sneaking up behind you.

Sarcasm is one of the most effective tools of the steel magnolia. She uses it as a way to express anger while playing it safe. By pretending to be funny a sarcastic person disguises her anger and discourages retaliation. If you respond to the sarcasm you may be accused of being negative, assuming the worst, or not having a sense of humor. "What's the matter—can't you take a joke?" may be the immediate response.

Sarcasm is an assault by misdirection and disguise. It is a way of attacking while avoiding a clearly hostile intent. Over time, individuals who use this tactic may convince themselves that they don't have aggressive feelings. They may come across as being shocked that anyone could misunderstand their pure motives and sincere intentions.

Sometimes steel magnolias will disguise their anger with a smile and a joke. You know what I mean—the sarcastic, not-so-funny joke that makes you cringe rather than laugh. The one that sounds humorous but carries a sharp, subtle barb. It gets the message across, but it doesn't leave you with many options. If you confront a steel magnolia, she will deny being angry. Proverbs has something to say about this response: "A man who is caught lying to his neighbor and says, 'I was just fooling,' is like a madman throwing around firebrands, arrows and death!" (Proverbs 26:18–19 TLB).

One writer has compared arguing with a steel magnolia to fighting with the Tar Baby of the Uncle Remus children's stories. Over time the Tar Baby gets you so mad you throw a punch, but, to your surprise, your fist sticks to him. Pummel him and he absorbs your blows as though nothing were going on. Of course that only tends to increase your frustration.[6]

Linda Brown has written, "When you become the butt of someone else's humor and then are urged to be a 'good sport,' you feel confused, frustrated and even angry. The other person inflicts wounds, and you're discouraged from responding or trying to understand why."[7]

If time after time it feels like there is a double message, there probably is. Don't ignore your discomfort, feelings of frustration, and confusion. If you don't feel listened to or cared about, you probably aren't. If you consistently feel put down rather than constructively criticized, that is probably the real intent. If a personal joke hurts, that could be an indicator that the joke was indeed meant to be a hostile barb rather than harmless fun.

What are some characteristics of steel magnolias?

Procrastination	Subtle sarcasm
Forgetfulness	Stubbornness
Fosters confusion	Obstructionism
Fear of intimacy	Makes excuses
Misunderstanding	Silent treatment
Sulking	Lies
Chronic lateness	Inconsistency
Ambiguity	Mixed messages
Carelessness	Resentful

WHERE DO WE GO FROM HERE?

One of the main reasons these three anger styles are unhealthy and don't work is that they involve a denial of our real selves. When we stuff, repress, suppress, deny, ignore, or hurl our anger, we are ignoring anger's potentially important message. We have lost touch with the primary emotion that triggered our anger.

Reactors deny their real grief and pain. Resentment and rage keep them from dealing with legitimate fears and hurts and limit God's ability to bring recovery and restoration. If we refuse to allow God to help us face the real issues of our lives, how can we understand, forgive ourselves, forgive others, or grow?

All three of the anger styles we have discussed thus far involve unhealthy reactions. They are usually an automatic, unconscious reaction to some real or perceived threat to our sense of significance, safety, or security. Each one of them is unhealthy. Each is dysfunctional. Each falls short of God's plan and purpose in giving us the gift of anger.

Fortunately God has given us a healthy option. God can help you trade your unhealthy, reactive style for a mature, healthy, and biblically sound way of understanding and expressing your anger.

THE MATURE (OR ASSERTIVE) RESPONDER

The healthy option is not an automatic reaction but involves a reasoned response. It is a way of responding that allows us to "be angry and sin not." It is the assertive response.

Unfortunately, the word *assertive* is often confused with the word *aggressive*. But there is an enormous difference between the two.

In *Smart Cookies Don't Crumble: A Modern Woman's Guide to Living and Loving Her Own Life,* Sonya Friedman has this to say:

> Assertion and aggression are not identical—do not believe any rumors to the contrary. Here's why: Assertion is like having the right of way at the wheel of a late-model Cadillac; aggression is like deliberately plowing into another car at a demolition derby. Aggression is hostile comments or jokes at another's expense;

assertion means using humor to defuse a volatile situation dip-
lomatically or to connect to another human being by a shared
sense of comedy. Aggression is a disregard for the consequences of your actions; assertion involves taking responsibility. Assertion is freedom from the persistent aggravation of a
recurrent problem; aggression re-creates the problems. Assertion is common courtesy; aggression means pushing others
around in their own lives.[8]

The mature responder is an assertive woman who has a
clear sense of who she is in Christ. Her emotions, mind, and
will work together and function in a balanced way. She can
express her opinions but doesn't need to put others down. She
delights in serving but isn't servile. She can be tough and
tender. She isn't reactive; she is proactive. She has taken the
time to look at, understand, and develop a healthy plan for
dealing with the God-given emotion of anger.

If the anger of the cream puff is characterized by resentment and the anger of the locomotive is characterized by rage,
then the anger of the mature responder is characterized by indignation. What is indignation? How does it differ from rage
and resentment? In his book on anger, Richard Walters provides a helpful comparison of the effects of all three emotions:
rage, resentment, and indignation.

Rage seeks to do wrong, resentment seeks to hide wrong, indignation seeks to correct wrongs. Rage and resentment seek to
destroy people, indignation seeks to destroy evil. Rage and resentment seek vengeance, indignation seeks justice. Rage is
guided by selfishness, resentment is guided by cowardice, indignation is guided by mercy. Rage uses open warfare, resentment is a guerrilla fighter, indignation is an honest and fearless
and forceful defender of truth. Rage defends itself, resentment
defends the status quo, indignation defends the other person.
Rage and resentment are forbidden by the Bible, indignation is
required. . . .

Rage blows up bridges people need to reach each other,
and resentment sends people scurrying behind barriers to hide

from one another and to hurt one another indirectly. Indignation is constructive. It seeks to heal hurts and to bring people together. Its purpose is to rebuild the bridges and pull down the barriers, yet it is like rage and resentment in that the feelings of anger remain.[9]

The mature response is a style of responding to anger without which this world of ours would be a much poorer place. What are some characteristics of a mature responder?

Responds	Careful	Indignation
Trusting	Healthy shame	Anger communicated
Responsible	Warm	Proactive
Interdependent	Motivated by love	Unselfish
Firm	I win/You win	Direct communication
Caring	Listens	Constructive

The mature responder is free to "speak the truth in love." The cream puff will often speak in love yet due to her overconcern for others may not speak the whole truth. Because she fears hurting someone's feelings or making waves, she may say only as much as she thinks the other person wants to hear or whatever will not provoke him. The locomotive is not usually concerned with what others think or feel, so she is more likely to speak the truth as she sees it. However, she rarely does this with love. She is much more likely to dump and run.

When provoked, the mature responder is less likely to immediately react without thinking but rather responds in a way that reflects discipline and thought. She has learned the value of anger. She has learned to be aware of and choose her expressions of anger. She is more likely to have trained herself to think, act, and feel constructively. She expresses her thoughts, preferences, and emotions directly to the other person in healthy ways that communicate a respect for the dignity and the rights of both herself and others. Her response is more likely to move her toward achieving her personal and relational goals.

Anger can be an invaluable tool in the hands of a responsible person. It is a force capable of being directed and used constructively. Aristotle acknowledged those positive aspects of anger when he said, "Those who do not show anger at things that ought to arouse anger are regarded as fools; so too if they do not show anger in the right way, at the right time or at the right person."

In the next chapter we will be discussing some proven ways in which you can learn how to express the God-given emotion of anger in ways that heal rather than hurt.

TONGUE-IN-CHEEK NAMES FOR THE THREE STYLES

One woman has proposed three new names for the three anger styles:

Cream Puff	= Timid Tulip
Locomotive	= Snapdragon
Steel Magnolia	= Venus's-flytrap

NOTES

1. For more information see Carol Zisowitz Stearns and Peter N. Stearns, *Anger: The Struggle for Emotional Control in America's History* (Chicago: Univ. of Chicago Press, 1986), 207.

2. "Women More Likely Than Men to Suppress Anger, Study Finds," *The Denver Post*, 25 January 1989, 4C.

3. Quoted by Carol Tavris, "Do Codependency Theories Explain Women's Unhappiness—Or Exploit Their Insecurities?" *Vogue*, December 1989, 220–26.

4. Susan Jacoby, "Why Is That Lady So Red in the Face?" *McCalls*, November 1983, 123–24, 205.

5. Scott Wetzler, *Living with the Passive-Aggressive Man* (New York: Simon & Schuster, 1992), 106.

6. Willard Gaylin, *The Rage Within: Anger in Modern Life* (New York: Penguin, 1989), 103–4.

7. Quoted in Deidre Laiken, "Hidden Anger," *Glamour*, March 1984, 274–75.

8. Sonya Friedman, *Smart Cookies Don't Crumble: A Modern Woman's Guide to Living and Loving Her Own Life* (New York: Putnam, 1985), 89–90.

9. Richard P. Walters, *Anger: Yours, Mine, and What to Do About It* (Zondervan: Grand Rapids, 1981), 17, 139.

CHAPTER TWELVE

Overreactions and Underreactions

One of the recurring questions we hear in counseling is "Can you help me with my anger?" Women say they get too angry or don't get angry enough, wonder if their anger comes too fast or too slow, say their anger hurts others, report that they feel guilt over their anger, say they take out their anger on the wrong people, say they become too aggressive, say their anger makes them sick, and report that they cry instead of showing their anger.

Anger has many means of expression. Do you feel good about the way you express your anger? Do you misuse it toward yourself or toward others? Are you wondering what to do with your anger? Let's consider some of the more typical ways anger is misused and what you can do about it.

OVERREACTION

Jean's concern about her anger reflects the way many women feel. "I don't know why I do it," she said. "It seems like my anger is an overreaction. I just seem to get more angry than any situation should merit. What can I do?"

Have you ever felt as though your anger is an overreaction? At times do you get angry at something insignificant, and even though you are aware of it you seem unable to do anything about it? Often such women are slow to even recognize their anger and its buildup. But they do recognize it and feel it. Often the anger builds up over a period of days, weeks, and even months, and then something minor happens at home or at work and there's an explosion. Overreacting people are usually reacting to the past rather than to what's going on in the present. That is something to keep in mind and perhaps post it in writing where you can see it.

If you tend to overrespond with your anger, try this: At the end of each day for a week or two inventory the times that you may have been annoyed or irritated. What drew forth an angry response from you?

Were there any times when you anticipated a problem with a family member or someone at work? Did you experience anger at any time over something you thought might happen but never materialized? Determine what you will say or do each time you feel irritated, so that you can handle the emotion immediately and not let it build. When you think about other people, before you assume that what they said or did was intentional, ask some clarifying questions. You may discover there was nothing intentional in their behavior or that they weren't even aware that what they did or said was a problem.

LOST OPPORTUNITIES

Cindy expressed yet another common difficulty with anger. "You know," she said, "there are times when I wonder if I'm angry and don't even know it. Sometimes I get angry, but it seems to take so long to arrive. Rarely does it come when the problem occurs. It's like I have a delayed fuse, and sometimes I don't even know that it's lit until I get angry. It's hard for me to experience anger. And I wish it would happen at the time I need it the most."

Many women are like Cindy. They regret lost opportunities to express their anger. Later on they can imagine what they would have liked to have said. They have the feeling that it might have been beneficial to have become angry at the time. Often the difficulty is that a slow anger responder isn't used to expressing anger in the presence of other people, or chooses not to. In order to feel her anger she may need privacy.

If you are like Cindy, schedule some private time so you can reflect on situations that happened during the day. Were there any incidents that might have triggered an angry response in you but didn't? What were your thoughts at that time, negative or positive? Were the other people fair at the time of the incident? When did you first become aware of your anger? What did you want to do or say at that time but didn't?

As you become aware of each incident, immediately take your emotional temperature to determine if you are angry. If you *are* angry, ask yourself, *What do I want to have happen because I expressed my anger?* Then express your feelings at that time. Doing it immediately can be healthy for your relationships and prevent a buildup that will be expressed sooner or later.

GUILT

Carol presented a unique conflict over her anger. "It isn't just when I express anger that I feel anger," she confided, "it's when I feel anger that the guilt starts. I end up feeling miserable over the fact that I get angry. But sometimes I need to be angry, and yet my guilt cripples my anger and keeps it from being productive. Perhaps I'm expecting that I should be more in control of my feelings. I wish I could control my guilt rather than have it control my anger."

Carol and others like her can learn to eliminate their guilt. It's important first of all to identify where the beliefs you have about your anger came from and whether they're accurate or not. Often our beliefs and values come into play and generate the guilt we feel. Make a list of the times when you either felt or expressed anger and what it was about. Determine whether your anger was justified or not. Formulate a statement that you will say to your guilt the next time it occurs. Give yourself permission to become angry when it's needed.

If you still tend to feel guilty, list three reasons for believing your anger is wrong and then three reasons for believing it is right. Each day give yourself permission to feel anger, but don't express it. By making the choice not to express your anger you will be showing that you are in control of it. Tell yourself that feeling anger is nothing to feel guilty about. Make a chart and keep track of the level of your guilt for one month to identify your progress. Develop a positive plan for and method of expressing anger so that you feel positive about its expression.

ANGER THAT HURTS OTHERS

Colleen was to the point as she discussed the way she expresses anger. "When I'm angry, you know it," she said. "So do the people who've upset me. I don't edit. I cut loose, and I don't care how they feel either. If they're hurt or put down, well, they deserved it after what they did or said to me. Sometimes other people in the same room feel my anger, but they could get out of the way."

Anger that hurts others is a problem. And not everyone is unconcerned like Colleen. There are those who realize that their relationships with family, work associates, and friends are deteriorating because of their overly direct anger attacks. They want to find a better way to express their anger. Also, too often their anger attacks are directed at the the other person's character rather than what he did. Their anger is seen not as anger, but as aggression, and that's the problem. Five steps will help you change this problem expression of anger.

- Think back over a time when you were overly angry with someone. Perhaps it was your husband, your child, one of your parents, or someone at work. Don't give any regard to what he or she said or did. Think about what you said, what you did, your nonverbals, and your gestures. Imagine that you were the other person. How might you have felt receiving your anger?
- Select two of your anger encounters and write down what you could have said to make it a constructive event. Focus on what the other person did and what you would have preferred him to do. Imagine yourself telling him only what he did that was unacceptable, why you didn't like it, and what you would have preferred.
- Notice how you felt about yourself, the person, and your response. Was it a better feeling than what you experienced before?
- Apply Ephesians 4:26a and Proverbs 16:32 to your new response. Does it fit?
- Make a commitment to yourself, to God, and to one other person as to how you will respond the next time you are angry.

MISDIRECTED ANGER

Kathy told me of pattern of hers that had plagued her for years. "It's like I'm on an archery range, and every time I shoot at the target I miss it and hit the target next to it. I was angry at my son the other day, and yet I took it out on his sister. I guess I wasn't even aware that I was angry at him until I exploded, and then I had to deal with the problems my anger created between myself and my daughter. This has happened at work as well. I'm often not aware that I'm angry with another coworker, and yet later on I'm griping my head off about him! I guess I was angry but took it out by griping." Kathy was describing two ways of misdirecting your anger: griping about others and taking out your anger on the wrong target.

The first step in correcting this misuse of anger is to figure out the reason you're reluctant to let out your anger directly at the person you're angry with. Is it his position of power or authority, a fear of his anger, or a fear of his rejection? Has this been your usual way of responding over the years? Is this the style you use only with family or coworkers or just certain kinds of people? What do you gain by not expressing your anger directly? What do you lose by not confronting directly? What would it take for you to be willing to express your anger directly to the person who angered you? Would you be willing to commit yourself to expressing your anger to that person on the next three occasions? When you express your anger (and this is applicable for all these problem responses) you might want to state the underlying reason for your anger (whether it be fear, hurt, or frustration) as well as stating what you would prefer the person to do differently in the future.

PRESERVED ANGER

A serious anger issue described by Teri is shared by many other women. "I'm a keeper," Teri said. "Unfortunately, somewhere over the years I've picked up the idea that anger should never be shared with others. So I've learned to keep it to myself and contain it. Stuff it would be a better word! I guess that's why I'm so thin. My stomach has taken the brunt of my anger. I knew this a long time ago, but I was still willing to put up with it. It seemed a small price to pay for not creating a scene with my anger."

Teri is like many whose body has become a dumping ground for the toxic waste of buried anger. Depression, ulcerated colitis, elevated blood pressure, hypertension, and upset stomach are just a few of the physical symptoms that occur when people absorb their anger. Teri knew about it and was willing to pay the price. Many women don't know about it and still pay the price.

What can you do if you are like Teri? First, if you have a number of physical symptoms as well as unshared anger, consider the possibility of a correlation between your anger and your symptoms. Be sure to discuss this possibility with your family physician and ask him to recommend literature and books on the subject. Keep a written record of your physical symptoms and your anger to see how the two connect. When you become irritated at home or at work—or wherever—keep track of how much time it takes for your body to begin responding to your anger.

Once you have identified the correlation, become aware of your anger sooner each time. Identify the beliefs or experiences that cause you not to express your anger toward another person. Select appropriate healthy responses from this and other chapters to learn to use in place of stuffing your anger. Practice, rehearse, and implement those new steps.

CONTROLLED BY OTHERS' ANGER

Linda described an interesting scenario. "My problems start when others get angry at me. I don't like it and can't handle it too well. I get along fine with my family and the others at work, but let someone get angry at me or let me know they are displeased in some way, then watch out. I come on strong—too strong. And usually the other person is taken aback and confused. At work I've had people tell me I need to learn to control myself and save that reaction for home. And at home I'm told that I should be nicer to them than anyone else and ought to save my angry reactions for work. It's as though I have to be perfect at home and perfect at work, and that expectation makes me angry too. They can't see their contribution to the problem. It's their anger that I'm responding to in the first place."

Many of us have difficulty responding to others' anger, and our initial response is a defensive posture coupled with the offensive stance of being aggressive. Sometimes we may be feeling that others shouldn't expect us to be perfect. But if we blame their anger for activating our aggression, it could be we are expecting them to be perfect too.

Some steps you can take will help. One is to think about what you're doing. How do you feel about yourself reacting to another person's anger? Do you *want* to become angry? After all, isn't that what you dislike in the other person? There is probably nothing you can do to keep others from becoming angry, so why not give them permission to do so? When they respond in anger, there are several things you can do: (1) just listen and ask clarification questions, (2) reflect back what you heard them saying and feeling, (3) let them know you want to think over what they've just said for a minute, or (4) tell them you want to hear what they have to say and can understand their being upset at this time. Whatever approach you take, plan and rehearse your new response a number of times.

THE TEARS OF ANGER

Two more anger expressions are major problems. One of these responses is something both women and men have expressed frustration over when it occurs in a woman—crying to express anger. This response is especially confusing to a man. Crying comes in many shapes and sizes. Sometimes it's just the feeling of choking up and not being able to talk. Sometimes its having your eyes fill with tears. Some persons will avert their eyes or mumble that there's a speck in their eyes as they wipe them. Others simply find the tears pouring forth. You may find it easier to cry in some settings than others. For most people, it is easiest to cry at home and the most difficult to cry at work.

Many adults, especially women, express their anger in tears. Perhaps the illustration below best expresses it:

> Tears that spring from anger appear to emerge from frustration that what one is saying isn't being heard by another. Such tears may also embody grieving that one's ideas are rejected by another out of hand, before they've been given a fair hearing (literally). They may incorporate fear and anger that the other person does not really want to hear what you're saying.
>
> Tears of anger and frustration at not being heard have been shed for centuries. Irving Stone, in *The Agony and the Ecstasy,*

gives us his understanding of a time early in Michelangelo's life when he had become aware of his passion for sculpture and might have thrown his energy into convincing his skeptical friends that sculpting is an exciting, vital art. Stone writes that one of Michelangelo's friends, Jacopo, "hooted" as Michelangelo spoke of his love for sculpting. . . Stone continues to envision the scene . . .

> Jacopo jumped down from his perch. "Sculpture is a bore. What can they make? A man, a woman, a lion, a horse. Then all over again. Monotonous. But the painter can portray the whole universe: the sky, the sun, the moon and the stars, clouds and rain, mountains, trees, rivers and seas. The sculptors have all perished of boredom."

Tears of frustration well in Michelangelo's eyes. Another friend picks up the attack:

> "Has it ever occurred to you that the reason there are no sculptors left is because of the cost of material? . . . Who would provide you with stone, who would support you while you practiced on it? . . ."
> Michelangelo turned away. If only he knew more. Then he could convince them of the magnificence of fashioning figures in space . . . Without another word, he walked down the cool marble steps, away from the Duomo, over the cobbled streets to home.

Within this story Michelangelo perceives clearly that he is not going to be heard. Tears come to his eyes.[1]

For some people it is easier to cry than to show their anger. For others the intensity of their anger frustrates them so much they are tongue-tied. This new frustration, coupled with the initial frustration, leads to the tears. Some people give themselves permission to cry but not to show anger, so the anger is channeled into crying. Have you ever heard the expression, "I was reduced to tears"? That is the ultimate sense of frustration.

If this is what you do, here are some suggestions. First, let others know that you tend to cry when you become frustrated or angry, and that in time you will learn to become more direct with your anger. Let them know that you need a bit of time to compose yourself, and then you'll be all right.

As soon as you begin to feel something, listen to it. Immediately after you have cried, analyze what happened, what was said, how you reacted, and what you felt—whether it was anger, fear, hurt, insecurity, or frustration. The next time a situation occurs at home or at work and you feel yourself beginning to choke or tear up, excuse yourself and go into another room. Let your tears out and then identify your true feelings at that time. When you return, don't apologize for your tears, but instead state what you were beginning to feel. Mention that the next time you might cry or you might be able to come out with your real feelings.

Spend time visualizing how you want to respond with your anger the next time. Imagine yourself saying, "I'm upset over . . . ," or, "Right now I'm angry . . ." Practice in advance will make it possible to move from tears to your true feelings.[2]

There is one last difficulty that infects the work atmosphere as well as our homes. It is chronic anger.

CHRONIC ANGER

Perhaps you've struggled with chronic anger over the years. Or perhaps you've had to live with an individual who is in a state of chronic anger. Either way, you can testify to the major impact people with chronic anger have on those around them. Chronic anger has been defined as a pattern of thinking, acting, and feeling in which the individual actually looks for and/or prolongs his anger. This pattern is the opposite of the one followed by anger-avoiders. A chronically angry person is often oversensitive to anger cues. Its as though she pays selective attention to them and welcomes the opportunity to react with anger. Her antenna has been programmed to hunt out and respond to any stimulus that will kick off anger. And because she is overly conditioned to the possibility of becoming angry, she underreacts to cues that would lead to her becoming happy, joyful, or fearful.

After she is aware of the factor that can trigger her anger, she moves into the excitement phase, and her mind fixates on the sensations and thoughts that accompany chronic anger. Her anger is activated and concentrated, which lessens her ability to think calmly and clearly about what is taking place. The more she focuses on her anger, the more it builds. A woman with a pattern of chronic anger tends to let anger propel her into impulsive and/or exaggerated action. When that happens we often say that she is out of control. Often the anger flows into a rage response. Trying to talk a chronically angry person out of her anger does very little except to feed it.

Chronically angry people cannot or will not withdraw from their anger. They tend to brood and dwell on past hurts and slights. Either their anger is on the "high" button or it's on the "simmer" button. There is no relief from their anger, for a chronically angry person never completely lets go of it.[3]

This type of anger response is extremely costly. A chronically angry person's interpersonal relationships are poor and her other emotions are stifled because anger crowds them out. There are a number of reasons for chronic anger, however.

- *Chronic anger is a signal that something is seriously wrong.*

Whatever is wrong could be a legitimate concern, but unfortunately the anger itself usually does not tell us what the problem is. If you are a chronically angry person and you feel anger beginning to build, you might find it helpful to say, "I am starting to get angry, but I need to take it slow and discover the message of my anger. Who knows? It could be a false alarm."

- *Chronic anger is sometimes a person's attempt to resolve some of his life problems.*

Using chronic anger as a means of resolving difficult life problems may seem like a good idea, but it is usually counter-productive. Anger distances us from other people rather than drawing them closer. It can actually compound our difficulties. If it seems to solve a problem it probably hasn't. Other persons have probably been intimidated.

- *Chronic anger is usually a long-term habit.*

Habits develop because the person has received some sort of benefit from that behavior. Unfortunately, the value of the anger could have been in the past, but now that it has developed into a habit it's become a leftover without much of a function. It only creates problems. Remember that habits do not usually engage your mind. They are a reaction. Anger is actually controlling a chronically angry person's life. For people who want to feel like they're in control, that's not a pleasant thought.

- *Chronic anger is sometimes used for the purpose of gaining control over others.*

Controllers often use anger as a power play. Some believe it's the only way to stay in control or get others activated. This type of anger is usually referred to as "instrumental anger" rather than the emotional state of "expressive anger." It has one basic purpose—to gain control over another person or situation.

Instrumental anger has extremely negative effects within a family situation and can cripple the work environment. It is a deliberate attempt to intimidate others and creates a glaring deficiency in the person's ability to relate in a positive, healthy manner. The result is a socially defective person. But he usually doesn't like to hear this or admit it.

- *Chronic anger sometimes represents an attempt to gain status in the eyes of others.*

Some people have learned that they can elicit respect, gain status, or draw out admiration when they are willing to risk overpowering others, especially those in a position of authority. They're referred to as "hotheads" or worse, but they don't mind the label. It gets them the attention they want. But in order to maintain the recognition and respect of others, they need to keep looking for reasons to become and stay angry. They can't afford to let up or rest from their anger.

I have seen teenage girls as well as women in their thirties and forties actually boast about their ability to intimidate. But often inside, especially among older women, resides a deep longing and sadness over their inability to develop the softer, positive, loving relationship skills that would cause others to want to be close to them.

- *Chronic anger is sometimes used to maintain physical and/or emotional distance from others.*

People who find it difficult to accept closeness and intimacy may use chronic anger as a means of keeping others from getting too close to them. It's as though they are carrying a "no trespassing" sign or a "beware of me, I bite" placard. Intense anger will actually remove people from your life, even though that might not have been your original purpose. Some people want to keep others away for a while or at certain times, but that isn't the message people hear. They hear, "I want you out of my life forever. Keep on going!" The buffer zone chronic anger creates keeps you protected but isolated at the same time. If you become angry because others don't reach out when you want them to, that may intensify your anger, which pushes them farther away just when you might want them around.

- *Chronic anger is sometimes used to hold a relationship together.*

There are couples who argue from morning to evening. Their relationship is held together by this tension. It's the old phrase, "I can't live with you, and I can't live without you." The pain these couples experience and the example their behavior gives their children is unfortunate. The children learn that intimacy is only obtained through conflict. If one individual started responding without being angry the relationship would probably collapse, because the couple wouldn't know what to do without their anger.

- *Chronic anger is sometimes used to defend against shame and real or perceived threats to a person's self-esteem.*

When you feel shame you also feel deficient, inferior, worthless, and useless. You end up feeling like a fish someone caught that's too small or the wrong kind—and you're not worth keeping. The most typical response against an attack on your identity is rage.

Have you ever felt the humiliation that occurs when another person makes a point of trying to shame you? He might call you names or itemize all your mistakes at work in front of the other employees. Each time you're shamed it goes into your storehouse of memories. When the next incident occurs your reaction is not just to the current situation but also to the memory you have built up. That leads to resentment and a sense of seething bitterness. Your memories keep churning for weeks, months, and in some cases I have seen, even years. The response I have witnessed in counseling is almost as though the inciting incident occurred that very day.

Some people who experience rage against shame become batterers. Believing that they have the right to attack because they were attacked first, they believe they are justified in what they are doing.

- *Chronic anger is sometimes used as a defense against experiencing other feelings, such as fear, sadness, and love.*

People who use anger this way may not even know that that is what they are doing, but nevertheless they have become much more comfortable with their anger than with sadness or fear. If a person is afraid of the closeness that often accompanies love, anger will soon take care of of that problem.

- *Chronic anger is sometimes an expression of the feeling of righteous indignation.*

Our world has so many problems and injustices we believe we have the right to be angry. *We* should *be angry,* we think. Someone has to attack those who hold different and inferior viewpoints. So we justify what we are doing on moral grounds. But we may not be simply fighting for a moral cause, but for the feeling of our own superiority. Some people may even follow us and our crusade. Sometimes anger of this type seems right and proper, and other times it is way off base. Cynicism and contempt permeate our expressions of anger. Unfortunately, this type of anger tends to work for some people, who override the opposition and appear to win.

- *Chronic anger is sometimes used as a means of making a person feel activated.*

This last purpose of anger has almost an addictive quality. Because anger contains an abundance of energy it helps some people who ordinarily live a dull and colorless life to become activated, or it gives them the experience of a "high" because of the adrenaline rush. These people look for reasons to become angry and even seek out anger to receive a thrill they would ordinarily never experience otherwise.

Perhaps chronic anger is not a part of your life. It could be that it is reflected in someone else, such as a family member or employer. Think for a moment about the purposes for anger we have discussed. Can you think of some examples for each one? Identify three of those that might be common in your life.

EXPLORING ALTERNATIVES TO CHRONIC ANGER

In *Anger, Alcoholism and Addiction: Treating Anger in a Chemical Dependency Setting*, Ronald T. Potter-Efron and Patricia S. Potter-Efron say that anger is

- A signal that something is wrong

- An attempt to solve some of the problems in your life
- A long-term habit in your life
- A way to gain control over others
- An attempt to gain status and admiration
- Used to keep others physically and/or emotionally away from you
- Used to hold a relationship together
- A defense against shame and threats to your self-esteem
- A defense against other feelings in your life
- Used to hold a position of righteous indignation
- An indicative response that puts excitement into your life

They discuss angry habits you may have, both verbal and nonverbal. Those could include frowning, glaring, snapping your fingers or hitting your palm against your thigh, yelling, swearing, slamming doors, chopping the vegetables into minute pieces with a knife.[4]

If you have this tendency, answer this question: Do you want to explore the possibility of learning to react in another manner? I'm not asking if you want to change, because you could be experiencing a lot of benefit from your anger (even though there are greater benefits when you learn to moderate your anger), or you may not believe you could possibly change. The first step in dealing with life in a new way is to consider the possibility that there is a different way to respond to the world. As you consider that, think about what you could replace your anger with so that you would have an alternative.

Once you have a picture in your mind of a different way to respond, remember that in moving ahead you are not totally giving up your usual way of responding. You are just putting it on the shelf for a while so that you can explore another way of handling the causes and purposes of your chronic anger. If your new way does not work after extensive attempts or it doesn't bring you greater benefits, you can always discard it and go back to your previous pattern.

I realize that that is easier said than done, and yet it is possible. Look carefully at the other sections of this book, which give you practical steps for changing and implementing new responses. Many people have made the switch; otherwise we would not even be considering the possibility. Keep one thought in mind. If God can see you changing and becoming a different person (and He can), why not grasp His perception of you and make it your own? Begin to think of yourself as person who is not chronically angry. Create a vision of what you can become rather than what you have been.

> Vision is the ability to see God's presence, to perceive God's power, to focus on God's plan in spite of the obstacles . . . Vision is the ability to see above and beyond the majority. Vision is perception—reading the presence and power of God into one's circumstances. I sometimes think of vision as looking at life through the lenses of God's eyes, seeing situations as He sees them. Too often we see things not as they are, but as we are. Think about that. Vision has to do with looking at life with a divine perspective, reading the scene with God in clear focus.
>
> Whoever wants to live differently in "the system" must correct his or her vision.[5]

NOTES

1. Jeanne Plas and Kathleen Hoover-Dempsey, *Working Up a Storm: Anger, Anxiety, Joy and Tears on the Job* (New York: Norton, 1988), 104–5.
2. Ibid., 254–87. Adapted.
3. Adapted from Ronald T. Potter-Efron and Patricia S. Potter-Efron, *Anger, Alcoholism and Addiction: Treating Anger in a Chemical Dependency Setting* (New York: Norton, 1991), 39–41.
4. Ibid., 85–101. Adapted.
5. Charles Swindoll, *Living Above the Level of Mediocrity: A Commitment to Excellence* (Waco, Tex.: Word, 1987), 88, 94–95.

CHAPTER THIRTEEN

What Can I Do About My Anger?

Every time I lose my temper and yell at Tom or the kids I feel like a total failure. I promise the Lord and myself that it will never happen again—but it does."

From this statement what would you guess Anna's the anger pattern was? Do you think that she's a cream puff, a locomotive, or a steel magnolia? If you guessed cream puff you are right. However, when I review this illustration with women's groups most guess that Anna is a locomotive.

It is true that locomotives are more likely to lose their temper and yell. But when a cream puff has been under enough pressure long enough she will often find herself "losing it."

Anna was the mother of four children and had been married to Chuck for fourteen years. She was a kind and gracious woman, loved by her husband and children and respected by her friends. When in our first session she told me, in a calm, soft voice, that she needed help in dealing with her anger I was a bit surprised. She told me that she had been raised in a home with an angry father, who made clear that he was the *head* of the house. "I don't mean head in the healthy and biblical sense of the word," she said emphatically with a hint of bitterness in her voice. "I mean that he ran the house and everyone in it with an iron fist. I promised myself that when I grew up I would not be an angry person like my dad."

Anna continued, "I remember Dad saying, 'I'm the man, and God has made me the head of this house.'" Anyone who questioned or disagreed with him was equated with someone who would question or disagree with the One who had placed him in the position of authority in the home. And who in their right mind wants to disagree with God?

Like Laura in chapter 3, Anna grew up believing that being a good and godly woman meant being quiet, submissive, compliant, complacent, and anger-free. Women, like children, were best seen and not heard. That's what she was told, and that's what she saw modeled. "Mom was a kind and gentle woman, but I never once heard her disagree with Dad." Whenever she even got close to disagreeing, Anna's Dad would give her mom "the look"—and everyone knew what that meant.

Anna met Chuck at a Christian college. She was a freshman, and he was a sophomore. They fell in love, dated for two years, and were married in his senior year. They had their first child, a girl, ten months after their wedding and in the next four years had three more children. Due to the birth of their first child Anna wasn't able to complete her college education.

After Chuck's graduation he went on for his law degree and joined a large law firm. For the first several years he worked long hours, and the family life centered around his schedule and needs.

"Even though at one time I had three children in diapers I never thought that what I did was that important," Anna told me. "After being with the kids all day long it didn't seem fair that I was always the one who got up with them at night and was always the one who changed their diapers. Yet I felt guilty for feeling that way and never said anything to Chuck."

It wasn't that Chuck was a selfish or bad husband. It wasn't that Anna didn't thoroughly enjoy and value being a stay-at-home mom. In fact just the opposite was true. The problem was that they had both come from homes that were ruled by the "don't think," "don't talk," and "don't feel" rules. They had both come from homes where the ideas, opinions, and needs of the women were clearly inferior to men. In their childhood they had learned those lessons well.

"At first I never expressed my needs to Chuck," Anna said, "because I don't think that I was even aware of them." As she started to become aware of them she tried to ignore them. When she could no longer ignore them, she worked hard at spiritualizing them. "I really believed that if I was sincere enough and prayed hard enough the hurts and frustrations wouldn't bother me any more." Her problem wasn't that she prayed. In fact that was one of the healthiest things she had done. Her problem was that she stopped there and didn't put feet to her prayers.

"By the time I realized that I could no longer run away from my feelings, it was almost too late." Anna and Chuck had become stuck in a relational rut and were well on their way to becoming married singles. Her health had gradually been getting worse, and her doctors couldn't find any physical causes for her problems. Toward the end of our work together Anna remarked, "Looking back now, it's clear to me that my loving heavenly Father used my marital and physical problems to get my attention."

Although Anna had come for help in dealing with her anger, that wasn't where we started to work. I started by helping her to establish a biblical foundation for who we are in Christ; what it means to be made in the image of God; what it means to have a personality; and how God has designed our mind, will, and emotions to work together in balance and harmony. I also gave her some specific insights into our emotions. At this point she had the tools to begin to understand her God-given emotion of anger and to begin to change her deep-seated anger patterns.

Anna's purpose in coming for counseling was to get some help in understanding and learning some healthy ways to deal with her anger. In the remainder of this chapter I'd like to recount some of the specific, practical steps God used to transform the role of anger in Anna's life. Anna learned that in order to change deep-seated anger patterns she needed to take steps at three different times: (1) before she got angry, (2) while she was angry, and (3) after she had been angry.

BEFORE YOU GET ANGRY

When is the best time to deal with your anger? The best time to deal with anger is before you get angry. That's right, before you get angry. Why? Because we need to learn how to seize opportunities to deal with discouraging, frustrating, and painful situations before we reach the boiling point.

It is easier to be clear and objective when you plan ahead. Your perspective is less likely to be clouded by emotion. Many people have found that if you wait until you are angry to try to understand and deal with that emotion, it is too late. Here are five important questions to ask yourself before you become aware of the fact that you are experiencing anger:

- *Is my anger a problem?*

Just because you get angry once in a while doesn't mean that you have an anger problem. Anger is a God-given emotion that is a normal part of everyday life. So far we've seen that healthy anger has tremendous potential for good.

Anger does become a problem when we don't understand it or allow it to serve its God-intended function. It becomes a problem when we deny, suppress, repress, stuff, and ignore it. It becomes a problem when we don't listen to it, but instead allow ourselves to be used, taken advantage of, or even victimized.

Anger can become a problem when it gets out of control and moves into more destructive emotions, such as hostility, rage, and aggression. It becomes a problem when we continue to allow ourselves to be puppets of past patterns rather than using the resources God has given us to redirect the energy of this powerful emotion. It becomes a problem when we haven't disciplined ourselves to express anger in healthy and constructive kinds of ways.

• What are some indicators that I might be angry?

In chapter 11, which dealt with anger styles, we saw that anger can come packaged in many different shapes and sizes and can hide behind many different masks. Due to its negative reputation and people's tendency to deny it, anger would win the prize as the emotion "most likely to be mislabeled" (see chapter 4).

This tendency is especially applicable to those with the cream puff anger style. Since Anna considered herself a "certified cream puff" I encouraged her to make a copy of the word list found at the beginning of chapter 11. For a two-week period of time I asked Anna to put a check by each word that described what she was experiencing.

Anna found that for many years her anger had been disguised by terms such as *aggravated, annoyed, cranky, exasperated, grumpy, out-of-sorts,* and *touchy.* By doing this simple exercise she knew that whenever she experienced any of these feelings she also needed to consider the possibility that they were a cover for anger.

• When am I most likely to be angry?

In addition to identifying indicators that we are angry, it is essential for us to know when we are most vulnerable to experiencing anger. For two weeks Anna kept an Anger Log (discussed in chapter 5). By faithfully using this simple tool she realized for the first time that in certain times and situations there was an increased likelihood that she would experience anger.

Anna discovered that she was most vulnerable to anger during the two-hour period before and after preparing the evening meal, on Sunday mornings while she was trying to get the entire family ready for church on time, when Chuck came home late without telling her, and when anyone in the family failed to follow through on something she was counting on his doing.

By identifying these "danger zones" she was able to prayerfully prepare her mind and her heart. This simple exercise helped Anna to decrease the power of potentially explosive situations and thereby to gain some control over her emotional response. If this is the only suggestion you apply in this chapter, I think that you will be surprised at how helpful it will be.

• *What is my anger pattern?*

For many of us, anger starts as a negative feeling toward something or someone. At the outset we need to learn how to take hold of that feeling and make the emotion of anger captive to the obedience of Christ.

In chapter 11 we identified three unhealthy anger styles: cream puff, locomotive, and steel magnolia. Understanding your primary style helps you to identify immediately what you don't want to do. It also points you in the direction you need to go to be able to experience and express anger in ways that glorify God and help you to become the woman He wants you to be.

In addition to identifying your anger style, it is also important to identify what your personal indicators are that you are getting angry. Sometimes we are the last ones to know when we're angry. I have a friend whose dog knew he was angry before he did. When Allen spoke in a certain tone of voice his shelty would put her head down and slink off into another room.

How do you know when you are getting angry? How do your children or your spouse know when you are getting angry? How do your friends know? Do you speak with a louder voice? Do you talk faster? Does your face get red or pupils larger? Do you start to perspire? Do you have a churning sensation in your stomach? Do you feel like throwing or hitting something? Do you want to run and hide?

What is your personal anger profile? When you are angry does your body get more tense? Does your pulse increase? Is it more difficult for you to concentrate? Do you become increasingly preoccupied with what is making you angry?

If you are experiencing anger that's good. Your emotions are operating the way God designed them to operate. Now the question becomes, "What can I do with my anger?"

We can learn how to be more effective in the future by better understanding the mistakes we have made in the past. Mistakes can be our greatest teachers, and, since we've already made them and paid for them, there is no additional emotional cost to using them as a learning device. I repeat: emotionally it doesn't cost us anything to learn from the past. But it can cost us a lot *not* to!

It is important to identify your personal anger indicators in advance. The best way to do that is to look at your past experience. By keeping the Anger Log you will be able to gain invaluable information about your personal anger pattern.

It is also helpful to illustrate what you have discovered by drawing a bell-shaped curve. A sample is given on page 266. Notice that I have placed what looks like a series of road signs on the front portion of the curve. Each of the road signs represents one of my personal anger indicators. The curve represents my anger. As the curve gets steeper the intensity of my anger increases.

On Anna's anger curve (page 267) the first personal anger indicator is the feeling of wanting to run. The next indicator is a sense of irritation. At this point she is aware of an increased heartbeat and a tendency to speak more quickly. By the time she reaches the frustration level she is also talking more loudly, is more negative and critical, and is on her way to the stage of yelling at people and labeling people. After Anna drew her personal anger pattern, I encouraged her to keep a copy in her Bible. I suggested that each time she opened the Word she glance at the drawing of her personal anger curve and offer a prayer of petition for God's help in dealing with her anger.

An Anger Curve

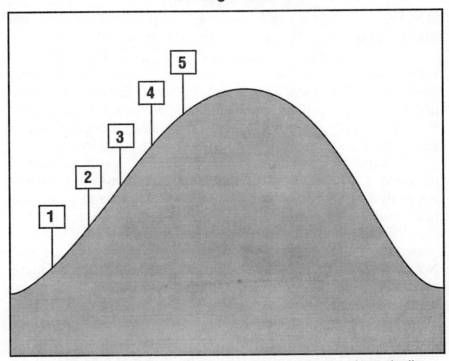

If the anger is caught at step 5, or at step 4, and so on down the line, the emotion does not get out of control. The energy can then be invested rather than spent.

Anna's Anger Curve

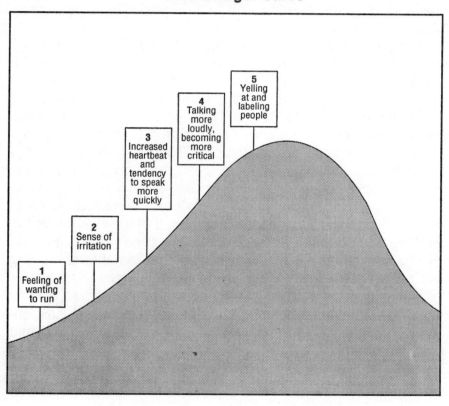

- *What are the benefits of dealing with my anger?*

At this point you may be tempted to say to yourself, *Working on this anger stuff is a lot more work than I had anticipated. Is it really worth it?* Well, only you can answer that question. Many people have found that one of the most helpful ways to answer that question is to remind themselves of the benefits of understanding and learning how to appropriately express their anger.

If our desire is to become the persons God wants us to be we will make the time to learn how to make our anger work for us. Hebrews 12:15 says, "See to it that no one misses the grace of God and that no bitter root grows up to cause trouble and defile many" (NIV). It is easy for a bitter root to grow up in our lives. Some people think they are doing the right thing by not dealing with or dwelling on the past. There're partly right—it *is* a good thing not to dwell on the past. But there is a big difference between not dealing with the past and not dwelling on it.

I think that the best way to answer the question concerning the worth of dealing with one's anger is to let some of the women we've interviewed and work with speak for themselves. We've asked many women, "What are the benefits of dealing with your anger?" Here are some of their answers:

— Understanding and dealing with my anger has enhanced my physical, emotional, mental, and spiritual health
— It has given me an increased source of energy to make the hard choices
— It has improved the quality of my marriage
— It has strengthened my relationships with the kids
— It has alleviated my fear of someone else's anger
— Now my children have a healthy model for this God-given emotion
— It helps me keep things in perspective
— The appropriate expression of my anger has helped others better understand me and what is important to me

— It helps me clarify and protect personal boundaries
— It helps me to protect myself physically and emotionally
— It has given me the power and courage to remove myself from the victim role

WHEN YOU GET ANGRY

As soon as you become aware of the fact that you are experiencing anger, you can take five simple steps that will help you make anger work for you rather than against you.

- *Acknowledge the fact that you are angry.*

This sounds simple, but for many people it is easier said than done. Anna could easily say that she was aggravated, annoyed, cranky, exasperated, grumpy, out-of-sorts, or touchy. Over time she saw that these were often code words for her anger. "It's much more comfortable and acceptable for me to say I'm annoyed or grumpy than to say that I'm angry."

If you are at all like Anna and find it difficult to say the "A" word (anger), you can be comforted by the fact that you have a lot of company. One of the most effective ways to work through this barrier is to start by silently acknowledging your anger to yourself. Then when you are alone and are aware of being angry, say to yourself out loud "I think I may be angry." If you have no doubt about it, simply say, "I'm angry!" Feel free to let your volume and tone of voice accurately reflect the intensity of your anger.

Then find someone you feel safe with and begin to share your anger with him or her. It may not be someone you are even angry with. You'll find that the simple act of acknowledging and talking about your anger with someone will decrease your discomfort and fear.

It rarely helps to "try hard" to stop being angry. What does help is to acknowledge that you are angry, identify the root causes, and redirect your energy away from attacking a person to attacking the problem.

- *Have I put first things first?*

Once you have acknowledged that you are angry, before doing anything else ask yourself if you've put first things first. When dealing with emotional issues it is tempting to find out what technique or gimmick someone else used and rush off to try, often in one's own strength, to do the same thing.

What do I mean by putting first things first? I mean that you should take the problem to the Lord in prayer. He created us, redeemed us, and has given us His Spirit to help us do in His strength what is often impossible for us to do on our own. Instead of turning on your husband or your children, turn your eyes to Jesus. Focus on what you do have, on your many blessings, on God's faithfulness, and His many promises to you.

In 2 Corinthians 10:5 (NASB) Paul exhorts us to "[take] every thought captive to the obedience of Christ." I don't think it does any injustice to the intent of that passage to suggest that we also need to get into the habit of taking every emotion captive to the obedience of Christ. This is especially true of the emotion of anger.

At the outset we need to set aside focused time to take all of our concerns, including our struggles with our emotions, to the Lord in prayer. In Psalm 42:4 David talks about pouring out his soul, and in Psalm 62:8 David wrote, "Trust in Him at all times, O people; pour out your heart before Him; God is a refuge for us" (NASB).

If you are frustrated, hurt, discouraged, and experiencing anger with someone, talk to the Lord about it, first in silent prayer and then perhaps even out loud. Ask God for His help and His guidance. It is foolish to try to do this in your own strength. Take advantage of the power of the Holy Spirit. In James 1:5 we are told that if we lack wisdom we only need to ask for it. In 1 Peter 5:7 we are told to cast all of our concerns on Him "because He cares for you" (NASB).

Many people have found the following simple prayer to be of help.

Dear Lord, Thank you for creating me in your image with the ability to experience and express the emotion of anger. While sin has damaged and distorted anger in my life, I thank you that you have promised to be at work within me both to will and to work for your good pleasure. I thank you that you can cause all things to work together for good and that I can do all things through you who strengthens me. I ask you to help me to change my anger patterns. Help me to experience and express this emotion in ways that are good and that bring honor and glory to you. Amen.

• *What are the causes?*

Now it's time to look for the causes. Notice that I said *causes* and not *cause*. As we said in chapter 4, anger rarely has only one cause. It is usually the result of a combination of factors. It is also important to remember that anger is almost always a secondary emotion. It may be an indicator that something is wrong with the decisions I am making or in the way I am allowing others to treat me.

When considering the possible causes of the anger, it is important for us to rule out two categories of causes. First of all, we must make sure that our anger is not due to sin or selfishness. That's right! One of the main effects of sin is to make meeting our own needs rather than doing God's will the most important thing in the world. When we put ourselves first we will inevitably end up last. When we put Him first (Matthew 6:33) He will take care of everything else.

Because we are all sons and daughters of Adam and Eve we are born selfish. We want what we want, and we want it when we want it. When we don't always get our way, when we aren't treated the way we think we should be, when we see others get something we think we deserve, it is easy for us to experience anger. If our anger is due to sin or selfishness we need to identify it, confess it, seek forgiveness, and ask the Holy Spirit for practical steps we can take to change that part of our lives.

The second cause that is important for us to rule out is that of oversensitivity. Whereas anger is an alarm, if we allow ourselves to become oversensitive that anger can easily be a false alarm. One of my good friends recently built a new home and had an alarm system installed. The first week he and his family lived there he received eleven calls at work letting him know the alarm and gone off. All eleven alarms turned out to be false alarms.

He finally discovered that the sensitivity levels for parts of the alarm system were set too high, thus creating the false alarms. If our sensitivity levels are set too high we can take offense when none is intended. We can look for slights when they aren't really there. We can assume the worst when it may not be true.

Once you've ruled out sin, selfishness, or oversensitivity, you are ready to learn how to identify the causes of your anger. At the beginning Anna found this to be a difficult step. It is not always easy to discern what might be causing our anger. However, over time and with some faithful observation, record keeping, and utilization of her Anger Log, Anna discovered that the primary sources of her anger were frustrations she had failed to deal with when they arose. "I kept on telling myself 'It's not that important!' when obviously it was."

If you have kept an Anger Log, you already have a list of the most frequent and thus the most probable causes of your anger. If you seem to be stuck and can't figure it out I'd encourage you to go back to chapter 4 ("Why Women Are Angry") and reconsider some of the categories we talked about there.

In addition to identifying some specific causes for her anger, Anna also uncovered factors that were in a more general way increasing her vulnerability to frustration. One of the main factors was physical exhaustion that came from the high levels of stress she allowed herself to be under. Another factor was the perfectionistic demands she placed on herself and others. She had been raised with the "enough is never enough" philosophy, and so performance always fell short of expectations.

One final factor Anna identified related to the gender issues discussed in chapter 4. During one session Anna stated, "I want you to know that I'm not a feminist, but at the same time it's frustrating to be treated as inferior, not very bright, an airhead, or like a slave simply because I am a woman."

Your situation may be much different than Anna's. In fact it probably is. But the steps God used to help Anna change her dysfunctional anger patterns can also be effective for you.

• What is the healthiest way for me to respond?

Moving to this step means that you are aware of the fact that you are angry, have committed your situation to the Lord, and have identified at least a couple of the causes of your anger. At this point the obvious question is, "Now what do I do?"

First you must determine if there is anything that you *can* do. What do I mean? Well, in life there are basically three kinds of situations: (1) situations you can control or change, (2) situations you can influence; and (3) situations you can do nothing about.

A great many people experience increased frustration (and thus increased anger) in trying to change or influence situations they can do nothing about. If your cause falls into this category, your only choice is to give it to the Lord in prayer as often as necessary, and turn your attention to things you can change or influence.

If your situation is one you can change or influence, get out a sheet of paper and make a list of your options. Don't worry about how practical your ideas are, just get loose and fill the sheet with as many constructive alternatives as you can think of. This may go slowly the first two or three times, but once you get the hang of it you will be surprised at how creative you can be.

If you've decided that a response is appropriate, what are some healthy ways for you to respond? First of all, determine who you need to talk to, when the best time to talk to them is, how can you communicate with them in the way they are most likely to receive favorably, and how long a time frame you have.

A good rule of thumb is to deal with a problem as soon as you become aware of it and have had time to choose how you can best express your feelings. Anger can vary in its intensity. If you are experiencing a mild anger you can usually deal with the situation on the spot.

However, if you are experiencing a moderate to intense degree of anger it is usually wise to wait until you've taken time to more thoroughly think and pray the matter through. In Proverbs 16:32 we read, "He who is slow to anger is better than the mighty." Why? Because the power and energy can be focused and directed. The verse continues, "And he who rules his spirit, than he who captures a city" (NASB).

Ecclesiastes 7:9 says, "Do not be eager in your heart to be angry, for anger resides in the bosom of fools" (NASB). The person who has learned to take the time to ponder and prayerfully consider important issues is the one who is best able to not only weather, but to even make progress in, the midst of a storm. A strong head wind can reveal your weaknesses, or it can call forth your strength.

God's word clearly teaches that a patient spirit provides an opportunity for greater clarity and wisdom. To be "hasty in spirit" is similar to experiencing "vexation of spirit." To grow vexed or to become agitated in a time of distress only makes matters worse.[1]

It is always best to express your anger at the source of your hurt. If you have bought into the myth that anger always destroys relationships this may be difficult for you to do. The only way to pull the teeth out of that lion of fear is to do it. Challenge the misbelief. Risk speaking the truth in love. Anger rarely keeps friends apart. It is what we choose to do with the anger.

Choose to nurture a spirit of forgiveness. At some point we must choose to let go. Ephesians 4:31–32 is a *must* in regard to anger and forgiveness. I have worked with people who seemed to relish dwelling on the cause of their anger. But it's not enough to *think* forgiveness. Go to him/her and *say* "I'm angry, and because our relationship is important to me I'd like to tell you why." If the other person isn't available or won't listen, write him a letter stating and clarifying your feelings.

Be open to being responsible for the way your life is running. Be open to God's teaching you what you can learn about yourself in this situation. God's promises, power, and grace are sufficient. He has given us all we need to deal with our own emotions. It is our responsibility to do something about our own pain.

- *Now that I've decided what to do, where do I begin?*

Once you have decided that you need to communicate your anger and you have decided on a healthy way to express it, the next, and for many the most difficult, step is actually doing it. That is sometimes easier said than done. That is why it helps to take the first step with someone you can trust.

Anna decided that, although she experienced anger with a number of people, the best and safest person to begin to develop her new skills with was her husband, Chuck. In your case, I would encourage you to find someone you can trust and start with her or him. The following story, taken from a book by Janet L. Kobobel, *But Can She Type?*, provides a great illustration of how the process can proceed.

Then God placed a friend in my life who recognized my advanced case of controlled emotions. I was sensitive to everyone's feelings but my own. Wayne kept telling me I could say anything to him. Then one day he promised to phone me later when we both had more time to talk. I had had a tough day and wanted to tell him. But he never called.

I decided to test the water and expressed dismay the next day. Wayne accepted it and apologized for not calling. Gee, that was pretty easy.

A few weeks later, I was explaining a deep hurt to him, and he responded in what I considered a cavalier fashion. That really hurt. I got mad. So I lambasted him with the gale force of my anger and hurt, listing all the specifics. He received it all and acknowledged how right I was and how wrong he'd been.

Immediately my face fell. I realized, once I'd vented my anger, that I had castigated Wayne not just because his comments were so upsetting but because I was angry at God, another friend, and my boss. (It had been a bad week.) Wayne just happened to say the wrong thing at the wrong time and ended up receiving my railing for all the Bad Guys in my life.

His response to my mumbled apology was a hallmark in my emotional growth. He smiled, touched my arm, and said, "Janet, you don't trust our relationship enough to really believe it's okay to be angry. We're seldom isolated in our anger. I can handle any degree of anger you can give out, and I was wrong in what I said."

So, with the encouragement of a caring friend, I found more freedom to express my anger. And I learned to make it articulate ("Why did you say _____? What I needed to hear was _____"). I not only vented an authentic emotion, but we also ended up closer friends who trusted each other more.[2]

A few days after you have communicated your anger and discussed the relevant issues with a friend, take a few minutes to get back to him. Reconfirm your commitment to him and to developing an increasingly healthy relationship. You can do this with a word, a touch, a hug, a note, or a call. This can serve as an important reminder that regardless of the surface struggles, who he is is important to you. It is because of his value to you that you are willing to risk pain. It is your love and appreciation for him that makes the relationship worth working on, fighting for, and fighting about.

AFTER YOU'VE BEEN ANGRY

Perhaps you successfully navigated that emotional rapids. Or perhaps you were more successful than you were in the past, but still need to work on it. Whatever the result of your putting into practice the five steps listed above, you're not quite finished yet.

● *What have I learned from this experience?*

In order to complete the learning process, it is important for you to ask yourself, "What have I learned from this experience?" One of the most encouraging aspects of being a Christian is that, whatever our experience, good or bad, with God's help we can learn from it. If you have been a Christian very long you have learned that Romans 8:28 is true. God carefully recorded the experiences of many men and women in the Bible. For over two thousand years God protected the record of those experiences. Why? So that we could learn from them.

- *What do I know about this experience?*

The last step in dealing with anger is to discover all you can about your experience. What went well? What was different from the usual pattern? Were there any positive surprises? What could you have done differently? Over a period of several months, Anna, Chuck, and their children began to see noticeable changes in her anger style and pattern. They were able to see God's faithfulness in clear and practical ways.

TAKE ACTION

Draw a couple of blank anger curve illustrations and do one on yourself. Then have your spouse or child, or a friend, do one on you.

NOTES

1. See H. C. Leupold, *Exposition of Ecclesiastes* (Grand Rapids: Baker, 1978), 154–55; and Franz Delitzsch, *Commentary on The Song Of Songs and Ecclesiastes* (Grand Rapids: Eerdmans, 1970), 318–19.
2. Janet L. Kobobel, *But Can She Type?* (Downers Grove, Ill.: InterVarsity, 1986), 93–94.

Appendix

The more than 2,400 completed surveys at the time of this writing represent a cross section of responses from women from over twenty states across the United States and approximately fifty surveys from British Columbia, Canada. The responses were gathered in churches, conferences, colleges, and businesses. The age range of the respondents was from eighteen to ninety-two. Twenty-eight nationalities and twenty-four denominations were identified.

The following is a sampling of some of the responses to the survey question, "If there is any one question that I could have answered about anger, it would be . . ."

- How can I get angry and not do damage to my husband and children? How do I take back what I've said sometimes when it is said in anger?
- How can I deal with someone else's anger?

- How do you express anger in a godly, loving way? Or don't you?
- What is the difference between healthy anger and harmful anger?
- What is the relationship between anger and hatred? Can there be hatred without anger?
- How do I validate myself when I'm angry?
- Why is this world full of so much anger, and why do we permit it?
- If God is love, how do you explain all the wrathful situations He initiated and condoned (i.e, in the Old Testament)? If all that rage and anger was OK in the religious/spiritual world back in the OT days, then why is it not OK today?
- How can you prevent anger?
- How to deal with it and make it go away.
- If everyone had the love of God in their hearts, would there be anger? (And wars?)
- Why, as hard as I try, can't I control the anger I feel when I know I will be sad for a time after?
- Why is it important to express your anger instead of stuffing it?
- How do you know when your anger is due to selfishness or so-called "righteous anger"? Is there a line?
- How can I better help my family and friends handle their anger in a positive way?
- How do you teach your children about anger—different types? Abuse and how to deal with it appropriately?
- How do you learn to hush some anger that does *not* need to be vented?
- Even though I know about anger, why can't I get past expressing anger in such a destructive way?
- Why do we express anger so easily when other emotions can be so hard to express?
- What is the real definition of anger?
- Is anger a sin?

- Why does anger have to have such a lasting, negative effect on human behavior, especially on the recipient?
- How can I resolve conflicts without feeling "stupid" or "illogical" and without losing physical control of myself?
- Why is anger usually negative in Christian circles?
- Why are the majority of people afraid to express anger?
- How can a man who loves a woman express anger through verbal and physical abuse?
- How can one eliminate anger altogether?
- When would it be beneficial to express anger?
- How can I control my anger without being a doormat?

Selected Bibliography

Caplan, Paula J. *Don't Blame Mother: Mending the Mother-Daughter Relationship.* New York: Harper & Row, 1989.

Cook, Kaye, and Lance Lee. *Man and Woman: Alone and Together.* Wheaton: BridgePoint, 1992.

Dobson, James C. *Straight Talk to Men and Their Wives.* Waco, Tex.: Word, 1980.

Forward, Susan, and Joan Torres. *Men Who Hate Women and the Women Who Love Them.* New York: Bantam, 1986.

Hayford, Jack. *Taking Hold of Tomorrow.* Ventura, Calif.: Regal, 1989.

McKay, Matthew. Peter D. Rogers, and Judith McKay. *When Anger Hurts.* Oakland, Calif.: New Harbinger, 1989.

Oliver, Gary Jackson, and H. Norman Wright. *When Anger Hits Home: Taking Care of Your Anger Without Taking It Out on Your Family.* Chicago: Moody, 1992.

Oliver, Gary J.; H. Norman Wright; and Rita Schweitz. *Women Facing Life's Demands: A Workbook for Handling the Pressure Points in Your Life.* Chicago: Moody, 1993.

Olson, Kathy. *Silent Pain.* Colorado Springs: NavPress, 1992.

Piaget, Gerald W. *Control Freaks: Who They Are and How to Stop Them from Running Your Life.* New York: Doubleday, 1991.

Seamonds, David. *Healing Grace.* Wheaton, Ill. Victor, 1988.

Sehnert, Keith W. *Stress/Unstress.* Minneapolis: Augsburg, 1981.

Tannen, Deborah. *You Just Don't Understand: Women and Men in Conversation.* New York: William Morrow, 1990.

Witkin-Lanoil, Georgia. *The Female Stress Syndrome: How to Recognize and Live with It.* 2d ed. New York: Newmarket, 1991.

West, Sheila. *Beyond Chaos: Stress Relief for the Working Woman.* Colorado Springs: NavPress, 1992.

Wetzler, Scott. *Living with the Passive-Aggressive Man.* New York: Simon & Schuster, 1992.

Wright, H. Norman. *Always Daddy's Girl: Understanding Your Father's Impact on Who You Are.* Ventura, Calif.: Regal, 1989.

————. *Chosen for Blessing.* Eugene, Oreg.: Harvest, 1992.

A companion to *Pressure Points* has been written
by Gary J. Oliver, H. Norman Wright, and Rita Schweitz.
It is *Women Facing Life's Demands:*
A Workbook for Handling the Pressure Points in Your Life
(Chicago: Moody, 1993).

Moody Press, a ministry of the Moody Bible Institute,
is designed for education, evangelization, and edification.
If we may assist you in knowing more about Christ
and the Christian life, please write us without obligation:
Moody Press, c/o MLM, Chicago, Illinois 60610.